CLASSIC MORITA THERAPY

Shoma (Masatake) Morita, MD (1874–1938) was a Japanese psychiatrist-professor who developed a revolutionary four stage therapy process. He knowingly critiqued psychoanalysts who sanctioned an unconscious or unconsciousness (collective or otherwise) that resides inside the mind. Significantly, he advanced a phenomenal connection between existentialism, Zen, Nature, and the therapeutic role of serendipity. Morita is a forerunner of eco-psychology and he equalised the strength between human-to-human attachment and human-to-Nature bonds.

This book chronicles Morita's theory of 'peripheral consciousness', his paradoxical method, his design of a natural therapeutic setting, and his progressive four stage therapy. It explores how this therapy can be beneficial for clients outside of Japan using, for the first time, non-Japanese case studies. The author's personal material, collected while training in Japan and in her subsequent practice of Morita's phenomenological therapy in Australia and the United States enhance this book. LeVine's coining of 'cruelty-based trauma' generates a rich discussion on the need for therapy inclusive of ecological settings. As a medical anthropologist, clinical psychologist, and genocide scholar, LeVine shows how the four progressive stages are essential to the classic method. The first 'rest' stage is at the core of recovery for clients who have been embossed by trauma.

Since cognitive science took hold in the 1970s, complex consciousness theories have lost footing in psychology and medical science. This book reinstates 'consciousness' as the dynamic charge of Morita therapy. The case material illustrates the use of Morita therapy for clients struggling with the aftermath of trauma and how to live creatively and responsively inside the uncertainty of existence. The never before published archival biographic notes and photos of psychoanalysts Karen Horney, Fritz Perls, Eric Fromm, and other renowned scholars who took an interest in Morita in the 1950s and 1960s, provide a dense historical backdrop.

Peg LeVine is a clinical psychologist and medical anthropologist and specialist in trauma, genocide, and cultural studies. She has a permanent research affiliation with the Center for Advanced Genocide Studies (Shoah Foundation) in Los Angeles, and is an associate professor adjunct in the School of Medicine at Monash University in Melbourne, Australia. Peg directs the Classic Morita Therapy Centre for training and therapy. As a sculptor of clay, wax, stone and bronze, she reimagines the grotesque in her figurative work.

CLASSIC MORITA THERAPY

Consciousness, Zen, Justice and Trauma

Peg LeVine

Routledge
Taylor & Francis Group

LONDON AND NEW YORK

First published 2018
by Routledge
2 Park Square, Milton Park, Abingdon, Oxon OX14 4RN

and by Routledge
711 Third Avenue, New York, NY 10017

Routledge is an imprint of the Taylor & Francis Group, an informa business

© 2018 Peg LeVine

British Library Cataloguing in Publication Data
A catalogue record for this book is available from the British Library

Library of Congress Cataloging-in-Publication Data
Names: LeVine, Peg, 1952- author.
Title: Classic morita therapy : eco-consciousness, zen, justice and trauma /
    Peg LeVine.
Description: Milton Park, Abingdon, Oxon ; New York, NY : Routledge,
    2017. | Includes bibliographical references.
Identifiers: LCCN 2016044688| ISBN 9780415790505 (hbk) |
    ISBN 9780415790512 (pbk) | ISBN 9781315213088 (ebk)
Subjects: LCSH: Morita psychotherapy. | National characteristics, Japanese.
Classification: LCC RC489.M65 L48 2017 | DDC 616.89/14—dc23
LC record available at https://lccn.loc.gov/2016044688

ISBN: 978-0-415-79050-5 (hbk)
ISBN: 978-0-415-79051-2 (pbk)
ISBN: 978-1-315-21308-8 (ebk)

Typeset in Bembo
by Apex CoVantage, LLC

For Akihisa (Aki) Kondo

FIGURE 0.1　Morita Shoma (1874–1938). Photo taken approximately in 1932. Printed with written permission from Mishima Morita Hospital Archival Library.

CONTENTS

ACKNOWLEDGEMENTS

Those who encouraged and contributed to this book have participated in upholding the integrity of Morita therapy in its classic form. Foremost is Akihisa Kondo, MD (1911–1999), whose mentorship between 1989 and 1999 remains incomparable to others in my professional development. Kondo invited me often to the office of his sensei, Takehisa Kora, MD (1899–1996), a disciple of Morita where we had lively discussions on the complexity and design of Morita practice. I met Kora's patients during various stages of their therapy in his garden hospital (Kora Koseinn Morita Hospital) where there were woodcarving, painting, and calligraphy studios. On one occasion, Kora and Kondo considered the future of Morita therapy inside and outside Japan and pondered ways to fortify and preserve Morita's theory of consciousness and intended therapy, particularly after they passed on. As feared, Kora's garden hospital practice was dismantled after his death and his successors were unable to carry on his practice there, though a small memorial archive library remains at the former site.[1] At that foreseen time, Kondo sensei told me this.

> As our next generation, your charge is simple and not so simple. Just practice Morita therapy as Morita intended. Find the right natural place and the place will support you. Keep to your kendo practice and side-step those who exclude you. The hawk sees what is and is not from the slightest movement. A hawk-eyed therapist finds Morita therapy. Look after your energy; practice, supervise, read, reflect, sculpt and write. Advance by a steady presence.

Since his death, I find traces of Kondo sensei and the wideness of his world when least expected. Just this morning I opened R.H. Blyth's book, *Zen and Zen Classics* (1964a), and found a dedication to Kondo and a forward by Kondo's other friend, Frederick Franck, author of *The Zen of Seeing: Seeing Drawing as Meditation* (1988) and *Zen and Zen Classics: Selections from R.H. Blyth* (1978). Suddenly I recalled how

Kondo described Franck's New York country, arty property, which he believed was a prototype for a Morita therapy centre and training institute.[2]

Others have cushioned my felt isolation that comes from holding firm to Morita's ecological, sequenced therapy. In Melbourne, Australia, David Chandler, renowned Cambodian historian, scholar, Emeritus Professor, poet, and humourist provided essential challenges and editorial advice. Of equal generosity in Melbourne is Graeme Smith, psychiatrist, Emeritus Professor, psychoanalyst and art collector; his commitment to the ethics of case formulation bolsters the field of psychological medicine. In Daylesford, Peter O'Mara, poet – artist – teacher – political activist brought his one-word grit to many pages. Throughout this project, Di Clifton – psychiatrist, trauma therapist, oil painter, and rose gardener – has been my essential 'sister' and ally.

In Japan, Yoshio Matsuda comprehends the true nature of Morita therapy like no other therapist. Over the years, Naoki Watanabe has been a most generous colleague and fellow explorer; he made possible our pilgrimage on the Shikōku trail. Go Nonaka turned up at uncanny moments to assist the richness of the history in this book. In fact, he served as editor to the final book on Morita therapy by Chihiro Fujita (1923–2014) – which was released the year Fujita died. Go's commitment to Morita is unfaltering.

Across the globe, foremost, Brian Ogawa has been my visionary friend, colleague, and accomplice in safeguarding Morita's original therapy as other scholars reconfigure Morita therapy for counselling practices.[3] From Boston, Christopher Ives, scholar of Japanese and religious studies, and Zen and ethics, gave princely, rich exchanges. He provided the kanji and literal translations in the *Glossary of Terms*.

In addition to Morita, I dedicate this book to three other renegade pioneers, Akihisa Kondo (1911–1999), Karen Horney (1885–1952), and Thomas Szasz (1920–2012). During the final writing stage of this book, Szasz died. As a young university student, *The Myth of Mental Illness* (Szasz, 1961) increased my awareness of human rights and mental health, globally. Throughout my career, I have witnessed mental health professionals justify use of treatments that confine, dispirit, and disempower those who live in compromising systems. Morita moved his theory into a holistic practice by *not* positioning the mind against body, body against mind, or humans above Nature. I am fortunate to have a small community of practitioner-scholars who practice and supervise from this perspective. For us, Morita therapy (as Morita intended) remains revolutionary.

While not an exhaustive list, the following have enriched my capacity to pen this book.

In Japan: Akihisa Kondo, Takehisa Kora, Yozo Hasegawa (Seikatsu No Hakkenkai), Toshiko Kondo, Katchi Netonai, Chihiro Fujita, Naoki Watanabe, Go Nonaka, Yoshio Matsuda, Jinroh Itami (Meaningful Life Therapy), Rei Ota, Yukiko Seto, Keiko Miyasaka, Kenji Kitanishi, and research assistance from the Okamoto Foundation. I am grateful to Yoshito Koizumi and the Mishima Morita Hospital's Memorial Archive Library, and to the resources of Mr Hoshino, secretary to Engaku-ji Temple in Kamakura, and to Fumio Hatano who has generously verified historical dates from Morita's personal diaries, and the generosity of Kei Nakamura.

More to home, Heather Levine-Chesler and Macahla (Maki) LeVine roomed upstairs with me in the Kondo's home in their childhood. Their elegance, kindness and fortitude are ever-present—as are Louis, Sophie and Hannah.

In Australia: David Chandler, Robert White, Graeme Smith, Peter O'Mara, Dianne Clifton, Dale Hurst, John Mercer, Yoshimi Matsuda, Tibor Hegedis, Vic Bolger, Johannes Schonborn and Jude Spencer, David Chong, Rob Peterson, Michael Crewdson, the spearheading by Lucinda Knight, and paddock residents at the Classic Morita Centre (CMC) – the late Tsuki, Yuki, Pueblo, Moses, and Pokey.

In the United States: Brian Ogawa and Jon Frew have been steady on the frontline over the twenty years of my Morita practice. Christopher Ives has been a most valued scholar and fellow advocate for the protection of Morita's core lining. I am grateful to the late Richard DeMartino, Nancy Slater, William Cole, Ann Lammers, Thomas Kirsch, Suk Choo Chang, Audrey Glenn, Don Marshall and the University of Puget Sound, Lou Sagatov, Sayon Syprasoeuth, Douglas Ingram, Dey Young, and my two brothers of generous spirit – Thomas LeVine (photographer who restored archive photos of Morita), and Joseph LeVine.

In Cambodia: Bhoomi Kumar and colleagues at Chum Neas Children's Hospital in Takhmau, Lina Huot, and Sotheara Chimm.

In Germany: Walter DMoch psychiatrist and master of *kyūdō*.

In France and Lao PDR: Didier Bertrand as cutting-edge ethno-psychologist and dear friend. I am grateful to Rémi Bordes who advanced 'the meaning of silence' in Morita therapy for anthropologists and psychotherapists in France.

In the United Kingdom: Roger van Zwanenberg, Matt Bickerton and MyTime staff. A special appreciation for Anthony Stadlen and colleagues at the *Inner Circle Seminars* on Daseinsanalysis and Existential Psychotherapy in London – and for their respectful inclusion of Shoma Morita.

In India: Rajesh Kotecha, MD, Chakrapani Ayurveda Clinic and Research Center in Jaipur.

Notes

1　In order to assist the bibliography, Japanese and Chinese names are referenced according to English language protocol; surnames are cited last.
2　This dedication reads as follows: 'For Claske, Lukas and my revered Friends Abbot Kobori Nanrei and Kondo Akihisa.'
3　LeVine and Ogawa formed the *Morita Therapy Foundation* which replaced the *American Institute of Morita Therapy*. In 2015, Global interest led us to collaborate in workshop activities across residential therapy and outpatient counselling, while holding to the integrity of Morita's experiential and paradoxical modality.

PERSONAL PROLOGUE

This book departs from being a standard text on the theory, practice and efficacy of psychotherapy in order to unearth the essence of Morita therapy. In part, what I have written is informed by twenty-five years of practice, and a decade of case-based reflective supervision in Morita therapy. Shoma (Masatake) MORITA, MD (1874–1938) developed a system of therapy that responds to our deep longing to live an authentic life. To this aim, he respected the disquiet that accompanies our imminent non-existence. Each time I administer the four stages of Morita therapy, I stand in awe of its transferability across cultures and ecological settings. Inside or outside Japan, nature is nature – regardless of flora, fauna, or constellations in the night sky.

While moving through the sequenced therapy, clients gain the ability to feel contradictory feelings without panic – a rare experience for those who live with imaginations ruptured by cruelty, dread, and confusion. This body of work on Morita therapy is directed towards therapists and clients who seek a therapy that relaxes symptoms, while simplifying how to live creatively and responsively inside the uncertainty of existence.

Overall, psychotherapists who contact me for supervision grapple with the erosion of complexity and elegance in therapies being endorsed by their professional boards. And while their clients may exit treatment with fewer symptoms, they fall short often of living the lives they can imagine. At the time of this book's publication, I remain the sole Westerner who practices Morita's ecological and phenomenological therapy as he meant. For me, this situation is an isolating privilege since colleagues committed to training and practising as Morita intended are an endangered species.

As I was mentored formally in the tradition of Morita therapy under the supervision of Akihisa Kondo, MD (1911–1999), the pages that follow bring forward this knowledge. Dr Kondo graduated from Jikeikai University School of Medicine in 1949 with a dissertation on the *Comparison of Morita Therapy with the Ideas of Freud and Horney*. His understanding of Morita's unique theory of consciousness and method of therapy came from Morita's disciple, Takehisa Kora, MD (1899–1996), and from his Zen practice.

Prior to his medical degree, Kondo received a law degree from the Imperial University of Tokyo in 1935. Overall, his engagement in psychoanalysis, Zen, and Morita therapy and his capacity to separate and overlap their respective elements was matchless. Noteworthy is the paper Kondo read aloud on April 20, 1952, 'Intuition in Zen Buddhism', at the American Institute for Psychoanalysis interval meeting in New York City. This paper moved to publication months later under the same title in *The American Journal of Psychoanalysis* (1952, Volume XII, p. 10–14) under the editorship of Karen Horney.

> Twenty years ago a Japanese psychiatrist named Dr. Kora introduced a therapy of neurosis, which has been proved to be effective in our country. It is a kind of shortened Zen training.
>
> *(Kondo, 1952, p. 14)*

Kondo told me that following his public presentation the audience engaged him in a lively discussion about Morita therapy. Later that same year, Jacobson and Berenberg published a paper entitled 'Japanese Psychiatry and Psychotherapy' (*American Journal of Psychiatry*, 1952). While this paper is often credited in the literature as being the first introductory paper on Morita therapy in the United States, we can see that Kondo first introduced Morita therapy to an American audience in his spoken paper, which was followed by its publication.

During my research on Morita therapy in the 1970s and 1980s, Kondo's articles and his reverential tone inspired my request for his supervision. I first approached him in 1986 after working in the United States with American Vietnam Veterans and refugees from Cambodia, Laos, and Vietnam. In that era, survivors of genocide and war had few options outside Western medicine and occupational therapy for relief from trauma. Mental health specialists who were meant to care holistically for them often prolonged their suffering. Also, in those days in the United States, people from Southeast Asia were pigeonholed into one culture, despite differences across political history, geography, language, traditional rituals and health practices, religions, and cosmological perceptions. I sought to find a reliable therapy less dependent on language, with methods that assist complete rest of mind and body with less reliance on medication for symptom relief. While searching the globe, I noted consideration being given to indigenous therapies in North America, New Zealand, and Australia but found none grounded in medicine. My persistence was rewarded when I located a treatment indigenous to Japan that met the criteria I had set – Morita therapy.

When I first wrote to Kondo to ask if I could receive his training and supervision, his reply was less than engaging. I wrote again to ask if I could be a Morita patient of his in Tokyo so I might experience, first-hand, the four stages of Morita therapy. In those far-off days, I was living in the Seattle region and our correspondence was penned in ink and posted. Trans-ocean time between letters led to a pleasing, reflective exchange. Eventually, all was agreed. After two years of correspondence, I became a Morita inpatient in the Kondo Clinic in 1990. In a typed letter, Kondo described the relevant details.

December 4, 1989

Dear Dr. LeVine,

First of all I wish to apologize to you for my most impolite delay in answering your letter. The main reason is, since you are seriously considering to experience the pure Morita therapy here in Japan, it was necessary for me to make some alteration in the interior of the room where you are supposed to stay while you are under training, so that you may not feel so uncomfortable as a foreigner during the period of training for about four weeks. As you well know, the therapeutic course of Morita therapy consists of four periods, each period being about a week . . . Miscellaneous items will be discussed with you and decided later after your arrival, however, the following information is provided for your consideration. (1) First Period: A week of secluded life; (2) Second Period: A week of light work; (3) Third Period: A week of heavier work; (4) Fourth Period: A week for spontaneous social activities.

Sincerely yours,

Akihisa Kondo, MD

On January 30, 1990, in a letter that was more intimate in content, Kondo wrote to me about the seclusion stage of Morita therapy.

Dear Peg

. . . Of course, as you well know, the initial period in Morita therapy is meaningful. It is a sort of self-confinement period, in which a patient, separated from any dependent method has to suffer from, struggle with, confront his (her) own anxiety all the way by himself (herself) until he or she becomes exhausted, feels bored with the futile fighting, becomes tired of being idle in rest alone, and begins to feel his (her) spontaneous desire for activities, the expression of life force.

Sincerely yours,

Akihisa Kondo, MD

The very moment I was invited to enter his clinic, I rearranged my life to make that happen. Finally, after years of dissatisfaction with Western psychological practice, through the polite, brazen supervision by Kondo, I found a remarkable pathway into the classic practice of Morita therapy. Our meetings initiated in me a profound potentiality that I am beholden to, and about, to this day.

Personal account of Morita therapy traditional experience

Initially, I had set out to record my own phenomenological experience as a self-study. However, to my surprise the first stage of complete rest had an unexpected impact on me. You see, I entered residential Morita therapy five years after my husband, Stephen, died from brain cancer. By behavioural and cognitive standards, I was seen by friends, family, and colleagues as vibrant and fully engaged in life with our young daughter. I had been in brief therapy, too, the year after Stephen's death in want of reducing the haunting images in my dreams that I knew were related to a lived tragedy.

Through Morita therapy, my artistic ability gained traction. During the fourth day of complete rest, without fully understanding how, I released myself to exhaustion. For years, my body had encased the trauma aftermath in spite of my mind's integrity. The repercussion was a parched, creative core. Rest accompanied sleep; sleep accompanied rest. Until then, I would wake mid-way through dreams of the grotesque. By the end of Stage One, I could evolve my dream, lucidly, and offset the real with the surreal. I felt fortified. This awakening was *not* about me or about acceptance or resolution over my own past. Rather, Morita therapy increased my capacity to experience most fully the depths of longing for that which no longer exists. I worked sculpting material more deliberately when forming figurative images – connecting metal to stone.

In the end, I discovered that emotions were mine to be felt and claimed without a witness. I am secure in this fact. I did not try to make sense of any of the therapeutic experiences intellectually. While difficult to express in words, this wholesome sadness holds a sacred place in my body in its own right as part of my vitality. Perhaps related to this internal shift, the indelible, zombie-esque images of Stephen that infiltrated my dreams diminished dramatically – while his normal body and voice returned, sometimes. To this day, this is so. Herein I experienced, first-hand, the enduring, integrating power of Morita therapy in its original and classic form.

Following my residential experience, I began to explore the use of Morita therapy for clients who live with traumatic aftermath. During our first supervision session, Kondo discussed his observations of me as well as the key criteria that led him to move me from Stage One to Stage Two. Not long after, I entered a formal mentorship so that I might eventually take on clients and test the transcultural capacity of Morita therapy beyond my heuristic study.[1] That which Kondo termed 'pure' Morita therapy, I call 'classic' Morita therapy.

Consciousness and supervision

Overall, Kondo provided training in body and mind synthesis. He recommended that I study and practice *kendo* (the way of the sword) as an art form rather than a competitive or combative experience. Kondo thought one could enhance *peripheral awareness* by refining body-mind training. *Taitoku* means 'body obtain' or 'to know through one's body'. *Taiken* means experiencing with one's whole being. Most

FIGURE 0.2 Takehisa Kora (left), Akihisa Kondo (right), 1992

essential to Morita therapy is the way *taitoku* is drawn upon by therapists themselves when assessing the safety of clients in the seclusion, rest stage of therapy. Through the course of treatment, clients build their *taiken* and *taitoku* capacity.

LeVine: How does taitoku happen?
Kondo: Ah, the alignment of the body-mind in Nature is critical to one's capacity to grasp reality as it is.

After three years of clinical training in Japan and the United States, noting that Kondo travelled twice to the northwest of the USA, Kondo concluded that I was ready to practice with my own clients. This endorsement occurred just around the time I was migrating permanently to Australia. Following this validation, I conducted a single-case study to determine the cultural transferability of the four-stage treatment outside Asia. I administered the therapy to a 34-year-old Australian man in Melbourne, Australia in 1992. In a generous show of support and as reliability assurance, Kondo came to Australia and provided direct supervision during the client's seclusion, rest stage. I presented the outcomes of that first case at the Second International Congress of Morita therapy in Fukuoka, Japan in April of 1993 (LeVine, 1993).

At that time, and throughout my training, Kondo assisted my development of what I call *therapeutic poise*. Principally, the therapist assumes a stance that involves right-mindedness as demonstrated by an accomplished archer in *kyūdō* (Japanese

FIGURE 0.3   Kora (centre), Kondo (R), and LeVine (L), 1992

practice of archery). The archer does not focus the mind on a target or meditate on the moment; rather she or he applies attitude through one fluid body and breath movement.

> rational thinking gives way to feeling and intuition, the thoughts are quieted, and the technique merges with the blood and breath, becoming spontaneous and instinctive. The archer's body remains completely relaxed, yet is never slack . . . In this state it can be said that the arrow exists in the target prior to release . . . This is true, right-minded shooting.
>
> *(Onuma, 1993, pp. 1–3)*

Again, attaining such perceptual acuity is one way of enhancing the therapist's capacity to assess a client's condition in the first and second stages of therapy when there is little to no verbal exchange. In this way, the therapist gets glimpses of a client's demeanour by observing gestures and body movements. How a client picks up a stone and tumbles it in her hands reveals much.[2]

This book acknowledges with deep respect the experiential and clinical wisdom that has been passed on to me. As part of my supervision sequence in Tokyo, biannually I engaged in two three-week supervision intensives. In addition, Kondo travelled to Melbourne, Australia to supervise my Morita practice and reviewed regularly the context, content, and process of therapy. When in Tokyo, he included me in some of his clinical case study sessions held at his clinic. Training approaches

to Morita therapy inside and outside Japan vary – from short-term classroom lectures that lead to a certificate, to case-based intense study with supervision. In this
regard, it is fair to say that Kondo's method of direct case-by-case supervision with
prescribed readings influenced my practice. Being aware that some have referred to
Kondo's orientation as a Zen-Hornian dynamic stream of Morita therapy, it is more
accurate to say that Zen and Horney's analytic reflections informed the complexity of Kondo's practice, but did not lead it. When he administered Morita therapy,
Kondo practised it as Morita had designed, and as Kora had mentored him to do.

Kondo spoke often to me about the marginalisation he endured by Japanese
colleagues after he returned from New York in 1953; this history is described in
Chapter Three. He spoke of a particular turning point that led him to prioritise
publishing in non-Japanese sources.

Peg: Sensei, I notice that you began publishing on Morita therapy and Zen
inside the United States in 1951. After that period, less of your writing
moved forward into Japanese journals.

Kondo: Yes, at that time Japanese psychiatrists and psychoanalysts were most interested in adopting Western ideas, and not so interested in advancing oriental
ideas. You see, after I returned from New York I had submitted a book to
a Japanese publishing company, but another influential person who had
published with this company told the publisher he would not publish again
with them if my work appeared in print. The publisher phoned me in the
lateness of the night to tell me his dilemma. Then and there I made my
decision to write for an American audience on Morita therapy . . . much as
Suzuki was doing in the United States with Zen at that time.

(Kondo and LeVine, February 1, 1998, audiotaped
discussion, Kondo clinic, Tokyo)

Retrospectively, I wish I had inquired more and documented better the inclusion-
exclusion dynamics between psychiatrists in Japan that Kondo endured after New
York. I recall our train trip in November 1991 from Tokyo to Kyoto to attend an annual
Morita Therapy Congress. Just before entering Kyoto station, Kondo announced to
me that this was to be the last time he would attend a conference by the *Japanese
Society for Morita Therapy*. He asked me to continue to attend as a placeholder for him.
During our long discussion, I came to understand his predicament and decision; he
encouraged me to step away from debates on the modernisation of Morita therapy
and to just practice, record, and train professionals in the traditional method. (In 2017,
I formally withdrew from the Japanese Society for Morita Therapy to concentrate
exclusively on the classic method).

In 1997, Kondo and I generated guidelines for training that are now in use at the
Classic Morita Centre (*CMC*) in Australia. After Kondo sensei's death in 1999, I came
to believe that few existed who would safeguard Morita's original method and natural
context for therapy. Then, in 2012, just when I thought this manuscript was complete,
I received an email from filmmaker, Go Nonaka, who learned of Ms Seto. She was

FIGURE 0.4 Yukiko Seto (1914–2012)

(Photo by LeVine, 2012)

the life long attendant in Morita's home in Komagome. She assisted the family as well as Morita's patients.[3] At ninety-eight years of age, Ms Yukiko Seto (1914–2012) agreed to be interviewed and filmed in her home in Tokyo on February 26, 2012. For this I am grateful to the most sensitive arrangements by Go, her attendants, and the presence of Naoki Watanabe to assist translation.

We conversed for nearly five hours, including an outing to a restaurant near her home. Ms Seto told me that she read Morita's book in a library when she was just entering high school, and later acquired her own copy. In fact, she read aloud a passage from Morita's book that she kept near her bedside. She detailed Morita's descriptions of *shinkeishitsu* (anxiety-based disorder) and how his writing assisted her health and sense of determination to meet him. Until reading Morita, she considered herself a misfit. Soon she could appreciate her sensitive nature and out-spokenness as a girl. She told me how she had written to Dr Morita on numerous occasions because she wanted to become his patient initially in order to be cured of her panic attacks. Ms Seto confided in me about her tragic childhood and health condition, which I was informed later led to the amputation of her leg at a young age. At that time in history, she endured the cultural fact that she would most likely not marry due to this disability – a resignation that explains, in part, the meaningful contact provided by Morita, his family, and patients over the course of her life. Shortly after meeting, Morita invited Ms Seto to live in his home and assist his wife and son in daily activities, including some of Morita's administrative and practice tasks. She found that his Tokyo, natural setting gave her a sense of 'making a new start'. Following the death of Morita's wife, Ms Seto became Shoma Morita's carer and assistant until the day he died.

Ms Seto told me personal and unique stories about Morita and his practice that I have woven into this book. Her comments were refreshing and descriptive rather than clinical. She portrayed Morita as an original thinker, and as a kind and discerning human being. I knew from discussions with Kora and Kondo that Morita studied and practised kendo. Ms Seto confirmed this fact. I learned from her that Morita had practised kendo in his youth. For his clinic, he trained a pet monkey and adopted two more monkeys that he engaged strategically with his patients. I was unable to determine fully whether Morita chose monkeys because they hold a significant place in Zen art and lore; I follow this Zen thread in the second chapter. Similarly, Morita engaged in bonsai art, and often placed a bonsai tree outside a patient's door. Ms Seto told me, 'Morita let patients recover by living in an ordinary place, day in and day out, until their worries were in the past. He found silent ways for patients to feel kind-heartedness. For me, this was a rare experience.'

I inquired further about Morita's engagement in Zen, and listened for her descriptions rather than her opinions in this matter. Ms Seto said that Morita called a Zen Buddhist priest to visit his home and tend to his wife's funeral rites in 1935. Overall, the 1930s was a heart-wrenching period for Morita with the death of his brother, son, and wife. It was a time when Morita became weak and frail. She told me how Morita did not elevate one activity over another; tidying a drawer, and grooming a monkey were as essential as writing and publishing to him.

She gave me a copy of her favourite photograph of Morita; I later obtained permission to copy and publish the original photo from the Mishima Morita Hospital Archive Library. This image is presented as the first plate for this book. I agree with Ms Seto that this image captures Morita's avant-garde style from around 1935. I am aware through my direct contact with Ms Seto that Morita treated women equal to men in his practice; he did not attribute any particular illnesses to women such as hysteria, which for the 1920s and 1930s was refreshingly unusual. As far as I know, Ms Seto was the last surviving person who knew Shoma Morita in his private and professional life. She died on June 20, 2012 – not long after I met her.

Following that mighty day with Ms Seto, my felt sense of Morita's tie to Zen resurfaced and badgered me. I reflected on whether I should include Zen in the title of this book. I remained ambivalent due to the inferential evidence I was uncovering. At that time, too, I was supervising the phenomenological study by a PhD student who was investigating the essence of Zen in Morita therapy (Mercer, 2015). Reliable evidence had yet to be gathered. I returned to others' writings on the matter and sought English translation of 'Morita and Zen' (p. 166) from a small section in Akichika Nomura's (disciple of Morita) *Critical Biography of Shoma Morita* (1974). I remained hesitant in forming a conclusion even when keeping abreast of John Mercer's research.

Once again, just when I thought this book was publication ready, Go Nonaka appeared in his uncanny way just after I gave a paper on consciousness at an annual 2015 Morita Therapy congress in Tokushima.

At that time, I had intended to make a solo walk on more of the 88-temple circuit on the Shikōku Pilgrimage. However, not long after my arrival in Japan, Go pressed me to find Morita's house on Shikōku Island as it is under threat to be torn down and he believed I would discover something there. How could I not go? With the kind mapping by him and two other Japanese colleagues, Naoki Watanabe and Keiko Miyasaka, I set out by train to Kōchi from Tokushima, which lies south on the island. I arrived on October 17, 2015 and made my way to Morita's family grave, birth town, and home place where he had practised. (Images of his house and floor plan are in Chapter Three.)

I remain moved. For me, this erosion of Morita's estate was tantamount to bulldozing the Museum of Sigmund Freud at the distinguished *Berggasse 19* in Vienna where he lived from 1891 to 1938. Unmistakably, an international campaign would be mounted to preserve Freud's place. While standing in Morita's eroding gardens, I pondered deeply the depth of European and urban-centrism that drives theories and mental health practices. I offer my field notes from this Morita pilgrimage as visceral evidence of Zen.

Field notes from Morita's home in Kōchi (LeVine, 2015)

Shikōku Island, Kōchi (October 17, 2015). *Dry air hits mountains; shadow spotted garden. Wall of stone in pieces. Engraved boulder shows the front gate. Overhead, Black bird's wings clack like wood. Brown leaves fill spaces between what once was. I squeeze inside the Western wall to the front door. The wooden gate holds the garden of the main house. A cut-out oblong window offers a view for my face and camera. I see into Morita's inner garden – into HIS GARDEN. I hear my voice. 'Kare sansui. The answer has always been here.' Morita's inner garden struts off the wooden veranda – remnants of this Zen stone riverbed garden. Kare sansui – OVERGROWN ZEN is alive. Finally I conclude unwaveringly. Nature and Zen nourished Morita and his therapy.*

FIGURE 0.5   Stone garden at Morita's house in Kōchi, 2015

(Photo by LeVine)

> Shikōku Island, Kōchi (October 19, 2015). *I ponder recent history I came to learn on this trip. If Morita had lived beyond 1938, how would he have made sense of suffering inside Kōchi on July 3, 1945? This was the day the United States sent 129 aircraft to bomb and flatten nearly 50% of this city – his community. Just one month later came Hiroshima and then Nagasaki – whereupon Kōchi receded from global memory. So what will become of Morita's practice site that sits in this forgotten city?*

I return to contemplate Kondo's Zen garden and the presence this gave to my supervision. We met often with his doors open to that garden. Had it not been for him, I would not have been trained in the pure Morita method inside or outside Japan. Professionally, Kondo defied the male hierarchy that remains embedded in Morita therapy organisations in Japan, Zen practice, and academia – alongside many of our psychotherapeutic modalities that are considered to be evidence-based. I am clear that his relationship to Karen Horney and his spirited wife and artist, Toshiko Kondo, shaped his broadminded standpoint.

No longer can I ponder aloud with 'Aki' Kondo on the essential Nature of Morita therapy, or discuss our respective cases, and therapeutic context and process. I still call upon sounds and images from his mentorship: the elegant pause, the sound of 'ahh, I see' – followed often by the stroke of one word on paper – with a profundity that runs as deep as the indigo ink that filled his fountain pen.

FIGURE 0.6   Akihisa Kondo (1911–1999)

Notes

1 My heuristic account is published in Japanese with notes on Morita's use for treatment of trauma (LeVine, 1991).
2 Kondo and I completed the foundational guidelines for Morita therapy practice, training, supervision, and research in 1997. These core standards guide the activities at the *Classic Morita Centre (CMC)*.
3 This stirring interview is credited to the kind arrangements by film artist and producer, Go Nonaka, the generous nature of Dr Naoki Watanabe, who travelled to Tokyo to provide the first two hours of translation, and camera donation by Australian film and photo artist, Tibor Hegedis. I am grateful to Ms Seto's aides – Reiko Ura and Kumiko Kobayashi.

INTRODUCTION

Morita therapy is perhaps the only reliable mental health treatment in the world designed deliberately to bring clients inside the rhythm of our natural environment. To move a client to gawk at a sliver of the moon suspended somehow, somewhere above in blackness that is blacker than when the moon is full – stirs the therapeutic exchange for a Morita therapist.

An overriding aim of this book is to unearth the essence of Morita therapy and the range of human experience it addresses. Shoma Morita (1874–1938) designed the therapeutic milieu deliberately to advance his paradoxical and experiential method of therapy. These pages pull Morita's practice back to its bare bones to illustrate the eco-biopsychosocial stimuli that advance wellness. A comprehensive study of the history, phenomenological theory and experiential nature of Morita therapy is meant to overshadow discussions on its efficacy. By detailing the fundamentals of this distinctive therapy, researchers, practitioners, and consumers will be better able to discern what Morita is and is not.

This century is critical to the preservation of Morita therapy. As violence and discrimination displace people across the globe and natural disasters generate environmental refugees, safe therapeutic harbours for whole person care are needed. Morita never intended a 'psycho' therapy *per se*. He did not set out to cure anyone's mind. Instead, he gave clients a restorative and dignifying place to dwell during therapy; in this way he assisted human rights in psychiatry.

Disconcertingly, some clinicians and researchers in various countries are welding bits and pieces of Morita's practice on to cognitive, behavioural, and mindful counselling modalities. While paradoxical constructs embedded in Morita therapy are useful in counselling, such as withdrawing symptom focus while fostering a practical attitude for ordinary daily life – they are just borrowed bits. In the current discourse on evidence-based research, internal validity is weakened each time Morita's treatment formula is deconstructed. In this regard, a key question begs to be asked. How far can Morita's progressive, ecological, and experiential-based therapy be parcelled or stretched – across inpatient and outpatient settings – before his sophisticated principles, methods, and use of natural space lose credibility, internal validity, and therapeutic capacity?[1] In order to protect the internal validity and integrity of Morita therapy, I have coined the phrase 'classic Morita therapy' so that Morita's original progressive, experiential treatment and use of natural space is no longer misappropriated, his therapy outcomes are not sold short, and clients get a chance for whole person restoration.

The uniqueness of Morita's experiential perspective is deservedly woven and finely rewoven throughout this book. The repetition is intended so that the reader keeps returning to the significance of Morita's basic principles. For example, his theory of emotions grounds his practice. For Morita, emotions are natural occurrences rather than symptoms of a so-called mental illness. Treatments aimed at rationalising emotions rarely honour our existential plight or show clients how to live safely inside our hardy-fragile human condition. We feel feelings according to our lived history. In this regard, it makes sense that the more challenging the experience, the more contradictory the feelings. A child or adult victim of violence, for instance, can feel sad, mad, and glad simultaneously. Morita therapy provides the therapist expertise to orchestrate structured and unstructured time, silence and engagement, and the safety of contained and open space for clients to experience all such feelings without passing judgement. In this way, feelings run their natural course and clients' worry over their own suffering eases. Therapeutic time is needed for this process and the therapist has a duty of care to monitor clients' distractibility and restructure therapy accordingly.

Morita shares the human justice perspective advanced by psychiatrist Thomas Szasz (1920–2012) in the *Myth of Mental Illness* (1961). Like Morita, Szasz defied the conventional psychiatry of his time. Szasz challenged the validity of the term 'mental' illness and its assignment to patients, which often determines the quality of their treatment. Ironically, he stood behind medical science by differentiating the human brain from its mental-emotional complex (Stadlen, 2013). For him, mental illness is a metaphor for feelings, behaviours, and/or beliefs judged to be unsound by institutional or social convention.

I gained greater understanding about the place of convention in Morita's life after seeing his signatures on calligraphies at the archival library at Mishima Morita Hospital in Japan. Morita signed some with the nickname he gave himself, *Keigai,* which means 'existing beyond the frame' or living outside the borders of convention.

Consciousness, nature and therapeutic agency

By setting anthropocentric assumptions to one side, Morita formulated a theory of consciousness that extends in all directions – peripheral consciousness. Literally, *mushojūshin* (無所住心) means 'the mind that does not dwell anywhere' (see Glossary). Most deeply, the span of Morita's consciousness resonates with indigenous perspectives globally.[2] In accordance with a justice perspective, by giving primary therapeutic agency to the ecological domain, Morita's formulation of conscious-ness releases clients from being solely responsible for their disorder. In keeping with Morita's ecological thrust, throughout this book nature is given an uppercase N when signifying the ever-present ecological life forces that exist with or without human presence. As we shall see in Chapters Two and Three, this view of Nature coincides with Zen. By contrast, references to the character (true nature) of a thing, phenomenon or person are placed in lower case, such as the nature of one's creative self, or the nature of time, or the curious nature of a cat or child.

Morita's consciousness theory privileges the creative easement that sits between marvel and doubt; such a view coincides with existential and psychodynamic prem-ises (Cooper, 2002). Morita agreed with the analytic notion that dynamic tensions in human relationships are essential to resourceful human existence. And like Freud, Morita allowed for what Calhoun (2004) has called 'accidental wisdom' inside the therapy context. Morita, however, brought the cosmological realm forward into his therapeutic field in ways that affirmed serendipitous moments as key therapeutic moments.

Existential psychotherapists, psychoanalysts, and classic Morita therapists address the suffering that is rooted in human existence. How do we live inside the dynamic, creative tension of feeling significant and insignificant, simultaneously? As this book will reveal, Morita designed his four successive stages to equalise the tension between the human desire for life and natural fear of non-existence. Herein, his theory of consciousness is behind the dynamic force that runs through the therapy process.

The next chapter discusses the crucial reasons for beginning therapy with rest and minimal stimulation. Throughout all the stages, Morita never withdrew his engaging presence, nutritional and varied food, animal and plant contact, and creative and purposeful social activity. Therapy gradually increases clients' embodiment of life force and body knowing (*taitoku*) by engaging them directly in Nature. Essentially, the sequenced therapy is designed to integrate one's soulful being (*kokoro*).[3]

Across the chapters, the reader is invited to dwell in the uniqueness of Morita and his therapy and to ponder it deeply. In a parallel way, Morita therapists stimu-late and reinforce a client's interest about the natural world. They carefully craft the use of paradox to increase clients' curiosity about the natural world of something like an oak. How is it that an oak tree is the last to drop its leaves in autumn? How does a small animal crack open an acorn? There and there they are refreshed. Such interventions require therapists to notice their surrounds and to notice what stimuli captivate clients' attention, naturally. There lies the evidence of the uniqueness of the client. Again for such capacity the therapist needs lots of training.

I recall a client who worried increasingly that her sleep was erratic before enter-ing the first rest stage of Morita Therapy. She expected sound sleep in spite of poor nutrition, absence of aerobic activity, and daily caffeine and alcohol intake. Rather than challenge her thinking on day one of rest, the therapist asked her to describe the colour and shape of food on her breakfast tray. Before leaving the room the therapist asked her to listen intently to the first bird song as light appears in the morning window and said that he would be inquiring about the bird's call at next morning's breakfast. When the time came, the client smiled and said she heard a raven first and then a magpie. By the end of week one, her waking and sleeping followed daylight night-dark patterns in the absence of coffee, wine and artificial light. She responded to the environment with refined adaptation. In stage two, she noticed an empty water bowl for an animal and filled it spontaneously.

> After the rest stage, I direct therapy so my patients experience the world through their senses – hear a broom sweep dried leaves, smell the damp dirt. These moments are recovering moments.
>
> *(Kondo in personal conversation, 1992)*

The closing chapter centres on the use of Morita therapy for people who have endured cruelty and trauma. All too often, in the fallout from trauma people's cycles are disrupted in waking, resting, sleeping, eating, socialising, exercising, playing, and working. Without offering purposeful rest of mind and body at the start of therapy, regaining balance of vital biorhythms is unlikely. Experiencing rest in a simple, safe place is beneficial for those with childhood trauma. At the end of Stage Two, many of my clients report that they have started to use their imagination in practical ways. It is as if their imaginations are no longer tainted by dread. And as an added feature, they can dare to imagine a world that existed before traumatic events compromised their childhood innocence.

Morita therapists do not teach or train the client in mindful focusing, meditation, or other techniques. It cannot be stressed enough that the experience of moving progressively through the four stages of therapy (as orchestrated by the therapist's clinical observations) prompts all the senses to engage in the aesthetics of day-to-day life.

A whiff of cinnamon sprinkled on toast can be a sensational delight.

Increasing clients' aesthetic awareness in their ordinary daily encounters is a goal of therapy. In this way, the persuasions of *wabi-sabi* embedded in the objects and spiritism of Japanese tea ceremony run through Morita therapy. '*Wabi-sabi* is a beauty in things imperfect, impermanent, and incomplete. It is a beauty of things modest and humble. It is a beauty of things unconventional' (Koren, 2008, p. 7). In particular, *wabi-sabi* is comprised of the metaphysical realm (wabi) and the material domain (sabi) and is often associated with Zen. Emptiness is like the space to be filled in an earthen teacup; space holds possibilities: 'the universe is in constant motion toward or away from potential' (Koren, 2008, p. 45). Undoubtedly, Morita's therapeutic distinctiveness holds a unique place inside the circle of key historical figures in the field of psychological medicine.

The rise and fall of Zen, Morita therapy, and Karen Horney's analysis

A collage of Zen networks resurfaced when I was engaged in archival research in Japan between 2013 and 2015. I returned often to the library of Kondo sensei that his widow, Toshiko Kondo, has preserved. The musty trace of Kondo's incense was moving for me as I reread his special collection of books, many of them autographed by such eminent figures as Erich Fromm (1951, 1959), D.T. Suzuki, Rollo May, Paul Tillich, R.H. Blyth, Richard DeMartino, Carl Rogers, and other humanistic scholars.

In those concentrated times, I traced several historical factors that have marked Morita's rise and fall internationally. As detailed in Chapter Two, Akihisa Kondo was supervised directly by Karen Horney, MD in New York in the early 1950s in her method of psychoanalysis. Through their association, Horney gained a keen interest in Buddhist thought (Horney, 1949, 1950, 1952). Over time, she gained the capacity to distinguish Zen from Buddhism (with no Buddha image to revere) through her discussions with Kondo in New York and later in Japan when she was introduced to Morita therapy more formally. When she visited Kyoto, along with Daisetz Teitaro (D.T.) Suzuki and Kondo she spoke with Genyu Usa at the hospital he founded (Sansei hospital). Usa and Morita had been friends and colleagues and Morita often stayed in a certain room at his hospital when he visited. According to Kondo, Suzuki formed an interest in Morita through his associations with Horney and her inquiries about Morita practice. It was not until Suzuki saw Morita's calligraphies at Usa's hospital when visiting with Horney that he approached Kondo to discuss Morita and Zen, specifically (personal taped conversation with Kondo, 1994).

By the end of her Japan trip, Horney's curiosity about Morita therapy peaked. And yet, she did not have enough life time to integrate Morita and her own psychoanalytic ideas about therapy and 'real self'. She died of cancer in 1952. After her death, Suzuki sought conversations with Kondo about Morita and Zen. Disappointingly, he did not pursue his Morita interests once he returned to the United States (personal correspondence, Kondo and LeVine, 1994).

As a note for historical clarification, Kendra Smith (1981) and Miura and Usa (1970) claim that Karen Horney developed an interest in Morita therapy in Japan in 1952 through her associations with Suzuki. Other scholars have written about her interests in Buddhism and spirituality from a Western perspective, while not distinguishing her grasp of Zen and related research on Morita (Walborn, 2014). In fact, Kondo told me about his experience of being interviewed by Susan Quinn who wrote the biography of Karen Horney (Quinn, 1988). He withheld giving her his personal photos that appear in this book as he re-experienced the American fascination with Suzuki that continues to overshadow his role in Karen's professional and personal life. After all, Akihisa Kondo and Karen Horney were both psychiatrists and analysts who continued to refine their analyses so that their patients could experience their authentic nature.

The fact is that Horney developed a philosophical interest in Buddhism and Zen through Suzuki. Akihisa Kondo introduced her to Morita therapy and the relevance of Zen for psychotherapy. Their discussions were focused on Morita, Zen, and psychoanalysis rather than Buddhism and psychoanalysis. The distinction is made in Chapter Two. Given Horney's death, Kondo and Horney could not fulfil their desire to publish together on this topic. In addition, scholars at the American Institute of Psychoanalysis moved away from discussing Horney's remarks on psychoanalysis, Zen, and Morita; outside contributions by Kondo, seminars and papers on the topic ceased.

FIGURE 0.7 The room in Kyoto where Morita stayed when visiting his friend, Genyu Usa

(Le Vine, 2012)

The essential environmental surrounds of Morita therapy

Morita's four progressive stages are secured by the places where they occur. Throughout therapy, the natural setting is omnipresent and its essentiality coincides with research on the physiological health benefits of exposure to restorative, green environments (Heerwagen and Orians, 1993; Suzuki, 2007; Frumkin, 2001). Many writers agree that in the Japanese practice of *shinrin-yoku* (forest communing), nature and natural settings can enhance cognitive functioning, boost the immune system, and reduce blood pressure, heart rate, and levels of cortisol.[4] The environmental surrounds of Morita therapy assist homeostasis in a client as much as the monitored rest without cognitive reframing, or the purposeful activities that progress from fine motor to gross-motor. It is in the spaciousness of a garden that clients place descriptive observations of the natural environment in their diaries. Akin to the *biophilia hypothesis* put forth by Edward Osborne Wilson in 1984 (Wilson, 1984; Heerwagen and Orians, 1993), Morita built his practice on the premise that an inherent emotional affiliation exists between humans and other living organisms. Morita therapy increases one's alertness to the breadth of aliveness that runs through natural habitats. In this way, allegiance is awakened to Nature regardless of culture (Hakeda, 1967; Kitanishi, 2015; Roszak, 1992).

The natural desire for life or *sei no yokubō* is stimulated in therapy. The literal meaning for *sei no yokubō* is the 'innate human desire to preserve the self', which is derived from 生の欲望. This is often represented as the desire for life in Morita discussions in English-speaking countries. However, emphasis is to be placed on the *natural* desire for life that is linked to our natural fear of non-existence and death.

Anxiety occurs when the even tension between natural desire and natural fear are out of balance. Morita therapy evens that tension.

Placing Morita justly in the history of psychological medicine

To date, ethnocentric points of view have confined Morita and prevented him from gaining the recognition held by his European and American contemporaries, including William James, Sigmund Freud, Wilfred Bion, Melanie Klein, Wilhelm Reich, Maria Montessori, Jean Charcot, Jacob Levy Moreno, Carl Rogers, G. Ivanovitch Gurdjieff, and Alfred Adler. To a certain extent, the cultural hegemony of West over East has been operating since Morita's days and long before Morita. In many parts, Westerners attribute an exotic or esoteric position to Eastern practices; similarly, many in Japan have come to believe the West offers therapies with the most reliable power, as seen by Japanese advocates of psychoanalysis and cognitive behavioural therapies.

But where would Morita therapy be today if the status quo were reversed?

Envision, if you will, that Japan's context-based language is the most prestigious in the world – akin to English in today's international marketplace. Likewise, make commonplace the Japanese calendar of sacred holidays with all the customary ancestral obligations and rituals. Honour Obon (season of the deceased) above Christmas, Hanukkah, and Ramadan. Elevate the status of Japanese psychiatric nomenclature when designing research that informs 'evidence-based' outcomes. Now give the anxiety disorders listed in the Diagnostic and Statistical Manual (American Psychiatric Association, 2013) subordinate status to Japan's classification of anxiety and phobic disorders. Embrace Morita's theories of peripheral consciousness and *mushojūshin* with as much diligence as theories on the unconscious. Train psychology, counselling, social work, and medical students in the art of assuming the *fumon* position.[5] Advance therapists in the use of silence as strategically as any verbal intervention. Revise cognitive restructuring methods to include the wisdom encased in complex emotion. Use paradoxical methods that strengthen the power of emotion, intuition, and experience. Shift the nuanced understanding of repression to *akirame*.[6] Reconceptualise community mental health by designing health clinics where patients engage collectively in sensate activities, such as planting vegetables, smelling herbs, caring for small animals, cooking healthful meals, watching bird flight patterns, painting, sculpting, and sanding wood. All in all, though not so transparent, ethnocentrism has run right through mental health research and practice since the turn of the last century.

Cultural bias pervades analyses of Morita therapy by many North American and European scholars. As presented in Chapter Two, I uncovered archival files of Fritz Perls (key founder of Gestalt therapy) in 2009 that refer to his trip to Kyoto in 1962. Among the documents were personal diaries that he penned when he was an inpatient at a Morita hospital. No biographer or Perls himself has written on his voluntary admission to a Morita therapy hospital in hope of overcoming his tobacco dependency. His abrupt cessation of treatment is described in Chapter Two.

More recently, Emmett Velten (2007) outlined Morita's notion of acceptance when making comparisons to Acceptance and Commitment therapy.[7]

> And Morita sounded very much like Ellis in saying: The best approach to Buddha or God is to remain obedient to the laws of nature, to accept the nature of causality, and to accept and appreciate one's own and another person's situation.
>
> *(Velten, 2007, p. 89)*

Acceptance as depicted here is not a goal in Morita therapy, in the Western sense of this term. Time and again, comparative analyses misplace time (King, 1968). For instance, might it be that Albert Ellis sounds a bit like Morita, since Morita's theory and practice were well underway when Ellis was a boy? In fact, Morita did not advocate instructing his patients to change their thinking. Action is the natural by-product of going through the stages. The momentum of the therapeutic stages is like choreographed movements in dance. Those who brand Morita therapy as a neo-cognitive behavioural therapy fail to understand this essential aspect. As stated throughout this book, Morita therapists are trained to orchestrate the four periods of therapy so that patterns of eating, sleeping, resting, imagining, thinking, emoting, playing, and working are recalibrated for health at an even natural pace.

As a way of engaging the reader in knowledge I acquired under Kondo sensei's supervision, excerpts from our personal conversations and letters are sprinkled throughout this book. It is my desire that the reader gain a sense of participation in a process that has directed my knowledge about consciousness, authentic self, Zen, and Morita therapy. The following exchange shows the flavour of our conversations.

Le Vine: What are ways a therapist fosters life force in a client?
Kondo: Notice what 'moves' your client.

This book has been born out of reflections on *just* therapy – in both senses of the word – and aims to centralise Morita therapy in the global field of psychotherapy. Morita's translated quotes are interspersed as excerpts from *Morita Therapy and the True Nature of Anxiety-based Disorders, Shinkeitshitsu* (Morita, 1928/1998), translated by Akihisa Kondo. As editor of this book, I wrote the *Glossary of Morita Terms*, which has been expanded for this manuscript.[8]

The reclusive tone that runs through case material is meant to reveal to the reader the egolessness that Morita brought to his therapy. The authenticity of Morita therapy rests in the width and depth of his consciousness system, the inclusion of context in case formulation, and the advancement of his ecological setting as a therapeutic domain.

Notes

1 It is advised that consumers research the authenticity and safety of practices at Morita therapy centres globally before seeking training or treatment.
2 Gausset, Kenrick, and Gibb (2011) detail the complexities in human rights law and anthropology on use of the terms indigenous and autochthōnous. Morita's views are in accordance with autochthōnous views on self – from whence self *(*auto) sprang from earth (chthōn).
3 *Kokoro* is sometimes rendered as heart-mind or body-mind-spirit. Herein, 'embodied spirit' is the omnipresent life force, not a spiritual or religious concept.
4 See especially Berto, 2005; Berman, Jonides, and Kaplan, 2008; Kaplan, Kaplan, and Ryan, 1998; Gladwell et al., 2012.
5 The Morita therapist is trained to assume a *fumon* presence with clients during therapy by keeping a cool-warm and aloof-available stance, particularly when clients seek a witness to their suffering. See *Fumon* in the Morita Glossary of Terms.
6 *Akirame* is the process of giving up when life is tough, which is often the consequence for those who have an 'under-developed will'. One gets caught in a cycle of wanting to go down hill, or giving up because one feels defeated; over time, frustration increases as one's access to and embodiment of life force is dashed.
7 See Chapter 7 in Velton (2007): *Hard Facts for ACT to Follow: Morita Therapy, General Semantics, Person-Centered Therapy, Fixed-Role Therapy, Cognitive Therapy, Values Clarification, Reality Therapy, Multimodal Therapy, and – yes, of course – Rational Emotive Behavior Therapy.*
8 Morita, S. (1998, translation of his 1928 publication). Kondo, A. (Trans), LeVine (Editor). *True Nature of Anxiety-based Disorders: Shinkeishitsu.* State University of New York Press, New York. (The reference 1928/1998 indicates this 1998 edited translation of the 1928 manuscript).

1

CLASSIC MORITA THERAPY INSIDE AND OUTSIDE JAPAN

Morita's progressive, staged therapy moves clients seamlessly through sequenced activities that engage them in the animate and inanimate domain. This sequenced therapy is perhaps the foremost *ecological-based therapy* in existence and includes a theory of consciousness that widens the therapeutic alliance to include Nature. Herein lies the power of the rural or garden therapy setting that includes and extends the human-centric domain.

Meiji backdrop to Morita's life and therapy

The era in which Morita theorised and practised in Japan (*Meiji Restoration*, 1867–1868) was subject to unique pressures; he was most influenced by the *Meiji period* (1868–1912). Herein, intellectual and social constraints were placed on Japanese people to adopt Western sciences, philosophies, and religions; all citizens were expected to assume State Shintoism and worship the emperor. With stresses coinciding with the aftermath of World War I, an avant-garde (*zen'ei*) movement was ripe for taking place in Japan in the 1920s alongside an artists' movement known as MAVO.[1] Believing in social transformation through art, 'They aimed to reestablish a connection they felt had been broken in the Meiji period (1868–1912), with the codification of autonomous "fine art" based on the Western model . . . Mavo artists chose to critique state and society as outsiders' (Weisenfeld, 2001, pp. 2–3).

An historian of Japan, Godart writes,

> Although Buddhism is now generally regarded as a religion, for Meiji Buddhists and philosophers this was not self-evident, because the word 'religion' was closely associated with Christianity in this period . . . Buddhism's foreign origin became problematic in this period of national unification. In the

FIGURE 1.1   MORITA, Shoma, approximately 1932

With permission from Mishima Morita Hospital, Morita archives

creation of a national ideology, centered around the emperor and justified by nativist myths, this foreign religion was interpreted as an anomaly in Japanese society.

(Godart, 2004, p. 2)

Similar to Morita in complexity and perceptiveness was Enryō Inoue (1858–1919), an influential writer in Morita's time.[2] Inoue chose to reclassify Buddhism as a modern philosophy so that it could be repositioned socially, advanced publicly, and aligned with science. In the Meiji period, the government forced separation between Shintoism and Buddhism. Perhaps as a show of European union, Inoue compared Zen to the philosophy put forth in Germany by Arthur Schopenhauer (1788–1860). Schopenhauer advocated preserving the ethical, artistic, and aesthetic forms of practice by arguing that the universe functions according to its own laws void of reason (Josephson, 2006). Relatedly, Zen-based art could be justified for the way it captured Nature in aesthetic form through clay, stone, paint, and ink.

Overall, the beginning of the Meiji period was a bleak time as temples were being closed or destroyed, objects of Buddhist worship were ruined, and monks and nuns were disrobed. One could ponder how the government participated in *ritualcide* through their enacted policies, too (LeVine, 2010). Inoue was under pressure to partition off Buddhist religion into 'Buddhist thought' just as Morita was cornered to present politically neutral ideas.[3] Morita's allegorical use of Zen, whether strategic or not, would have protected him from criticism. Similarly, Inoue persisted in formalising 'Buddhist philosophy' as a religion-oriented philosophy, while separating it from Christianity as a religion based on a 'doctrine of creation'. Similarly, as a Japanese scholar of psychological medicine, Morita persevered in maintaining a wider view of consciousness that involved the mind but was not bound to it.

This was the socio-political backdrop from which Morita formulated his less than conventional therapy. From a more intimate domain, Morita's personal experiences would have interacted with his philosophy on living according to Nature. During the time he was formulating his therapy, he endured the death of his brother, Tokuya, who died at the beginning of the Russo-Japanese war (February 1904 to September 1905). In his personal diaries, Morita wrote about his excursion to China by ship not long after his brother's death in April 1905. He sketched images of his journey and contemplated the Manchuria incident with political and existential persuasion (diaries examined at the Mishima Morita Hospital, Morita Archive Library, July, 2016).

Years later in 1911, Morita's son Shoichiro was born. Morita and his wife suffered tremendously when their only child, Shoichiro, died of a respiratory illness at the age of twenty. Morita and his wife kept their son's ashes for two years before bringing them to Kōchi, their family homestead (dialogue from Fumio Hatano via Go Nonaka).

After his son's death, Morita made arrangements with his sister and her husband to adopt their third son of four children so that he might have an heir. (His sister had married into the Tahara family.) Hidetoshi Tahara was born in 1919 and adopted as Hidetoshi Morita by Morita in 1935. He went on to medical school and became a psychiatrist in his own right. He directed the Mishima Morita Hospital (Mishima, Shizoku Prefecture, Japan) until his death in 1988. Shoma Morita's personal and professional artifacts, family photo albums, and personal diaries are archived and protected at Mishima Morita Hospital.

森田正一郎 十四才頃、

FIGURE 1.2 School photo of Morita's son at age 14

With permission from Mishima Morita Hospital, Morita Archives, 2016

In this sequence of tender experiences, Morita survived the death of his wife, Hisai in 1935. According to his diaries held at Mishima Morita hospital archives, he set her ashes to rest on June 10, 1937 according to ritual custom two years after her death (correspondence with Go Nonaka). As recounted by Morita's personal attendant Ms Seto, Morita called a Zen priest to perform the home services and ceremonial rites for his wife across the sequenced years of Japanese death rituals (interview, 2012).

Throughout my study into Morita's life and through my training and practice of his therapy, Morita's sensitivity to the natural landscape and rhythms of life has been overriding. While thumbing through Morita's diaries that were written during his youth, I saw how he used English language to capture remarkable beats of Nature (Mishima Morita Hospital Archives). The passage that I found in Morita's personal diaries at Mishima Morita Hospital (Morita archives) reveals Morita's artful sense-ability; his words pound out a rhythm in nature, 'rain bisha bisha'.

Foundations of Morita therapy

From the perspective of Morita, therapy space is meant to hold life dear and to honour suffering, simultaneously. Over time a person moves naturally from an unnatural to a natural state, rather than an abnormal to normal state (LeVine, 1994). Initially Morita designed his therapy to treat those diagnosed with *shinkeitshitsu*. This Japanese condition of anxiety emanates from excessive thinking whereupon clients over-focus attention on their physical and emotional discomfort and set their life course to get rid of distress at all cost.[4] Those with *shinkeishitsu* tend to: (1) judge and classify natural emotions and interpret anger and sadness as negative, and happiness as positive; (2) exert intellectual control over emotional experiences; (3) deny the cycles and natural changes of human nature (physical, emotional, and psychological); (4) panic about panic; (5) over-focus on uncomfortable thoughts, feelings, and body sensations; and (6) neglect and disengage from the animate and inanimate environments at large.[5]

Morita was interested in treating patients diagnosed with neurasthenia, a condition brought about by exhaustion of the nervous system. Symptoms of neurasthenia overlap with those found in depression, anxiety disorders, and post-trauma syndromes (Beard, 1869; Kleinman, 1980; T. Suzuki, 1989; Kitanishi and Kondo, 1994; Kitanishi, 2005).[6] Note that the original Japanese term, *shinkeisuijaku*, most closely represented Beard's description of neurasthenia at that time.[7]

It was after the Second World War that the term neurosis began to replace neurasthenia in Western literature, though neurasthenia continues to be used in Japan, and is part of the International Classification of Diseases by the World Health Organization. Neurasthenia relates to the Chinese culture-specific term, *shenjing shuairuo*, which means 'weakness of nerves'. A disorder linked to neurasthenia in the *Diagnostic and Statistical Manual (DSM-V)* is Undifferentiated Somatoform Disorder. In addition, Selective Mutism, which is regarded often as Kinetic Mutism in Japan, relates to a survival mechanism that shuts out stimuli when one is overwhelmed. Noticeably, in my own Morita practice, I find that neurasthenia describes most accurately symptoms related to a client's overtaxed biological system, particularly in the aftermath of complex traumatic experiences.

As Morita came to understand how symptoms are formed and perpetuated, he reclassified some psychiatric disorders prevalent in the 1920s in Japan. He coined the diagnostic category *paroxysmal neurosis*, which is a condition that resembles contemporary features of Acute Stress Disorder.[8] For Morita therapists, assessment is an on-going process across the four stages. In particular, a client's total immersion in the therapeutic environment is the process that alleviates symptoms over time. Morita differentiated neurasthenia from *shinkeishitsu* based, in part, on clients' character sensitivities. He noted how those diagnosed with *shinkeishitsu* are often self-contained, and are overly sensitive to minute body and emotion changes.[9]

Morita discovered the therapeutic benefits of secluded rest by sheer persistence when attempting to treat a woman who had been placed in a psychiatric hospital for an obsessive disorder, and had been released without improvement. He discovered that she responded, paradoxically, to a period of supervised seclusion. From that observation, he began to experiment with varied forms of rest for body and mind in various environments until he got the right therapeutic recipe for places and methods. He found that his progressive form of therapy in a natural environment was most effective for treating his patients. Fujita (1986, p. 24) comments as follows:

> The patient came to Morita, who tried hypnosis, persuasive techniques and regulation of daily activities, without success. Since Morita had exhausted his therapeutic resources, he left the patient alone for a while. Believing that he had abandoned her case as hopeless, the patient initially experienced severe distress and despair. However, this reaction was followed by an experience of courage wrung out of sheer desperation. The symptoms of mysophobia abruptly disappeared.

Morita continued to record the therapeutic processes that sustained the initial paradoxical response. He had seen improvement in his patients with hypnosis but without long-term impact. He found that his patients related to the therapist and the quality of the therapeutic environment, equally. Initial feelings of abandonment and anger by the client towards the therapist predict the client's renewed independence from the therapist – as long as the therapist leaves it alone and does not attempt to convince the client of anything. In this way, the therapist is expected to refrain from cognitive reframing. Once mental tension subsides naturally through clients' prolonged rest in a safe place, only then do they abandon burdening themselves to be symptom free. In this way, obsessive thinking subsides and the client finally gets to experience this released state of being.

Fujita (1986, p. 25) describes the essential period of secluded rest:

> All the subterfuges used to evade the self-confrontation were now unravelling. The resultant reaction was one of being left without protection, stripped naked.

Purposeful seclusion for a turbulent mind

Seclusion is purposeful in Morita therapy; it provides the initial impetus for client's curiosity about the natural world around them. By formally removing stimuli (phones, music, books, computers, pens and paper, and dialogue), the mind and body have a chance to rest and recuperate, clients can then notice movements outside the self. For those with complex trauma histories, a straightforward, non-pressured exchange between the client, therapist, and environment assists rest. In this regard, the first phrase of Morita therapy gives clients a running chance to recover from neurological, emotional, and cognitive demands that have led to their exhaustion. This is one reason that cognitive interventions are avoided when the client is in a vulnerable and exhausted state. I cannot overstress how the first stage requires mental rest, without any prescriptions to think differently or to meditate on anything. It is for this reason that Morita therapists assess if and when cognitive and psycho-educational interventions are beneficial; all too often, mind-engaging methods can lead to further turbulence of the mind and sabotage therapeutic outcomes. All too often the client rather than a therapist's timing or choice of intervention is deemed disordered.

It is essential to state that the secluded rest period in Morita therapy bears no resemblance to sensory deprivation. Jack Vernon (1963) was a pioneer researcher on the psychology of sensory deprivation (SD). In his book, *Inside the Black Box: Studies of Sensory Deprivation*, he provides a formative definition.

> The study of sensory deprivation involves the restriction of a man alone in a small cubicle where he can perceive neither light nor sound.
> *(Vernon, 1963, p. 15)*

In general, brief and strategic rest of the sensory system is critical to the successful progression of Morita therapy. It is noted, again, that credible Morita therapists never impose extreme isolation, neglectful confinement, testimonial-based interviews, induced catharsis, or quick-fix shocking methods of therapy. The client is free to leave the seclusion stage at any time and has access to natural light and sounds, and other environmental stimuli. The early therapeutic room for resting provides a limited stimulus field that never approximates total deprivation.[10] There are some extenuating cultural circumstances that can be accommodated in therapy. For example, a history is taken on traditional religious rituals and food restrictions related to health and religious protocol. Herein, the four stages can accommodate such observances as the Jewish *Shabbat* with acceptable food and candle lighting on Fridays, Christian prayer on Sundays, or the Muslim daily call to traditional prayer. However, activity during the seclusion rest stage is to be performed with the least physical effort. The room size allows for a positioned prayer rug for the standing, bowing, prostrating, and sitting that coincide with Muslim prayer – but the activity cannot exceed five minutes, five times a day. The boundaries of this activity are established prior to the client's entrance into treatment.

Interestingly, the majority of studies on beneficial and detrimental forms of deprivation occurred in the 1960s, before cognitive methods came into vogue – at a time when interest in Zen was high in the field of psychological medicine. Since that period, therapeutic studies have dwindled. Overall, formative literature can be found in *Sensory Deprivation: Fifteen Years of Research* (Zubek, 1969). For instance, Jones (1964) found that gradual sequencing of stimuli after deprivation increases motivation and drive, which has implications for clients' departure from depressive symptoms. Adams (1964) showed how brief sensory deprivation modified harmful behaviours in clients without instruction. Under experimental conditions, cognitive restructuring and low anxiety and arousal occurred as a response to perceptual isolation when subjects were briefed about the conditions beforehand (Culver, Cohen, Silverman, and Shmavonian, 1964; Jacobson, 1966). Brief sensory deprivation was therapeutic and calming for those diagnosed with schizophrenia, particularly when recipients had reprieve from over-filtering competing attention systems, such as radio, television, phone, or social demands (Gaines and Vetter, 1968). This may have carry over for those who struggle with the aftermath of traumatic experiences.

In Morita therapy, brief seclusion serves as a period of retreat from social and mental stimulation. The rest room is designed so that day and night variations in natural light and external sound infiltrate the resting space for client observation and awareness. Meals of varied tastes and colours are savoured and gradually appreciated. Paradoxically, therapeutic seclusion actually increases clients' attention to pleasing stimuli formerly ignored. The seclusion room provides a safe holding ground for clients who feel exposed to the fluctuations of their own emotions. When self is exposed to self in a safe environment without expectations being imposed by others, embodied insights (*taitoku*) are primed and therapeutic change is probable. In his article on Morita therapy and 'conceptus cosmicus', Hisaki Hashi (2013) discusses this concept of 'clear insight' as the body and mind that correspond with the environment. During Morita's initial quiet stage for mental and physical rest, the natural environment comes to the foreground and then recedes. Finally foreground and background merge and Nature is present reliably in one's field of vision; an increase in environmental reliance fosters insight for the client. Overall, trust increases in oneself, the Morita therapist, and the natural environment. In addition, the client's capacity to imagine without dread increases. Morita combined bed rest and seclusion after studying methods being put forth by American neurologist Silas Weir Mitchel (1829–1914) and Otto L. Binswanger (1852–1929), uncle to Ludwig Binswanger (1881–1966) who brought existentialism to the fore in psychiatry. Morita studied the therapeutic progression of his clients' recovery from withdrawal to full engagement in their social, physical, and natural environments (Fujita, 1986).

Morita therapy is designed to assist clients to gradually spread their range of awareness and functional relationships across the animate scape without prioritising people contact as more or less healthful. In this way, contact with animals, birds, trees, rivers, rock, mountains, and fish are just as essential in fostering human attachments. The full sequence of four stages acts as a springboard for experiential growth. In this way, clients get to experience the world that has always been before them as refreshing.

Classic Morita therapy does not rely on a therapist's interpretation or instruction about symptom reduction, or verbal dialogue about ways to feel good or happy. This is a significant difference between inpatient and outpatient care. In fact, Morita saw how clients' suffering increased dramatically when they labelled their feelings as negative, and aimed fiercely to get escape from anxiety, grief, or sadness, or how clients wrongly interpreted a state of happiness as an indicator of mental health. Morita therapy aims to break down clients' assumptions about feeling experiences being either positive or negative. Such a way of thinking leads clients to over-focus on escaping emotional facts that emerge from pure experience. Such emotional evaluation leads clients to become anxious about being sad, or leads physicians to overuse medication for the purpose of emotion regulation. Morita's study of human nature led him to create a therapy that assists clients to form an alliance with their emotions and the ever-evolving ecosystem at large. Following, clients stop evaluating their feelings, and observe how feelings change, rise, and fall naturally and in relation to each other – like patterns of rain-wind-sun-rain.

All too often, compromising life experiences interfere with people's judgement and habits for health promotion; they over-eat, under-eat, over-sleep, under-sleep, over-exercise, under-exercise, over-/under-socialise, smoke various substances, or drink alcohol excessively. On top of that they expect, if not demand, to feel well. Nearly one hundred years ago, Morita discussed how emotional angst and grief arise as natural responses to trauma and loss. Classic Morita therapy provides a safe place with extended time in which clients can emote naturally and return gradually to their diurnal rhythms of waking and sleeping, eating and hydrating cycles, and a balance of indoor and outdoor physical and social activities in a safe, contained environment.

The health philosophy developed by Morita resembles that of Wilfred R. Bion (1984) who claimed that an encounter into anxiety just might re-order us back to our own safe keeping.[11] As part of my supervision, Kondo and I would discuss passages from Bion's books. In our discussions, we were struck often by how Bion's view on memory born out of sensuous experience resembles Morita's perspective.[12] Clearly for us, Morita designed therapeutic stages that gradually and delicately engage a client's senses (during and after the period of rest and seclusion). The residential therapy awakens clients' experiences of elongated time in a safe place; in this way their sensory memory is restored and they no longer react to traumatic re-triggering alarms.

Therapeutic sequence of Morita therapy

Each one of the four stages of therapy usually requires five to eight days, though the therapist determines the length of the period as the client progresses. Morita strongly recommended a strict screening for clients before they undertake the first phase of treatment.[13] The intensity of reduced activity and social contact can be disorienting and risky for those harbouring suicidal ideation, acute psychosis, extreme dissociation, intellectual disability, substance dependence or impulse control challenges.

> Although I tried various therapies, including hypnosis for clients with anxiety disorders, I did not obtain results beyond the temporary relief of symptoms in clients. I also used the life-control method for many years and followed Binswanger's (1911) theory, only to find it manneristic, too theoretical, relatively impractical, and ineffective. Binswanger's methods deprived my clients of spontaneous activity. Initially, I tried to modify and extend these existing systems, but later designed my own method of treatment. In principle, my method of therapy requires residential care . . . My treatment involves four stages: (1) isolation-rest

therapy, (2) light occupational therapy, (3) heavy occupational therapy, and (4) complicated activity therapy in preparation for actual life.

(Morita, 1928/1998, p. 35)[14]

As a guiding paradigm, Morita therapists do not attempt to make changes to clients' emotions and thoughts, or to confront contradictions between what they think and feel. Rather, as clients move through the stages of therapy, their natural curiosity and desire to engage in purposive and creative activity with-all-their-senses become roused. Eradication of worry is no longer their goal as the foreground; their ideas are shaped by direct experiences while engaging in Morita's ecotherapy. It is after resting completely that clients gradually feel their opposing emotions simultaneously and without competition – such as pity and anger, and sadness and relief. They disengage from trying to harbour only one emotional state. This is the reason that reductionist statements by therapists, such as 'You must feel very angry', serve to limit the clients' experience of emotional capacity, depth, and spontaneous recognition.

Rather profoundly, clients' experiences across the four stages serve to challenge their faulty beliefs. Cognitive change does not come from verbal challenge, debate, or instruction by the therapist. The therapist does, however, nudge the client through the diary exchanges that begin usually in Stage Two. As emphasised throughout what follows, there is no meditation or here-and-now instruction in Morita therapy.

Paradox and fumon (不問) stance of the therapist

Fumon (不問) is integral to the methodological core of Morita's progressive therapy. This can be translated as 'not questioning' or 'non-questioning' (translation by Chris Ives, 2016; see Glossary). This unquestioning position taken by the therapist is assumed in her or his body stance. Paradoxically, the therapist assumes a warm, aloof presence and takes an approachable yet standoffish body pose. As clients experience the *fumon* stance taken by the therapist, their protests, inquiries, and interpretations about their own symptoms recede. Paradoxically, the therapist's consistency in stance assists clients to experience their impulses and 'self' entrapment, which increases their insight and self-adjustment to their own suffering.

A *fumon* stance requires a particular 'demotion of self' on the part of the therapist so that she or he can step aside and let therapy function according to Morita's design. Initially clients may feel let down by the therapist as they expect emotional coddling. The even presence of the therapist, however, builds trust. Over the course of the four stages, clients reset their expectations and no longer require the therapist to fix them or serve as the central person in their life.

Just as I received training at the Kondo Clinic in Tokyo in how to respond to the client's anger or dissatisfaction, so do those under my supervision. The therapist refrains from telling clients that they are responsible for doing anything; instead the therapist replies in an ambiguous way or with a koan-like question. For example, there was a client who on the second day of his secluded rest asked pressing questions to the therapist.

Client: I hate staying in this room alone when I feel restless. Can't you see that I am uptight? Aren't you going to do something or give me something to calm me down?

Therapist: I remain alert to your safety. Right now, I see that there are steamed, purple plums in this green bowl. I wonder how they taste when you are restless.

This intervention dares the client to engage regardless of felt conflict. In this way, therapy runs its experiential, natural course without the therapist's reasonable explanation. Thus, *fumon* facilitates the 'experiential core' of Morita's progressive therapy. Such agitated criticism on the part of the client is expected during the rest stage. Gradually, however, the client experiences the therapist's consistency as a kind, unshakeable rock − solid, available, and present. The therapist's presence can be likened to that of the *kuroko* − the masked puppet artist of Japanese *bunraku* (puppet theatre). Metaphorically, the therapist provides the motion, yet remains in the background. Thus, the paradoxical *fumon* positioning assists the therapist to be distant yet near, while providing the client a 'place' from which to review a life story when emotionality is charged in the client. In this way, they own their history and contemplate their future with practical imagination.

Clients usually report that they gain insight into the 'origins' of their thinking. Such a kind of insight, I contend, is partially due to the therapist's *fumon* stance that is assumed across the four stages. One client told me of his discovery in the first rest-seclusion stage. All in all, while insight is not the goal in Morita therapy, it is a usual outcome.

> At first I was furious with you for not talking to me about all the things I was thinking and how much I hurt inside. I wanted to walk out. And when you said that the room was my room to occupy or not occupy, I chose to stay − to spite you. You never imposed your words or reaction the way my father used to do. You were steady everyday and without words you were kind to me. When I said I was bored and asked for a pen and writing tablet, you said paper and pen would arrive in the second stage. You said I was free in my mind to imagine what I might write. I never thought of being free like this before. It is strange for me to feel free enough to feel all of my feelings.

Evolution of the four stages

The stages are designed so that Nature teases and advances a client's attention-field throughout the stages, even when one is indoors. A recent systematic review of nature-assisted therapies by Annerstedt and Währborg (2011) and research reviews of ecotherapy by Chalquist (2009) yield results consistent with Morita's advancements nearly a century ago.[15] This section shows how the therapist weaves the ecological field within, between, and across the four stages.

STAGE ONE (5 to 7 days) consists of seclusion, silence, and rest in a contained place. The room has windows that give hints of a landscape. The room is empty of stimulating items such as books, photos, or artwork with only a bed or futon for sleeping, pillow, blanket, and small bedside table. This stage intensely challenges clients' attachments to their symptoms, as well as their orientation to their feelings. Morita was consistent in his contention that the rest stage is the place where his therapy begins. In fact, D.T. Suzuki believed that the supine position maintained by clients during Morita therapy's seclusion and rest stage, void of medication or illicit drugs, boosts one's potential for awakening or enlightenment (Kondo conversation, 1989, Tokyo).

During the entire rest stage, clients are expected to remain in a supine position on the futon or bed in their rooms. No books, pens, papers, computers, televisions, music devices, or phones are allowed in the room. Clients are to remain quiet and are to remain on the futon or bed unless they go to the toilet or bath. Of course most are challenged the first three days. My clients in Australia and the United States often try to negotiate more mobility or verbal exchange, such as asking to sit in a chair because of a sore back or questioning the rationale for such a state of rest. With a *fumon* presence, the therapist listens to clients' critique of the environment and tells them they are free to notice all that arises and subsides during this resting stage. Clients often report that they are bored. The therapist may suddenly declare, 'Oh I just heard a cricket outside your window'. Then, she or he quietly leaves the room. Since the food arrives at nearly the same time each day, clients are told to notice the shapes, textures, colours, and tastes of food. In the first stage, meals are simple and nutritious, and delivered by trained attendants. Psychologists and physicians under supervision at the *Classic Morita Therapy Centre* deliver meals and take descriptive notes on what they observe in clients from the moment they enter the room through to departure. We take photos of the food tray so we might study the progression of eating patterns and ways a client stacks dishes on the tray. The tone in the room and smells of the room are recorded. In general, clients settle into even movements and increased alertness by the fifth day of the rest period.

Building a client's desire to participate in all life forms that surround them is an essential goal of therapy. In order to experience a sense of community that is not dependent on verbal exchange, clients look after the gardens, chickens, and pond life together; in later stages, they plan and cook meals together. At the late Dr Kora's hospital, for instance, clients in Stage Three chopped wood and maintained the wood heating system that provided hot water for general bath use. In this way they contributed to others' comfort. In some private hospitals in Japan where hot water is scarce, baths are taken three or four times a week in accordance with available resources.

Case formulation and observation criteria developed by Kondo at his former clinic inform practice and professional training at the *Classic Morita Centre*. A daily bath in the early evening is customary after day two of rest unless alterations to this pattern are indicated by daily assessment. A bath is preferred in the first stage as showers are too stimulating. Some clients perspire more profusely during peaks of distress or agitation in the secluded rest stage, which is common for those who ruminate over past trauma and betrayal. Bathing or showering is adjusted according to the circumstance. Overall the main task for those in Stage One is to remain silent in a supine position 24-hours a day, except for leaving the room to use the toilet or bath.

The entrance door and windows of the resting rooms are often semi-transparent (some windows graduate to clear glass that exposes the sky, roof, and tree tops, and change in shadows in the day). As clients become less absorbed by their emotional escape mechanisms, they begin to notice the simple details in their environment. For instance, they begin to notice coloured patterns on the skin of a peach, or feel the dimpled texture of an orange, the scent and grain of a tatami mat, or the arrival of a particular bird song after rain, or the absence of certain sounds just before a storm.

Doors are never locked. Clients can call for assistance at any time. Room windows admit natural light through the day, and muted sounds from the garden and surrounds shift throughout the day – cicadas, voices, car engines, laughter, and so on. In city environments, natural sounds have to compete with the sounds of trains, buses, sirens, and cross walks. Annoying at first to clients, sounds blend gradually into a larger urban rhythm by the fourth day, and clients notice that which they make foreground and background. By day five, most clients yearn to join the animate world, cultivated by the strategic life-tease that has filtered in from the outside.

Stage One is often mistaken or criticised as being one of stimulation deprivation. On the contrary, the environment is one of moment-to-moment stimulation. Self-reflection is an important phase in this stage, or what Kondo called the period of autobiographic or *self-rehearsal* when clients review past events in agonising detail so they may reimagine a different future. Gradually, however, they pull back from this analytic excursion. It is then that they notice the bird sounds or human activity outside the therapy room window with some curiosity. They begin to study natural and human-made sounds throughout the day. I find that a rural setting in Australia and United States offers new material for sensory stimulation – but nature areas can be included in small urban settings through bonsai gardens and aviaries, for instance. Over time, clients move away from intense self-reflection into their senses; smells, textures, colours, and tastes of food become enjoyable and stimulating. The feel of how a ceremonial teacup sits in one's hand is a beautiful thing. If someone is bored it is because she or he remains focused on acquired ideas about boredom.

Morita was intrigued by Freud's use of the supine position in psychoanalysis, and the related method of free association (Morita, 1928/1998). But Morita was more interested in how the reclining position on a bed or futon as a therapeutic method leads a client to wander freely in her/his emotions and thoughts in a timeless manner that is not possible in a 50-minute therapy session. To diminish clients' over-focus on self, the therapist designs environments that allow for extended time in a consistent space that is natural and nurturing.

During the four stages, clients rarely have contact with family members unless negotiated for cultural or developmental reasons – particularly in the first stage; family members are informed of this restriction prior to clients' entry into therapy. Though this may sound harsh and insensitive by some cultural norms, the goal is to give clients enough time in the therapeutic environment to rearrange the field of attachments, reduce chaos for the client, and impart broader relationships to community and nature.

Morita read about the rest cure developed in 1876 by S. Weir Mitchell in Scotland. Complete rest was being prescribed for those with neurasthenia, at a time when Morita wanted to determine an effective method for treating *shinkeishitsu*, but with a holistic framework. Morita wanted to determine if this rest method alone could effectively treat his patients' suffering. He found, in the end, that Mitchell's rest method was unrelated to his first stage of treatment or his philosophy of gradual and natural therapeutic change. As an historical note, Mitchell was influenced by Beard (1869) and adopted Beard's controversial 'electrotherapy' in his practice, which Morita came to reject. Morita read German articles and became aware of the work by the German neurologist, Paul Julius Möebius (1853–1907). Not only did Morita challenge the use of electrotherapy being prescribed by Möebius, he did not share the ideas put forth by Möebius on the 'idiocy of women' (Kondo, conversations, 1994). At that time, this view of women was criticised by German feminist author, Marianne Adelaide Hedwig Dohm (1831–1919). Overall, Morita considered electrical treatments too abrupt, while interfering with clients' return to their natural rhythms (neurological balance) of the human body and mind (author's interview with Kora and Kondo in 1993).

During the seclusion period, clients begin to wake naturally without a clock or alarm or sense of urgency about time. Hashi (2011) describes the first phase of Morita therapy as a period when the client experiences total relaxation in body and soul.

Overall, the first stage is designed to generate a new awareness of one's own rhythm of thought, emotion, and body functioning. Near the end of that stage, clients recognise better the natural shifts in daily energy over the course of a day. They notice how night falls. Morita therapists do not direct or interpret clients' histories, feelings, or thoughts in any of the stages.[16] Generally, however, therapists use silence strategically and make fine-tuned observations of their client with the purpose of leading clients to challenge their own interpretations. This orientation runs across all stages. Therapists make a study of clients' likes and dislikes, and record how finicky a client may be with changes or new additions to food on their tray. The therapist trusts the therapeutic time, place, and methods of therapy within and between the stages. Clearly, Morita designed therapeutic space and time and use of silence with a purpose – to assist clients to return to their natural rhythms of eating, sleeping, waking, resting, and moving. Slowly, clients re-engage with the social and natural world where they learn about rhythms of studying, working, lovemaking, playing, relaxing, napping, and so on.

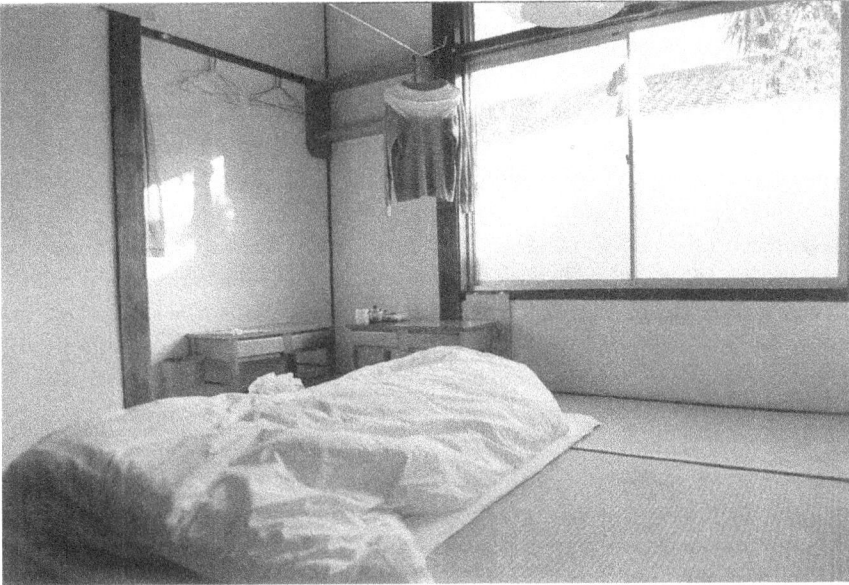

FIGURE 1.3   Stage One seclusion room with frosted windows

Permission from former Sansei hospital, Kyoto, 1998

Interestingly, studies in Japan on psycho-physiological changes that occur during the seclusion stage of Morita therapy show a re-balance in sleep-wake rhythms for clients diagnosed with anxiety (Komatsu, 1982; Masuda, 1986; Mori, Komatsu, and Masuda, 1986). This makes clinical sense because most often when clients enter the rest stage, they are often unaware of body sensation, or the nurturing capacity of the external environment.

All too often, clients struggling with past and/or current trauma detach from self, time, other, and place. These patterns become second nature. Paradoxically, in Morita therapy the de-emphasis on 'self' or analysis of past experience assists the client to re-place the self. Most often, people are less engaged in the physical and animistic environment when they attempt to escape from certain feelings. The secluded, silent period begins to break down the person's detachment tendencies, self-absorption, and urgency for relief, or 'separation anxiety in adulthood' as researched by Manicavasaga, Silove, and Curtis (1997). Ecological time is the therapeutic theatre. The first hot summer day the cicadas come out of the ground, the client is penetrated by their fresh song.

Particulars of Stage One

The therapist enters the seclusion room at least once a day, but sometimes twice or more depending on the safe state of the client. A trained attendant brings meals three times a day and charts observations about the client for the therapist. In this way, the therapist attends to the duty of care of the client through the day. The therapist and attendant intentionally keep conversation to a minimum when seeing the client. Again, the purpose of entering the room is to assess safety and hold a firm presence of *fumon* so that the client gains a sense of assurance that someone is near even when they are anxious; the client is encouraged to persevere with discomfort – while experiencing containment of rest alongside humane care. Diffused light from the window is essential to the rest environment.

As stated earlier, in this stage clients are not allowed to talk freely about their symptoms, feelings, or past history. In some Morita clinics, the attitude is cultivated that clients are in 'life training' together. This attitude resonates with the Japanese notion of *issho ni* (strength in togetherness). Clients stop comparing their suffering to others. At CMC, care is taken to assess the dynamics between staff and clients, as much as dynamics between residential clients, so that healthy adjustments can be made that assist the client therapeutically. In public or private psychiatric hospitals, the integrity of staff dynamics is rarely assessed or adjusted in order to maximise the best therapeutic milieu for clients. I was reminded frequently when in supervision at Kondo's clinic to make this kind of assessment a daily practice because Morita therapy is premised on a therapeutic ecosystem.

While some clients may take longer to engage after the rest stage, most experience a sense of aliveness when weeding an area in the garden, potting a bonsai, or washing a small rabbit, gathering quail eggs, making quill pens, learning archery together, or walking to a natural spring for water. Mostly, clients are meant to learn about another person's deportment based on direct observation, body intuition (*taitoku*), and experience of 'how' their fellow peers engage in work activity, play, nature, and the environment. In this way, clients become less judging of another's status, while becoming more confident of their own experiential knowledge of other people through silent observation.

As we have seen, the judging mind interferes with experiencing one's authentic self, pure emotion, and pure anxiety. Usually by the second stage of Morita therapy, the client notices how feelings of any sort operate under the same principles. Emotions mimic the changing, natural grey light, sky, and landscape. When clients notice moments of discomfort without assigning meaning, they break free from intellectual interpretations and begin to experience feelings as facts and respond accordingly. I once had a client who lived with a violent woman partner. He told himself to not feel intimidated or afraid because he was a man; he denied his 'emotion-as-fact' and interpreted fear as a weak emotion. Once he stopped interpreting how a man should feel, he attended to his own neglect and made a safe plan that eventually led him to leave the violent relationship in an ethical way.

In Morita therapy, there is no need for cognitive acrobatics since the client experiences a kind of 'isness' about her or his state without pushing or pulling to make it different. The stage of imposed silence in a safe context thrusts the client into fuller awareness of sensations in a context. Over therapeutic time, emotion and thought settle into a natural course – without meditation or medication. Kondo (1960) writes about the progression of the stages.

> In short, being deprived of all neurotic diversions . . . the patient realizes his capacity to endure and his tremendous urge for creative living. When a person is really hungry he does not demand a fancy meal. In the same way, the patient feels stimulated and satisfied by any trifling work or activity he can find after this period of inactivity, when he drops the neurotic demands he previously insisted on. Nevertheless, this second phase is a period of fluctuation. The old habit of mind comes back to trouble him. But he has had the fresh experience of liberation from it, he can clearly see his danger and . . . is advised not to be too much concerned with it, to just experience pain as pain, pleasure as pleasure, to get along with anything that comes up. He is advised to keep a diary so that the doctor can have more understanding of what is going on within the patient. In this phase, moreover, greater access to nature is encouraged.
>
> *(Kondo, 1960, p. 222)*

The therapist is trained to assess the readiness of the client to move to the next stage. There are certain signs that are indicators for this transition, with the first to second stage perhaps being most critical due to the abruptness of shifting from an indoor to outdoor setting and from physical and mental inactivity to activity.

KEY TRANSITION STAGE: The first day that someone transitions out of the secluded rest room to Stage Two, much supervision is needed. Muscle atrophy has set in and the person may be wobbly at first. Many clients have a tendency to move faster than their body dictates. For those who are used to vigorous physical activity before they enter Morita therapy, the therapist encourages them to synchronise their mind to their body. Many are used to pushing their bodies to new limits and have a tendency to override their bodies' messages. Therapists might model the pace they would like the client to assume by working alongside them in the garden without words.

The beginning of Stage Two is an essential re-embodiment period. The client is instructed to maintain slow and even movements with little strain. Also, this is the first time clients eat meals with others. They are asked to speak about the immediate environment. The therapist does not respond verbally to clients' complaints about their moods; this paradoxical dismissal assists the breakdown of a client's judging mind that tags emotions as negative or positive.

STAGE TWO consists of light repetitive work wherein the client is encouraged to go out of doors. This is the stage when the client has an opportunity to engage in the ordinary as an essential feature in day-to-day life. The front doorway, for example, may be laden with pine needles and twigs following a rain. Seeing this, a client sweeps them into a pile. By not judging the activity as 'work', clients are more likely to smell the fragrance of wet earth. These are simple moments of accomplishment that go unrecognised by clients often.

In the second stage, the client moves out of the rest room to reside in another room, sometimes with another client. In my own practice, I find this to be a most significant event for clients. They leave the history of internal struggle that they endured when in the secluded rest period. It is usual for a client to press the therapist or staff to explain what is going to happen next. Again, in a *fumon* manner, the therapist replies in ways that encourage clients to soften their overly inquisitive mind. During Stage Two the client is directed to limit conversation and avoid any talk of feelings or philosophy – the focus is on simple matters, such as securing the screen on the window so mosquitoes do not come into the room, or providing water for the rabbit, or noticing what leaves fall last in autumn.

Many clients had some hesitation about remaining for days in the secluded room. Day after day, however, they form a stronger attachment to the space and simple rest of mind and body. By the time Stage Two arrives, some clients ask me if they can stay in their room for all of the therapy. The therapist does not enter a discussion about a rationale for such, and invites the client to notice what happens to this desire when moving outside in Stage Two of therapy. In this way, clients begin to realise how their mind is calmer when they engage in ecological time in the rise and fall of the day; there is freedom in this realisation. The second stage often begins with a sense of hesitation or discomfort. This is natural. Yet once the person begins to engage in the natural environment in silence, interesting experiences happen.

During Stage Two, the therapist studies what interests a client naturally in the environment and actively tracks her/his curiosity. The therapist may give a client a book on beekeeping or flower identification if the client notices bees on flowers. Over time, clients observe that the more they partake in purposeful activity, the more quickly worrisome symptoms decrease. While sitting in silence and sketching movements in a garden, a client may notice the patterned sounds of insects or birds, watch the activity of an inchworm, or note the movement of the changing length of shadows on a hillside through late afternoon.[17]

In addition, during the first stage, the client's muscles atrophy due to the prolonged immobility. When moving outside to begin work in the second stage, they move more profoundly – which often leads to a re-embodiment as small and large muscle groups moving systematically. I strongly contend that this 're-embodiment process' is essential to the reduction in dissociation for those recovering from severe trauma.

It is at the end of the second stage that animal care often begins. In Japan today, small critters, such as a rabbit, turtle, fish, or bird, are residents in hospitals that clients nurture. In Australia, animal husbandry includes caring for a cat, a chicken, and farm animals, such as a goat, or sheep. Most uniquely, Morita used pet monkeys in his home practice. During my interview with Ms Seto in Japan in 2012, it was inconclusive whether Morita purposefully chose a monkey as a metaphorical source for client observation and reflection, or for simple companionship. The

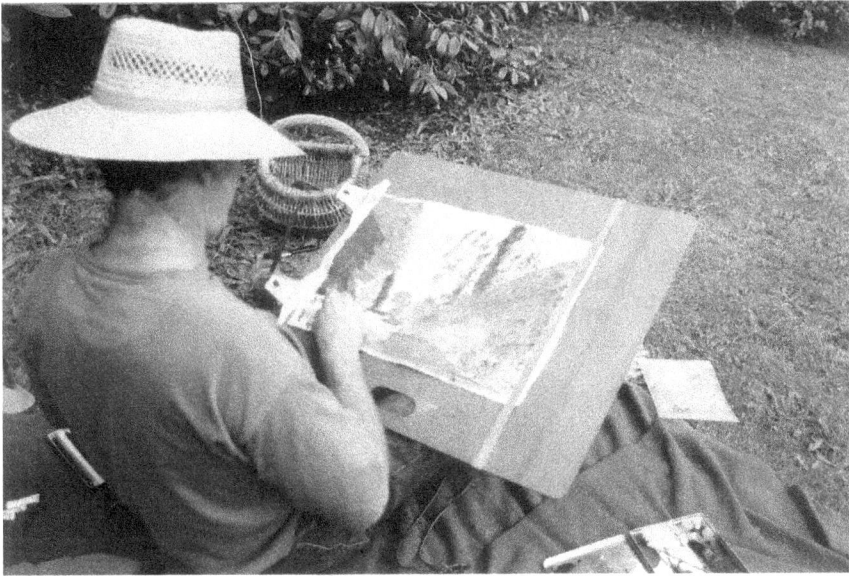

FIGURE 1.4   Stage Two: sketching the landscape. Classic Morita Centre (CMC), Australia, 1994

monkey is found in Shinto lore. Traditionally in Japan, people go to shrines to receive a red monkey charm to ward off illness, bad luck, or evil spirits. In Zen, too, attention is given to *Monkey Mind*, which is a restless mind that skips from one thought to the next.[18] And yet, monkeys are close to humans in form; they are known to respond to human emotion, and represent a creature free from social convention.[19] Regardless, such interactions increase experiences of safe intimacy.

STAGE THREE consists of labour-intensive work and descriptive diary writing, art projects, and communal meal preparation. In this stage, the client begins to speak aloud to others in the environment. However, talking is always restricted to tasks at hand. Though this may seem insensitive, the therapist is trained in how, when, and where to respond to the client's attempts to engage in emotional-based dialogues. One of my clients sketched an herb garden in his journal and wrote of his anger over deception by his lover. In response, I wrote: 'Show me where in the garden I might find your anguish about your lover's affair.' This client's reply, 'Of course, it is not found under a twig or leaf.' While my intervention may sound dismissive, it served to re-shape the client's perception about relationships. The garden does not play tricks or collude. In Morita therapy, clients are dropped into place and time. Far from outpatient therapy, classic Morita therapists do not ask clients to become mindful of the environment; the goal is to establish an intimate, interactive, and on-going relationship with Nature. Therapy is not about a hike in the woods; it is about sensing Nature that surrounds us moment-to-moment; the sky does not go away. All too often, people with excess trauma have the habit of taking on activities for

FIGURE 1.5 Transition Stage Two: Bonsai pruning. CMC, Australia 2014

the purpose of distraction, or forming social relationships is based on an exchange by exchanging stories of anguish.[20] I observe often how Morita therapy breaks this cycle.

Clients are encouraged to provide care to the environment on the premises (bird, sheep, rescued wombat, chicken, and fruiting tree). Clients in Stage Four may teach clients in Stage Three to prune roses.[21]

FIGURE 1.6 Bonsai, CMC, 2014

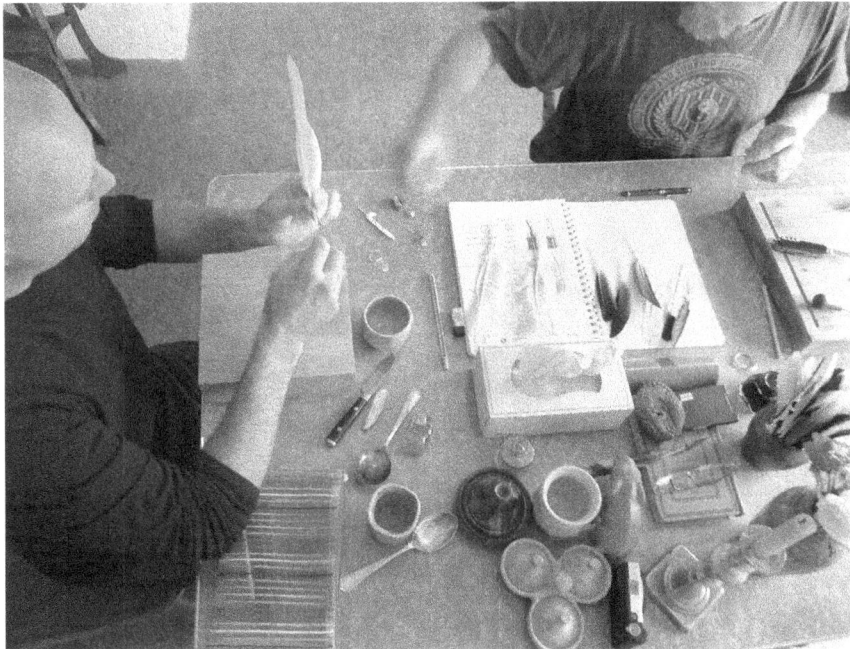

FIGURE 1.7 Collecting feathers and making quill pens. CMC, 2012

FIGURE 1.8 Transition to Stage Three; haiku composing with quill pen, CMC, 2014

FIGURE 1.9 Stage Three: Sheep ('Pokey') relating and herding, CMC, 2014

FIGURE 1.10   Early Stage Three, leather crafting (fine motor). CMC, 2014

Near the end of Stage Two and through Stage Three, clients write diary observations about what they see, hear, smell, touch, taste, and discover during the day. This might be about animals, insects, colour of soil, and wind patterns. Clients are encouraged to sketch scenery. Those with eye impairments are asked to focus on sounds, smell, or felt textures – such as describing the feel and scent of sheep's wool. A client can record sounds instead of images. The therapist collects the visual and/or auditory journal and makes written or verbal comments. If clients divulge personal history, they are re-directed to observe and record concrete activity in the natural environment. The purpose of this redirection is to minimise self-glorification or self-deprecation. The therapist's strategic comments shape the client's observations, and this exchange is a rehearsal for forming intimate relations from wonder-based shared experiences, rather than misery-based personal ones.

From a psychodynamic perspective, the writing exchanged between client and therapist generates 'object-relation' connections. My clients report often that they feel encouraged when opening their diaries and reading my handwritten comments; some have described this contact as comforting. Also, clients refer back to notes by the therapist during treatment and later at their homes. Within the diary, they take notes from readings on plant, rock, and insect identification, seasonal star constellations, or calligraphy and art. As the therapists track clients' interests, they

FIGURE 1.11   Stage Three: branch pruning (gross motor). CMC, 2014

FIGURE 1.12   End of Stage Three: on the archery range (fine and gross motor). CMC, 2014

select books, nature studies, or sound identification tapes for their clients to review, which reinforces their healthy curiosity about the world. One of my clients learned to identify four frogs by their songs in the pond; she plans to go pond exploring in spring in hope of recording the native 'peppered tree frog'. For her, this kind of treasure hunt nourished her spirit. When we evolve and hone our inquisitive nature and sources of wonder, we move along our creative grain. One prominent goal of Morita therapy is to bring clients to realisation of what Kondo calls their 'capacity and power for creative living with more spontaneity and genuine feeling' (Kondo, 1960, p. 222).

STAGE FOUR focuses on social cooperation and spans five to seven days. Often, the client in Stage Four teaches clients who are in Stage Three to use a potter's wheel, transplant a tree, or prepare a meal. This is the first time that the client travels away from the residential grounds (by walking or taking public transportation) to do communal errands, such as posting letters or buying groceries. This is the stage when the therapist assesses the readiness of the client to leave the centre. Over the course of this final stage, the client returns to the social world, but with the added perception of being refreshed by the environment – a literal shift in 'world' view. In essence, the evolution of moving through the stages is the therapeutic process that fosters wellness (Morita, 1928/1998).

The evolving stages of therapy offer a gentle system for treating people who have survived cruelty and trauma. The range of the therapeutic environment and methods is not confined to talking indoors. Morita therapists open out the animated world. The following is a diary excerpt from one of my Morita therapy clients in Stage Two (by permission).

FIGURE 1.13 Stage Three, stone wall, CMC, 2014

She (therapist) came to the herb garden where I was weeding, pulled a leaf from a plant and rubbed it between her fingers; she asked me to do the same. The smell reminded me of my auntie's tea. Then I noticed that I don't smell much of the world. I tried to tell her about all of this. She replied by taking a piece from the rosemary bush. She invited me to draw and colour the leaves of the herbs and to describe the scent. I don't think I've ever described a smell

FIGURE 1.14   Stages Three–Four, building project, Jikeikai Hospital, Tokyo

(LeVine, 2000)

before . . . I discovered that the rosemary scent stays on my fingers longer than the mint. Peg wrote a small note on the margin: 'For me, peppermint smells like a baby bird's piercing cry.' I begin to put sound and smell together I began to understand by experiencing.

(Diary, Morita client, 2002)

Therapists' criteria for progressing clients through the four stages of therapy

During the course of this progressive treatment, the therapist looks for concrete signs of progress from which to transition the client into the next stage. During intensive training and supervision, therapists learn to fine-tune their observational skills, particularly since the clinician cannot rely heavily on clients' self-reports in the first stage. Of course, suicide risk is continually assessed. The attendants who deliver meals to clients are trained in refined observational skills. In particular, attendants at CMC record observations (what they see, hear, smell, intuit) and maintain the dissociative symptom checklist that monitors client safety. It is noted that these observations can be used for outcome studies, too.

Assessment guidelines are necessary for observing clients across the stages of Morita therapy, which inform training and supervision at the *Classic Morita Centre*.

FIGURE 1.15 Stage Four. Meal preparation, CMC, Australia, 2014

Stage One: A client's intake of food and liquid is recorded; changes in posture and presentation are recorded at time of meal delivery and collection from the resting room. At the end of each day the therapist makes a visit to the client's resting room at dusk. The therapist asks, 'How is your physical health today?' Changes in facial expression, body posture, body odour, pace of movement, and so on are recorded soon after leaving the room. The therapist's intuition is recorded.[22] Daily peer review of all qualitative data is standard.

Stage Two: The therapist keeps records of a client's requests and comments; this is descriptive data. If a diary begins in Stage Two, themes are noted in drawings, sketches, and annotations. The diary consists of unlined paper in a bound sketchbook so that the use of space and stylised lines might show the uniqueness of the client; no interpretation is made of art since the therapist is simply curious about how the client interacts with different media. Therapists' comments are meant to increase the client's observations about the environment through descriptive writing, while decreasing the client's self-reflection and opinions. More changes are observed in the way the day is structured for clients when they are in the third and fourth stages, particularly as they engage with more intention in the outdoor setting.

Stages Three and Four: The therapist and attendants record 'spontaneous' responsive behaviours that tend to the natural and social world, such as tending to plants, small animals, and insects without the therapist's instruction, or assisting another client to do a task. Also, changes are recorded in the content and course of dialogue with other people in the therapeutic environment in Stage Four.

Over time as clients engage in the environment and make diary records, their hand writing and use of the space is often altered – with more spontaneous use of margins, lines, and shapes on the page. References to hardship drop off, and sketches are more finely illustrative, with added notes about sounds and smells in the environ as sensory awareness increases. The Morita therapist is trained to encourage expressions of wonder, such as 'The bird's nest in the bush is deep and the one in the barn is shallow with mud. I wonder which birds made these.'

The typical residential treatment ranges between 20 to 30 days. Though this concentration may seem long, when one considers that there is rarely re-admission following treatment, this time period is actually cost and time effective in the long run for clients.[23] Timetables vary slightly according to season. In the winter, clients rise around 7 a.m. (in summer they rise at 6:30 a.m.). In some residential hospitals in Japan, a signal or a series of wooden clack sounds indicate wake up time, mealtime, and bedtime (usually between 9 and 10 p.m.). Regardless of the location or season, daily rhythms of nature generate a sense of predictability and ecological community.

Overriding goals of classic Morita therapy

By experiencing a simple and safe environment, clients no longer become anxious about their symptoms. It is vital that the first stage of therapy meet the following goals: (1) to foster the client's experience of a safe containing place; (2) to decrease the urgency to solve anything; (3) to increase the client's capacity to endure discomfort and contradiction in feelings; (4) to decrease the client's urge to tell other people about their felt anguish; (5) to decrease one's attachment to symptoms; and (6) to increase the active observation of and participation in the ecological and social world (LeVine, 1994, 2008). Morita strongly recommended that on-going clinical assessment of clients be maintained, particularly since symptoms may increase, or new ones may emerge, in the first few days of seclusion before a dramatic decrease by Stage Three. Silence plays a role by decreasing the client and therapist's tone of therapeutic urgency to fix anguish. Morita states the following:

> If patients report that their headache has disappeared or that they feel refreshed, the therapist should explain that such a feeling is nothing but an expression of self-awareness. Good feelings are accompanied by their opposite, such as discomfort. If patients ponder over the type of work that will be effective for their condition, or search for something to do as a distraction from their suffering, they will suffer even more when they can not find suitable work.
>
> *(Morita, 1928/1998)*

Activity is to be directed towards an external purpose rather than to serve the self in its quest to feel more comfortable. When clients struggle to control emotion or cover up emotion by intellectual interpretations of what constitutes good or bad emotions,

FIGURE 1.16 Takehisa Kora: Garden path at Kora Koseinn Morita Hospital, Tokyo

(Le Vine film project, 1992)

they work against the 'emotional fact' that emotion has no valence (See 'Emotional facts' in the Glossary). Morita therapy provides an opportunity for the client to begin experiencing emotions before intellectual interpretation and judgement are applied (*arugamama* – isness).[24] Paradoxical interventions by the therapist assist this goal.

Through the sheer experience of progressing through the successive stages, clients' contradictions in thinking are recalibrated. This process coincides with the decontamination of emotions by the logical mind; emotions are freed from intellectual judgement during the course of therapy. Often, clients hold an intense conviction that justifies an emotion or an analysis about an event in their past. The stages of Morita therapy move a client to a state of simply feeling without any qualifiers or justifiers. In silent-seclusion, clients are given an opportunity to live without sounds and images from phones, computers, or televisions and to experience emotion most fully in its ebb and flow. Morita refers to this as 'isness' or 'suchness' as *arugamama*. In order to make sure the client does not feel abandoned, the resting room is designed as a context for seclusion, rather than sensory deprivation; in this way solitude is fostered rather than loneliness. The therapist's presence is essential to this outcome.

Morita therapy brings a client into intimate contact with the self and removes the need for pretence. This is akin to the Zen koan: 'Know your original face before you were born.' The entire four-stage treatment is designed to engage the client in Nature, which in turn, reveals how 'self' mimics nature (Fujita, 1986). It is from this state that the person appreciates 'emotion as fact' without an intellectual overlay, thus opening the natural desire for self-preservation and continuity, even in the face of anxiety.

> Sandōkai says, 'When each nature of the four cosmic elements – earth, water, fire, and wind – returns to normal, it is like a child who finds a mother: fire is hot, wind blows, water is cool, and earth is firm.' Delusion develops in a person who wants to feel coolness from a fire or warmth from water. When restored to the natural condition, one feels cold in winter, fears disease, dislikes uncleanliness, and sometimes feels shy in front of others . . . Desire does not exist if one returns to the origins of human nature.
>
> *(Morita, 1928/1998, pp. 91–92)*

As we have seen, Morita developed his practice after observing the erosion of inpatients' life force by psychiatric institutions in the name of mental health. Morita confronted what Karl Menninger called 'therapeutic nihilism' when referring to the state of mental health care in the 1960s.

> Psychiatric treatment has evolved through many stages – extrusion; ostracism; torture; execution; studied neglect; dreary maintenance; kindly care, mechanical, surgical, and electrical assaults of various kinds; and varied programs of work . . . the long era of therapeutic nihilism . . .
>
> *(Karl Menninger in Menninger, Mayman, and*
> *Pruyser, 1963, p. 402)*

Morita and Menninger challenged restrictive psychiatric practices and methods directed solely at symptom eradication. Morita, in particular, did not equate wellness with any specific emotional state. Overall, Morita set out to identify life-robbing environments and situations that compromise clients' health. He contended that a client deserves and requires being treated therapeutically inside a life-enhancing environment.

Notes

1   For an historical and political description of the Japanese art group that included book illustrations, paintings, architecture and writing, see *MAVO: Japanese Artists and the Avant-Garde, 1905–1931* (Weisenfeld, 2001).
2   For an overview of Inoue's life and thoughts review G.C. Godart (2004). Godart clarified these historical eras (personal correspondence).
3   For a comprehensive view of this period on the evolution of the schools of Zen and the lack of homogeneity within the schools themselves, see Michel Mohr (1998).
4   Yoshiyuki Koga (1967) compares Morita's term *shinkeishitsu* for neurotic features with *shinkeishitsu-sho*; the Chinese characters for 'sho' indicate disease, while *shinkeishitsu* suggests a transitory phase during one's capacity building. This is an example of Morita's positive attitude towards recovery.
5   See *Shinkeishitsu* in the Glossary.
6   For an historical overview see Philip Wiener (1956).
7   As an historical note, 'neurasthenia' was coined in 1869 by George Miller Beard to denote a cluster of symptoms: anxiety, fatigue, headache, sexual disinterest, depressed mood, and neuralgia – symptoms related to exhaustion of the central nervous system.
8   Paroxysmal neurosis presents as a pseudo-heart attack, and occurs when someone over-analyses fear and worry, feels the heart rate increase, and interprets this sensation of racing heart during distress as a cardiac disorder. Over attention to this cycle of 'racing mind=racing heart' perpetuates worry and panic.
9   As a cultural note, being extroverted in the Zen sense means being equally engaged with people and nature. Thus, someone might be walking and talking to a dog in the forest, noticing the sky, trees, and rock, while smelling eucalyptus leaves or picking up a stone and rolling it over in her/his hand; this is extroversion.
10 Even in a voluntary, deprivation situation, such as a cubicle or flotation tank, one hears auditory sensations in the body, such as a stomach growling, a nose sniffing, or the sound of a bone socket in movement.
11 W.R. Bion (1897–1979) was born in India and migrated to the United Kingdom at the age of eight. After obtaining his degree in medicine at University College London, he underwent training in psychoanalysis with John Rickman and Melanie Kline. Although he was Director of the London Clinic of Psycho-Analysis (1956–1962) and President of the British Psycho-Analytical Society (1962–1965), he worked in Los Angeles until his death.
12 Akihisa Kondo told me that he met often with an analytic group that discussed and debated Bion's ideas when he was in New York in 1951.
13 Originally designed to treat *shinkeishitsu*, Morita therapy has been broadened and found to be effective in treating a range of syndromes, including trauma-related anxiety and depression, existential anxiety, social and other phobias, eating disorders, various adjustment disorders, borderline features related to childhood trauma, and cancer repercussions (Nomura, 1963; Ohara, Aizawa, and Iwai, 1970; Fujita, 1986; Itami, 1986; Kitanishi, 1987; Kora, 1989; LeVine, 2003; Nakamura, 1995, 2002; Ohara, 1987; Y. Suzuki, 1987; Tamai, Takeichi, Tashiro, 1990; Tamai, Takeichi and Tashiro 1991).
14 This 1911 reference by Morita is from Binswanger, O. (1911) *Grundzüege füer die Behandlung des Geisteskrankheiten. Vorträge für Praktische Therapie* (Fundamentals of the Treatment of Mental Illness). Haft, 3.
15 Ecotherapy is active in Holland with over 600 'care farms' that include agricultural activities. Currently, there is a 'Green Agenda For Mental Health' in the United Kingdom. Research on mental health and engaging activities in green environments builds correlational evidence (Broocks, et al., 1998; Boucher, 2000; Burls, 2005, 2007). Burls and Caan (2004) link gardening to the experience of 'embracement'. Annerstedt (2009) links sustainable health development to environmental psychology practices.
16 In my own practice I often meet with clients post-treatment in my eco-setting, which stimulates and reinforces their discoveries and insights.

17 As an historical note, the early development of art therapy in Britain was influenced by 'moral treatments' whereby a period of rest cure with minimal verbal exchange was included (Hogan, 2001).

18 See the writing by Emiko Ohnuki-Tierney (1987).

19 See the organisation, *Helping Hands* and the therapeutic use of monkeys (www.monkeyhelpers.org).

20 This dynamic is often present in patients diagnosed with borderline features. Morita therapy breaks down the pattern whereby clients attach to people who live chaotic and dramatic lives.

21 Note that animal and plant care reflect the environment in which the person resides during treatment. For instance, at the Morita Therapy Center at Jikeikai University Hospital in Japan, there are small non-allergy prone animals such as rabbits, a small dog, homing pigeons, as well as citrus trees and regional plants. Whereas a country property offers parrots, herding animals, ducks, geese, an orchid of trees, and brilliant views of the Milky Way.

22 The underlying structure of communication in Morita therapy is less verbal than most forms of psychotherapy, which coincides with 'pragmatism' akin to that of the Chan Buddhist notion: *Never Tell Too Plainly*. Knowledge is transmitted rather than delivered or coached.

23 My primary engagement in Morita therapy in Japan occurred from 1988 to 2010 at the following sites: the late Dr Kora's private hospital in the Tokyo region (known as Kora Koseinn); the outpatient centre of *Seikatsu no Hakken* Organisation and discussions with the late Yozo Hasegawa; the late Sansei hospital in Kyoto, which I claim is a psychiatric institution rather than a therapeutic centre; Kyushu University hospital in Fukuoka; Jikeikai University hospital outside Tokyo; and the late Akihisa Kondo's home clinic in Tokyo.

24 An as-is emotional experience excludes 'acceptance of emotions'. 'To accept' means to acquire a mindset or orientation towards one's emotions. More accurately, *arugamama* means to experience the *isness* of emotion, without the mind's interference or goal to accept or reject.

2

MORITA, JAPONISME, KAREN HORNEY, AND ZEN

Zen is not opposed to social convention.
Zen is indifferent to convention.

(Kondo, personal conversation, 1997)

Images of Japan as 'other'

Oh, East is East, and West is West, and never the twain shall meet,
Till Earth and Sky stand presently at God's great Judgment Seat;
But there is neither East nor West, Border, nor Breed, nor Birth,
When two strong men stand face to face,
tho' they come from the ends of the earth!
The Ballad of East and West by Rudyard Kipling (1988)[1]

During the lifetime of Shoma Morita, exchanges flourished between Japan, Europe, and the United States about avant-garde art, philosophy, and literature. And though Kipling's line, 'Oh, East is East and West is West, and never the twain shall meet' remains popular, it is recited often out of context, which serves to widen the East–West divide. Perhaps as much as language, the strange and mysterious portrayal of Japan in Europe and North America has participated in perpetuating this divide.

In the mid-1800s, James McNeill Whistler produced his night (nocturne) series *Moonlight* and used binary colour themes from Hiroshige's woodblock prints to form his London landscapes, *Nocturne: Blue and Gold*.[2] In this same era, the performance art in *The Mikado* (music by Arthur Sullivan and book and libretto by W. S. Gilbert) was applauded when it opened as an opera on March 14, 1885 at the Savoy Theatre in London. At that time, Londoners sought Japanese icons – prints, kimonos, tea, masks, and fans. Similarly, Japanese *haiku* (17-syllable poems) and *renga* (chain poems) have been translated and studied for centuries, and often associated with exotic views on Zen. Exposés akin to Oscar Wilde's creation of Orientalism in 1889 and his famous quote 'the whole of Japan is a pure invention' have surged. Similarly, *Japonisme*,[3] a term coined in 1872 by art collector-writer Philippe Burty, reinforced Japan as exotic (Lambourne, 2007).

Foreign fascination with kabuki theatre, the tea ceremony, silk kimonos, ikebana (flower arranging), and Geisha houses was reinforced by Giacomo Puccini's opera, *Madam Butterfly*, which opened in Milan in 1904. The opera, by John Luther Long (1861–1927), was based on a short story of the same title. Neither Long nor Puccini had travelled to Japan.[4] In fact, Long was a lawyer in the USA and based the original story on his sister's accounts of living in Japan as the wife of a Methodist missionary. At that time, Nagasaki was a major international port city, ripe for the romanticised story of an American naval officer and local Geisha. Such stories fortified Kipling's *never the twain shall meet*.

Novelist Kenzaburo Oe, who received the Nobel Prize for literature in 1994, bemoans such international images of Japan. Patrick Smith (1997, p. 11) writes about a conversation he had with Oe:

> There is the old Japan of samurai and Zen gardens, and the new Japan of gadgets and efficiency. 'Between the two,' he once told me, 'there is a blank where the Japanese live.' . . . But one trait united these two extremes: at no point did Japan's occupiers try to see the Japanese as anything other than a reflection of themselves.

Those outside Asia often reference the ways of Japan as other – keys turn to the left, writing goes from top to bottom and right to left on the page, and Buddhist temples are designed to open into the landscape, whereas Christian churches are self-contained.

Morita practised in the Meiji era (1868–1912) and was impacted by the restoration events of 1867 and 1868. At that time, Japan was moving from an isolated agricultural nation to one with a highly refined rail system designed to link up the country. Alongside these national developments, Japan's colonising pace of activities matched those of France and other European countries. However, Japan was regarded as 'other' due to it being a leading non-Western example of imperial power, with particular undertakings around Japan's defeat of Russia by their armed forces in 1905, the Wars with China in 1894 and 1937, and the invasion of Korea in 1910.

All these factors contributed to the ebb and flow of global intrigue with Japan. In Morita's era, Europeans were fascinated with *ukiyo-e* (block prints of sensual relations) when Japanese artists gathered in Paris around the Surrealist movement in the early 1920s.[5] Around that time, Freud became popular inside Japan, and the Surrealist painter Takiguchi began relating psychoanalysis to art as he challenged the status quo in the Meiji period. The Japanese government remained increasingly intolerant of nonconformists, with crackdowns continuing through to 1941 when the legendary surrealists Fukuzawa and Takiguchi were arrested.

By the end of the 1930s, political and surrealist art, philosophy, and psycho-therapy (outside psychoanalysis) went underground in Japan. As mentioned earlier, Morita left his Chair at Tokyo Jikeikai School of Medicine to his protégé, Takehisa Kora, in 1937. However, Kora came to this post just as post-war Occupation was neglecting Japanese approaches to psychotherapy.[6] While Morita remained virtually unknown globally, his name became displaced inside Japan as psychiatrists across Asia turned their attention to Freud's theories and methods of analysis. It was not until the early 1950s when psychiatrist Karen Horney arranged a symposia on Zen and psychoanalysis in New York that Morita's name moved into American psychi-atric literature, paving the way soon afterwards for a brief resurgence of Morita's ideas in Japan.[7] The first formal reinstatement of Morita's work came in Octo-ber 1958 when the General Meeting on Psychopathology focused exclusively on Morita therapy; it was held in a Buddhist temple in Nagano. Following the meeting, the clinical journal *Seishin-Igaku* published a special edition on Morita therapy in July 1959 (Kondo, 1960).

The 1950s: Zen, Horney, and psychoanalysts converge in New York

The 1950s generated cultural exchanges between scholars, and a renewed interest in the phenomenology of consciousness. Early threads formed in March 1947 when Richard DeMartino met Daisetz Teitaro (D.T.) Suzuki while Richard was serving under the American Occupation Forces in Japan. Soon after, DeMartino entered the Engaku-ji Zen monastery to study under Suzuki (the temple Morita attended); he engaged in koan-like[8] dialogue with Suzuki's peer, Hisamatsu Shin'ichi (1889–1980). Between 1949–1952, DeMartino accompanied Suzuki on his scholarly trav-els to Hawaii, California, and New York (DeMartino, 1991).[9]

Existential philosophers brought a unique reflective process to the field of psy-chiatry in North America at a time when interests in Zen were also peaking. Prac-titioners and scholars reflected together on the true nature of anxiety embedded in the struggle to live one's authentic life. This was a time when Morita's name became known in certain circles, and scholar-practitioners wrote fiercely on what Paul Til-lich (1952) called the *ontology of courage*.[10]

As a kind of soirée, Paul Tillich, Akihisa Kondo, D.T. Suzuki, and Richard DeMartino gathered in various combinations with Karen Horney (1885–1952) for intimate discussions in her New York residence. Exchanges on Zen, Morita therapy, and psychoanalysis were insatiable for Horney, as was her desire to comprehend the difference between Zen and Buddhism (personal conversations with Kondo, 1990). Over time, their discourse stimulated the Terry Foundation Lectures given by Tillich at Yale University in 1952 (taped dialogues with Kondo, 1989, 1992).

> Nevertheless it is necessary for ontology of courage to include ontology of anxiety, for they are interdependent. And it is conceivable that in the light of the ontology of courage some fundamental aspects of anxiety become visible.

The first assertion about the nature of anxiety is this: anxiety is the state in which being is aware of its possible nonbeing.

(Tillich, 1952, The Courage to Be, p. 35)

At that time, psychiatrists in North America contemplated Zen and existential ideas about nothingness, death, being and non-being, and the natural angst that accompanies such possibilities. However, few grasped Zen as Zen.[11] Outside Kondo, Horney came closest to bridging the gap between Zen and psychoanalysis.

Horney was the earliest Euro-American psychiatrist interested in knowing about Morita therapy. Her fascination with Asian ideas and Buddhism began in the late 1930s (DeMartino, 1991).[12] Her focus on Zen peaked in 1950 when Suzuki received a grant from the Rockefeller Foundation and stayed in New York City. While lecturing on Zen at Columbia University, he met Horney. By a twist of fate, Akihisa Kondo received a 1950–1951 Fulbright Exchange Scholarship to study in New York City with scholars and analysts such as Norman Kelman (1924–1987)[13] and Kurt Goldstein (1878–1965), a German Jewish psychiatrist and pioneer in neuropsychology. Through Kelman, Kondo met Horney and eventually studied analysis under her guidance at the American Institute for Psychoanalysis.[14] Suzuki, Horney, and Kondo began meeting to discuss psychotherapy, authentic self, and Zen. Culminating from these associations, Horney travelled to Japan in the summer of 1952 with her daughter, Brigitte, and met with Suzuki, Kondo, DeMartino, and Morita psychiatrists, Takehisa Kora and Yoshiyuki Koga (1973).

Notably, Kora and Koga worked alongside Morita and are considered his disciples. In addition, Akitchika Nomura attended Morita's lectures in psychiatry and graduated from Jikei university in 1928. Nomura and Keiji Mizutani were mentored by Morita, too. Most significantly, Morita adopted his sister's son, Mishima, after the death of his own son. As his new heir, Mishima went on to become a psychiatrist; he carried on Morita's work and archived Morita's personal journals, calligraphies, and photos – some of which are presented with permission in this book.

Kondo arranged for Horney to have discussions with Kora and to give a lecture at Jikeikai School of Medicine; he translated her lecture into Japanese for this occasion. Of this lecture, Kondo wrote the following reflection in 1963, which is his typewritten, pre-edited paper that he gifted to me. This paper was published in 1991 as 'Recollections of Dr. Horney' in *The American Journal of Psychoanalysis*.

In expounding her basic idea about self-realization, the urge for self-growth, an optimistic, constructive idea against Freud's pessimistic one, she stated in her lecture that she found a very similar idea in Zen. She further referred to the similarity of her ideas with Morita's in understanding the importance of the patient's whole personality and emotional experiences. The increased understanding of Morita's ideas and his therapy clearly expressed in her lecture was the result of her intensive discussion with Dr. Kora, Dr. Koga, a disciple of Morita and myself in Hakone, a summer resort near Tokyo, where she visited before the lecture was given.

(Kondo, gifted unabridged version of 'Recollections of Dr. Horney')

FIGURE 2.1 Karen Horney and Takehisa Kora in Japan, 1952

(Gift to LeVine (incl. negative of print) from Akihisa Kondo)

Horney visited other Morita hospital settings in Tokyo and Kyoto, and discussed the complex nature of anxiety with key psychiatrists and Zen scholars (Kondo, 1983, 1992). Most scholars of Horney focus on the ways Buddhism rather than, Zen stirred new ideas about psychoanalysis for her (Quinn, 1988; Tro, 1993; Walborn, 2014). It is historically accurate to claim that Zen and Morita were equally stimulating for her. According to Kondo, Horney's overriding interest was in expanding psychoanalysis to be less dependent on analytic interpretations – a paradoxical task in itself – and an orientation directly related to Morita's philosophy. Horney moderated a discussion on Morita on 9 November 1952 at the Scientific Meetings at the New York Academy of Medicine.

> In her lecture to the Japanese psychiatrists, Horney expressed her ideas on the subject titled 'New Developments in Psychoanalysis'. She clarified her theory in contrast to Freud's, especially in connection with the basic difference of her understanding of human nature from that of Freud, namely the intrinsic human potentiality and urge for growth and self realization versus thanatos. She stressed the importance of paying therapeutic attention to the patient's personality as a whole and not to the symptoms, and also talked about the significance of the patient's emotional experience in therapy.
>
> *(Kondo, 'Recollections of Dr. Horney', unpublished paper, pp. 4–5)*[15]

According to Kondo, Horney came to comprehend Morita's consciousness while sitting in a Zen garden in Japan in the summer of 1952 – months before her

FIGURE 2.2   Karen Horney, 1952 in Dr Kora's hospital garden, Tokyo

(Gift to Le Vine from Akihisa Kondo)

death in New York.[16] Unfortunately, she lacked the time needed to determine how Morita's consciousness might augment her views on psychoanalysis. 'At the end of her stay in Japan, we talked about silence in analysis and stimulation by gardens that bring forward inner experiences of one's real life. The stillness in her was altered' (Kondo conversation, Tokyo, 1994).

Debate continues about Zen and Morita's consciousness.[17] To date, most scholars commenting on this topic have little to no operational knowledge of Morita's residential practice, or they equate Zen with Buddhism or a spiritual path (Leonhard, 1965; Kasulis, 1977, 1981; Smith, 1981).

In the early stages of her exploration, Karen Horney was equally interested in Buddhism, Zen and Morita therapy. During her Japan trip, Zen receded as she came to know more of Morita's theories and practice. Suzuki, too, took his first glimpse of Morita when he accompanied Horney to Kyoto to meet Genyu Usa, Zen practitioner and friend to Morita. It was at Usa's hospital that he saw Morita's calligraphies of Zen phrases. Somehow Suzuki did not fully digest Morita's insights before Horney's death, despite Kondo's first lecture on Morita at the New York Academy of Medicine, where Zen was discussed.

I took another research excursion to Japan in 2008 to re-interview Usa's surviving son, psychiatrist Shin-ichi Usa.[18] I sent him a section of this chapter so that he might comment on the historical content related to Horney's visit with his father; this is his follow-up letter, dated October 17, 2008.

Dear Dr. Peg LeVine,

Thank you for your kindness. This section of your book on 'Japanisme' gave me a feeling of the good old days. It is useful for us to walk in the history with Morita. In 1952, she (Horney) came to Kyoto. She invited my father, Genyu Usa, and asked about his relationship with Morita. She was in the company of Suzuki sensei, Akihisa Kondo, Richard DeMartino, Koji Sato, and Keiji Nishitani. However, in 1953, my father had another special visit from Suzuki. He looked around this hospital and talked to my father about Morita. This was Suzuki's first real point of contact with Morita therapy.

(Letter translated by Eiko Tamura)[19]

I recall a remarkable evening with Kondo sensei when he reminisced about a Zen garden in Hakone where he sat with Karen. 'Then and there I knew Karen embodied Zen.' He gave me this photo (Figure 2.3) and its negative and told me to publish it honourably one day.

It is noted that Keiji Nishitani (1900–1945) was a philosopher affected by Zen who lived during Morita's era. He studied under Martin Heidegger and was a disciple of Kitaro Nishida. Overall, he integrated existential thought, Zen, literature, religion, and poetry akin to Morita. Figure 2.4 shows a calligraphy by Morita from December 1927: "Reality lies not in a static fixed state but in motion, itself".

German philosopher Friedrich Nietzsche (1844–1900) is cited by Morita in another calligraphy from the Mishima Morita Archives.

Nietzsche said: South wind welcomes the North wind
A storm comes like a spiral.
In those situations, I go inside and remain calm in the eye of the storm.
But Morita says: The South wind is cool and the North wind is cold. The storm is scary. I have no time for such matters.

(Translation by Naoki Watanabe)

Morita slices through the cognitive notion that enlightenment equates to remaining calm in all circumstances. Stillness lies not in a fixed state of mind, either. In correspondence with Christopher Ives (July, 2016), 'slice' is a way of translating *danmen*, which describes Morita's teaching style. 'Rather, Truth is discovered dynamically in the diachronic process of a subject acting and evolving in time; truth is not an objective something that is found in a static slice of time/reality' (Ives correspondence, July 2016).

Through her dialogues with Koga, Kora, Kondo, and Suzuki, Horney's exposure to Zen and *danmen* persuasion was intensely rich, as was her introduction to Morita's philosophy and practice. Following Japan, she wrote zealously about psychoanalysis and the 'real self' from a Zen perspective, which took a different shape from her earlier writings on the 'idealised' self. Horney began to explore how her patients' distress is related to their natural desire to access and live according to their authentic self. Her conversations with Kondo explored this theme regularly.

Holding similar interests in Eastern philosophy and psychotherapy was Carl Gustav Jung (1875–1961), a contemporary of Freud, Horney, and an acquaintance

FIGURE 2.3 Karen Horney, 1952 in a Zen garden in Hakone

(Photo taken by Kondo and gifted to LeVine)

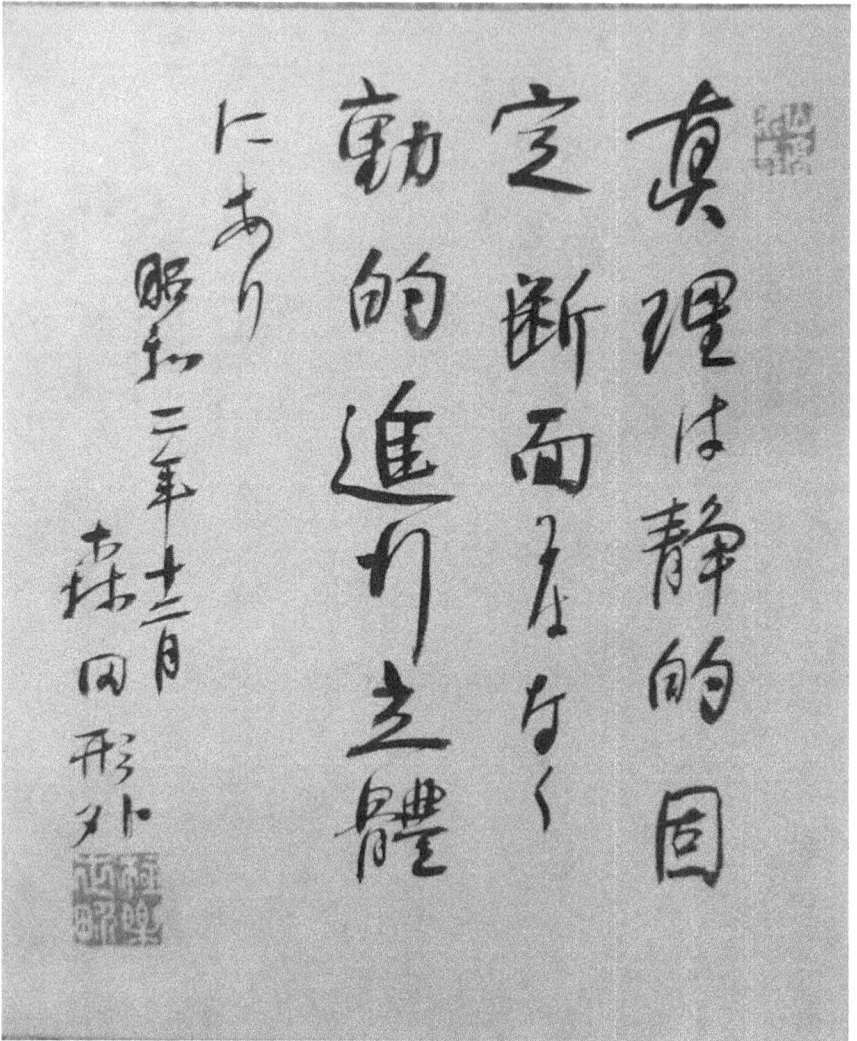

FIGURE 2.4 'Reality lies not...' December 1927. (Signed, Morita Keigai)

With written permission from the Mishima Morita Hospital Archives

of Suzuki. He contemplated the role of self in 'existential neurosis' (Jung, 1964). Jung but did not pursue Zen and psychotherapy as formally as Horney had done at the end of her life. According to Kondo, Horney had discussions with Suzuki about Jung's theory and its relevance to Zen. She reflected with Kondo on Freud and Jung's obliviousness to Morita's theory and practice and the true essence of Zen. 'It was this absence of awareness by Jung and Freud that made Karen most committed to bring these theories to the foreground of psychiatry' (Kondo, taped conversation, 1990). As we shall see in the following section, scholars maintained an interest in Eastern philosophy (Parsons, 2009), but constantly fell short of examining what Morita had integrated into his theory and method of practice.

> For Karen, the 'real self' is not hypothetical. One's authentic self exists despite a patient's lived history or culture. Too much suffering hinders one from experiencing authentic nature. She believed that therapists, too, gain pure intuition once they know their authentic selves. She was very interested in this intuition for advancing her analytic practice. You can only imagine our discussions about Morita and my delight to have truly known her.
>
> *(Supervision, Kondo with LeVine, 1992)*

Correspondence about consciousness: letters by James Kirsch, Carl Jung, and Akihisa Kondo

As happens when researching history, dangling threads often connect in coincidental or accidental ways. In early spring of 2009, the Jungian psychoanalyst Ann Lammers contacted me. She was in the final stage of researching four decades of correspondence between Carl Jung and James Kirsch for her book, *The Jung-Kirsch Letters: The Correspondence of C. G. Jung and James Kirsch* (Lammers, 2011). James Kirsch (1901–1989), who identified as Jewish, American, and German, established Jungian analysis in Tel Aviv, Berlin, London, and California. Relating to my work and our conversation, Lammers pieced together Kirsch's links to Akihisa Kondo and generously sent me a copy of the correspondence between Kirsch and Jung about Kondo on enlightenment (Lammers, 2011, pp. 239–242). In their correspondence, Kirsch describes for Jung the Satori (enlightenment) experience that Akihisa Kondo told him about during personal conversation. In this discourse, Kirsch described Kondo as his 'genuine' friend. Kirsch wrote to Jung on December 2, 1958.

> I would be very grateful to you if you could comment on this question of whether Satori, or any form of sudden widening of consciousness, could exist without some image, and also what this image-less state is to which Zen and also Indian Yoga so often refers.

In a self-enhancing manner, Jung replied to Kirsch on December 10, 1958.

> Many thanks for your kind and interesting letter of December 2. The satori experience of your friend Dr. Kondo is a typical mandala vision. If there are people in the East who assert that they've had an imageless experience, one must always remember that as a rule the report is extremely unpsychological. It's the tradition that such an experience is imageless, and therefore they say that the experience has been imageless. Not because they experienced it as imageless but just because it is the tradition.
>
> *(Jung, 1958, in Lammers, 2011, p. 238)*

After reading these letters, I was led to explore further the complex dynamics that prevented Kondo, Morita therapy, and Zen from full consideration by Jung and his associates. While Jung referred to Kondo as a psychologist rather than a psychiatrist, his reply to Kirsch was delivered as dismissal of Kirsch and Kondo's association. During a discussion on Jung and consciousness in 1989, Kondo told me that his companion and colleague, James Kirsch, might have extended his own ideas had he spent more time in Japan and less time empowering Jung's ideas. Rather than inquiring into Kondo's experience, or asking Kirsch more about his fascination with Kondo's ideas, Jung closed the doors – and whatever the dynamics between Kirsch and Jung, Kirsch did not venture further.

More puzzling is the fact that Jung was introduced to Kondo's ideas through Suzuki's references, though he may not have made the connections out of context. Kondo, too, knew of Jung via his dialogue with D.T. Suzuki in the early 1950s. I find it peculiar that Jung failed to recognise Kondo as the psychiatrist who was Karen Horney's protégé and as one very psychodynamically minded – particularly since Kondo was active in the *American Institute of Psychoanalysis* in New York. Giving Jung the benefit of doubt, there may have been a New York–California void or competition in scholarly exchanges at that time. Regardless, in the end, Jung replied to Kirsch by reifying his personal Mandala theory.

Kondo told me in fine detail of his first and second enlightenment. I like to imagine what might have happened had Jung (or Kirsch for that matter) inquired further. Jung would have found Kondo well versed in various Mandalas, including the famous Japanese Mandala on 'Contemplation', the *Tiama Mandala* that dates to 763 CE. Also, because Kondo had an affinity with Pure Land Buddhism, Jōdo Shinshū, and Zen, he knew all too well about ritual uses of various Mandalas. He himself contemplated the *Nembutsu Mandala* created by Shinran, the founder of Pure Land. Had I known more about this dynamic history when Kondo was alive, I am certain he would entertain wholeheartedly my question: 'I wonder sensei, what would Kirsch have contributed to psychoanalysis had he dismissed Jung's interpretation of your enlightenment and pursued his question exclusively on his own or with you?'

What is vital in the letter Kirsch sent to Jung about Kondo's Satori is Kirsch's reference to the *widening of consciousness*, which is the term Kondo used wholeheartedly. Jung bypassed this reference by claiming that 'people of the East' say they have an imageless experience because it is tradition to claim so. How I wish that Kirsch had taken Jung's reply back to Kondo for further exploration. Retrospectively, too, I wish I had followed some of the threads with James Kirsch and Akihisa Kondo while they were alive. Had contact occurred, Kirsch might have experienced the 'imageless experience' that arrives as one's consciousness widens.

In fact, I was in the early stages of intense supervision under Kondo when James Kirsch died in 1989. Kondo spoke fleetingly to me about this loss. While I have read correspondence exchanged between Kondo, Horney, Fromm, DeMartino, and other scholars and clinicians, I have only a handful of passing comments by Kondo about James Kirsch. After reading the letters exchanged between Kirsch and Jung about Kondo, I see more clearly how Kirsch was caught by Jung's treatise on the function of ego.

Kondo spoke to me, too, about the workshop on Zen Buddhism and Psychoanalysis that took place in 1957 in Mexico where Erich Fromm, D.T. Suzuki, and Richard DeMartino were key figures. In fact, as mentioned earlier, the renowned book *Zen Buddhism and Psychoanalysis,* by Fromm, Suzuki, and DeMartino (1960), was published from the proceedings of that workshop. Kirsch and Kondo were not invited authors, in spite of Kirsch's attendance at that conference. Significantly, a reprint of the paper from *Psychologia* (1960) that James Kirsch gave at that Zen workshop in Cuernavaca, Mexico was published in 2011 – a half century later. This contribution came from the collaboration between the journal editor, Richard Payne, and Thomas Kirsch, MD, Jungian analyst and son of James Kirsch.[20] In 1958, Kondo published, 'Zen in psychotherapy: The virtue of sitting' (Kondo, 1958b).

Kondo reflected on the direction Zen had taken in the United States following Horney's death in 1952:

> After Karen died, the freshness she offered psychoanalysis dissolved into a stagnant pond. Horney wanted to advance an analysis that leads a patient to 'authentic self'. We talked about Freud's induction methods and concluded he interfered with patients' imaginations by overinterpreting their material.
>
> *(Conversation with Kondo, 1990)*[21]

In his collected works, *Psychology and Religion, West and East,* Jung (1950) accounted for the role of paradox in fostering human growth. However, he did not extend his theory of consciousness widely into Nature, or develop a therapy with paradox as the core. It seems to me that a vital momentum for Morita therapy got lost during that Mexican workshop in which Suzuki, Fromm, and DeMartino came together to produce a particular US version of Zen, Buddhism, and Psychotherapy – I contend that they branded Zen and psychoanalysis—American style.

The time between 1950 and 1952 was a hit-and-miss era for Morita therapy. This was when Morita was given brief, prominent standing amongst key psychiatrists and scholars in the United States. The topical collection of articles in *The American Journal of Psychoanalysis* (1952, Vol. 12, No. 1) raised scholarly interest in Morita in North America. In particular, Karen Horney's article, 'The Paucity of Inner Experiences' (1952b, pp. 3–19), was followed by Akihisa Kondo's, 'Intuition in Zen Buddhism' (1952b, pp. 10–15).[22] On 27 February 1952, Horney read her paper before the New York Academy of Medicine at the Association for the Advancement of Psychoanalysis where she embraced Kierkegaard: 'For only if we no longer will the impossible do we have a glimpse of the possible – which gives us a sense of inner freedom' (p. 9).

The philosophy of Paul Tillich intrigued Horney. His interpretation of human existence harbours simultaneously an estrangement from and actualisation of essence. Horney appreciated how Tillich's ideas departed from other theologians and existentialists because he placed 'practicality and essential essence' side-by-side. Ian Wray (1986) comments on Tillich in *Buddhism and Psychotherapy: A Buddhist Perspective.* This notion of 'cultivation' by Wray resonates with

Morita's belief that cultivation of mind, not meditation by mind, returns one to a natural state:[23]

> The theologian Tillich argues that Christianity has been primarily concerned with the problem of justification rather than sanctification, that is, in being saved through the grace of God by believing in him . . . emphasis is reflected in the lack of Christian practices aimed at practical self-improvement . . . Spiritual exercises tend to follow a pattern of prayer and meditation, though these are very different from Buddhist meditation.
>
> *(Wray, 1986, p. 160)*

On October 22, 1952, Kondo was invited to speak at the meeting of the Association for the Advancement of Psychoanalysis at the New York Academy of Medicine. He gave an address on *Zen and Morita therapy* that Horney arranged and attended (personal conversation with Kondo). Following, Karen Horney was moderator for a discussion of Kondo's papers on Morita therapy at a meeting of the Association for the Advancement of Psychoanalysis held on November 9, 1952. [24]

While transcribing her Japan experiences into words for her last lecture, Horney was aware of her own frailty. She spoke to Kondo about her cancer and told him she wanted to organise a final lecture; her intention was to bring her knowledge from Japan into the culture of psychoanalysis. She told Kondo of her 'surrender' to Nature in the garden in Daigo Sanbō-in (Temple of Three Treasures in Daigo), which she visited twice with Kondo, DeMartino, and her daughter, Brigitte. 'Thereafter', Kondo told me, 'Karen no longer lamented about the length of her life.' As I write this, I reflect on something Kondo told me in 1998 as he was nearing the end of his life:

> The longer I live, the more I live the width of life rather than the length.

Shortly before her death, Horney asked Kondo to continue publishing from his understanding of psychoanalytic dynamics and the nature of consciousness; she feared that members of her institute would advance analytic training without honouring her desire to operationalise her 'realisation'. She expressed to Kondo, 'Who else will go to Japan with an inquisitive mind and follow on with this work? Find someone who can continue in this way.' Her collective experiences in Japan, from visiting Morita hospitals, talking with scholars, and sitting in Zen gardens were excursions toward, rather than away from, an essential 'dynamic' psychoanalysis that includes Nature. After her death, Kondo saw some of Karen's patients in New York before returning to Tokyo (Kondo, personal conversations, November, 1992).[25]

Most personally, Kondo recalled often his colleagueship and friendship with Karen Horney, and their profound stimulating discussions on original self, Zen, psychiatry, Morita therapy, and psychoanalysis. Whether in his office in Japan or her office or apartment in New York, or along the streets they walked together, they discussed how Zen might inform psychoanalysis. Perhaps without enough historical information, most biographers link Horney to the Buddhist scholar, D.T. Suzuki. While Suzuki offered invaluable discussions on Zen, Akihisa Kondo was the psychoanalyst, Zen practitioner, and Morita therapist who engaged in dialogue about clinical practice with Horney. To date, biographers have said little about this relationship. Kondo spoke to me candidly about a biography on Horney (Quinn, 1988). He granted Quinn an interview when she was researching Horney's travel in Japan. Kondo told me that the biographer's interests fell short of tracing Horney's transformation at Daigo Sanbō-in temple in Kyoto, much less Horney's interests in Kondo's and Morita's ideas on authentic self.[26]

It was not until decades after her death in late 1952 that Horney's lectures were gathered into a book and edited by Douglas Ingram (1987): *Karen Horney: Final Lectures*. This most vital book marks the summit of Horney's personal and professional evolution.

Alongside Akihisa Kondo, Richard DeMartino (1922–2013) was privy to Karen Horney's deeper thoughts. He speaks intimately about her desires in the following passage:[27]

> But right down to the closing months – even days – of her life, Horney continued to think and to rethink. As she did, she gave every evidence of a steadily intensifying interest in Zen, and in her personal life, she was developing a closer and closer relationship with Suzuki – as, in her professional life, she was with Kondo. No one can ever be sure, of course, what the final outcome would have been had she lived several years longer. However, at least to this observer, Horney's overall path and the overall path of Zen were moving steadfastly toward a greater convergence rather than divergence.
>
> (DeMartino, 1991, p. 280)

This passionate era of dialogue on Zen, Morita, and psychoanalysis had its last unveiling in the 1953 edition of *The American Journal of Psychoanalysis* (Volume XIII) with *In Memoriam: Karen Horney, MD September 16, 1885 – December 4, 1952*. This edition featured Akihisa Kondo's 'Morita Therapy: A Japanese Therapy for Neurosis' (pp. 31–37), with descriptions of Morita's four stages and excerpts from a patient's diary. Also included in that edition is the work by Zen scholar, Alan W. Watts, 'Asian Psychology and Modern Psychiatry'. Watts wrote:

> therapy is not the increase of conscious control over the unconscious by the ego. It is rather an integration of conscious and unconscious, preparatory to a type of living, thinking, and acting which in Zen Buddhism is called mushin (mu 'no', shin 'mind'). Mushin is a kind of 'inspired spontaneity.' It is the art of making the appropriate responses to life without the interruption of that wobbling and indecisive state which we call 'choosing.'. . . In Western psychology, free association – the nearest thing to mushin – has a different objective. The Freudian or Jungian analyst is primarily interested in what associations, symbol, and other diagnostic materials are produced in

free association. In Buddhist psychology the point of interest is rather that spontaneous images and symbols are produced.

(Watts, 1953, pp. 29–30)

Though cultures apart, Morita and Horney challenged Freud's theory of repression and neurosis, while advocating a broader discourse on disorder that allows social and environmental influences. After Horney's death, Morita therapy became nearly invisible in the United States as a viable therapeutic option, despite the sprinkling of articles that continued to appear in the psychoanalytic journals in the USA, such as Kondo (1961) and Kora (1968).

Just at the end of her life in October, 1952 when Horney asked Kondo to speak on Zen and Morita therapy to the New York Academy of Medicine, Jacobson and Berenberg (1952) discussed Buddhist influences on Morita therapy, while providing statistics from Kyushu University in their article in *The American Journal of Psychiatry*. This brought dialogue about Morita therapy forward from theory into practice and research. Meanwhile, Takehisa Kora (1955) published an article in a French journal, which brought Morita's theory and practice into the European domain. Kondo (1960) commented on Morita and Freud:

> At approximately the same time as Morita was active, Freud's theories and analytical methods of treatment were introduced into Japan and utilized by some groups of therapists . . . Following Freud, Marui emphasized the libido theory, stressing the importance of the patient's past experience, traumatic childhood experiences and other Freudian ideas. Morita, on the other hand, in accordance with his own understanding of neurosis, stressed the importance of a change in the patient's attitude here and now through the realization and reorientation of his own basic life force. He did not pay much attention to the patient's past experiences, nor did he approve of the libido theory, though he acknowledged the place of sex as an expression of human life force.
>
> *(Kondo, 1960, p. 223)*

I have chosen to emphasise Morita, Horney, Kora, and Kondo as pioneers and conscientious objectors given their tenacious pursuit of a natural, humane, and sustainable therapy. When considering the general assumptions of their time, that 'mental disorder' is contained in the individual, they advanced theories on the impact of social and environmental contexts on wellbeing. Mournfully, after Horney's death, Morita therapy became nearly invisible in the United States as a viable psychiatric treatment. While an unfortunate setback, a sprinkling of articles in the USA in the late 1950s, 1960s, and 1970s kept Morita's name active in psychological medicine, and religious and Zen studies (Fromm, Suzuki, and Martino, 1960; Fujita, 1967; Ikeda, 1971; Kelman, 1959a, 1959b; A. Kondo, 1958a, 1958b; K. Kondo, 1976; Kora, 1965, 1968; Kora and Sato, 1958; D.T. Suzuki, 1975, 1977).

In a similar vein, Zen scholar, Masao Abe (1915–2006) engaged with the New York City stream of psychoanalysts from 1955 to 1957, just three years after Horney's death.[28] Her institute, however, was building its own momentum, while scholarly interests in Zen and psychoanalysis were slowly fading and transforming. Abe brought an interfaith perspective to this dialogue, which may have dampened the potential for Morita's advancement in the United States. His associates included Paul Tillich, Akihisa Kondo, and D. T. Suzuki.[29] According to Kondo, Abe knew of Karen Horney's trip to Japan with Suzuki and DeMartino in 1952, and her drive to comprehend Zen related to Morita's ideas of authentic self. In one of our discussions, I asked Kondo how it was that Suzuki or Abe did not discuss or endorse Morita publicly.

Le Vine: I can't help but contemplate the years just after Horney's death. How it is that Japanese Zen scholars in New York did not mention Morita in their publications. How is it that someone in the American Institute of Psychoanalysis did not track Horney's interests on authentic self?

Kondo: A curious question. Karen and I spoke often about Morita, psychoanalysis, Buddhism, and Zen, but she did not have enough life time to reliably stimulate others on this topic. Other scholars had their ideas already shaped around particular schools of Zen more exclusively.

Le Vine: By this, do you mean those connected to the training by Kitaro Nishida in the Kyoto school, like Suzuki and Abe?

Kondo: Yes, in part. You see, at that time in New York City, scholars were building their American reputations and gaining a respectful following of students. I imagine they were caught by the excitement of this. And quite simply, at that time Morita sat outside the frame of consideration by Japanese Zen scholars in the United States. Direct lineage was too important. While Morita was attuned to the philosophy of Kitaro Nishida, he was not attached to any stream. The student of Nishida's, Shin'ichi Hisamatsu,[30] was associated with Abe and Suzuki in Kyoto. Even Richard (DeMartino) was in this lineage. Although I was a Zen practitioner, I was not attached to any one school, which could be a reason that Karen and I could explore contradictions and links between psychiatry and Zen in most lively ways. She pressed to know about Zen and Morita therapy from the standpoint of real self so she could assist her patients to this end.

(Personal conversation, Kondo, January 1992)

Nonetheless, while striking few chords in the United States, Horney's contributions seemed to revitalise Japanese and American interests in Morita therapy. A major thrust for Morita therapy inside Japan came in 1958 when Norman Kelman (psychoanalyst in New York connected to Columbia University and protégé of Horney's) met with Takehisa Kora in Japan to discuss Morita therapy. In 1959, Kelman contributed an article on 'Psychotherapy in the Far East'. As mentioned previously, at that time, the General Meeting on Psychopathology focused exclusively on Morita therapy; its session was held in a Buddhist temple in Nagano in October, 1958. In July 1959, the clinical journal *Seishin-Igaku* published a special edition on Morita therapy. As profoundly, on May 14, 1963 in Tokyo, D. T. Suzuki presented on 'Zen and Psychiatry' at the Joint meeting of the American Psychiatric Association and Japanese Society of Psychiatry and Neurology. He would have been exposed to the work of Akichika Nomura who presented on Morita therapy at that same meeting.

Soon after in March 1963, Harold Kelman published 'Oriental psychological processes and creativity' in the *American Journal of Psychoanalysis*. Approximating Morita's thesis but without reference to such, Kelman (1963, pp. 67–68) calls for 'the creating of a new form of cosmic consciousness, so urgent in our world today . . . what emerges are spontaneity, absolute subjectivity, pure consciousness, an aspect of the all, of cosmos, of Reality.' That which he referenced as the 'unique contributions of the Oriental Psychological Processes' relates directly to Zen and Morita's theory of consciousness (conversations with Kondo, 1989). Indeed, this was an effervescent period in psychiatry for Morita-related précises, Zen, and expanded notions of consciousness.

The 1960s to 1970s: Morita therapy and Fritz Perls

Few know that Frederick (Fritz) Perls (1893–1970) was a Morita therapy inpatient before he developed Gestalt therapy. In his autobiography, *In and Out of the Garbage Pail* (1969), Perls writes about the coining of 'Gestalt therapy' in 1950, and the development of his methods between 1964 and 1966 in the United States. He wrote often about his impressions of Zen. And yet Perls and his biographers have omitted a vital part of his history. Perls became a Morita therapy inpatient in Kyoto in 1962.

Perls went to New York in 1946 and soon after met Erich Fromm and Karen Horney (from whom he sought therapy), while being influenced by Harry Stack Sullivan's perspective on mental disorder and how events disrupt an individual and her/his relationship to the environment. Though it is recognised formally that Perl's interest in Zen was stirred by his relationship to Paul Weisz, this was also the era when Karen Horney's fascination peaked regarding Zen and Morita therapy – before Perls went to Kyoto, Japan (conversations with Kondo, 1998).[31] While reflecting on these facts, I pondered over the failure by Perls to write or state anything about Morita therapy. Paradoxically, with muted associations to Morita therapy alongside claims to having an alliance with Zen, the silence by Perls about his own encounters begs the question about some of Gestalt therapy's theoretical development, as well as his interpretation of Zen.[32]

None of Perls' biographers has mentioned his Morita inpatient stay. For instance, Jack Gaines (1979) cites William Quinn's account of Perls' hospital stay in Japan but makes no reference to Morita:

> He had a friend in Japan who was an abbot of a Zen monastery. The abbot put him in a hospital. He was there for several days, and he made a serious effort to stop smoking. Each day the abbot would pay him a formal visit in his formal attire. Fritz felt very serene. Then, after 3 or 4 days, he suddenly

exploded – smashed up furniture, just went completely berserk. And as he was watching himself do this, he thought, 'What? What? Is this me, tender little Fritz?'

(*Gaines, 1979, p. 115*)

We know that Perls' attending psychiatrist was Shinichi Usa, the son of the Zen priest, Genyu Usa. Sansei hospital was founded in 1927 at a Zen Buddhist site – a place where Morita stayed when he was in Kyoto. The 'abbot' was a Japanese psychologist and scholar of Zen, Koji Sato (1905–1971), who was the editor of *Psychologia: An International Journal of Psychology in the Orient*. Sato (1959, 1964) wrote on Zen, psychology, and enlightenment. In fact, Sato was an associate of Genyu Usa and Takehisa Kora. It was Shinichi Usa who agreed to treat Perls without fee out of felt obligation to his father, friends, and associates. A synopsis of Fritz Perls' inpatient stay was presented by Usa at the 12th World Congress of Psychiatry in Yokohama in 2002.

In 2008, I interviewed and filmed S. Usa on two occasions with the generous assistance of Naoki Watanabe. Not only did Usa speak candidly and at length about Perls, he had preserved the hospital records from Perls' stay from May 31 to June 4, 1962. Usa spoke frankly of his treatment of Perls during *Morita Therapy: Its Transcendence of History* in the symposium on 'Transcultural Psychotherapy' at the 12th World Congress of Psychotherapy (Yokohama Japan, August 26, 2002). Figure 2.5 is a copy of the Sansei hospital admission form for Frederick Perls.

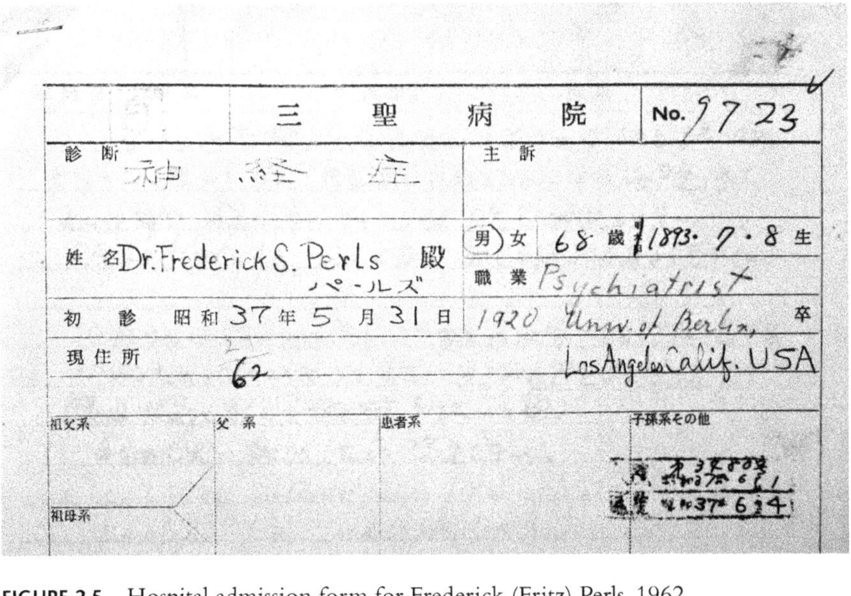
三 聖 病 院 No. 9723
診断 神経症
主訴
姓名 Dr. Frederick S. Perls 殿
パールズ
男 女 68 歳 1893・7・8 生
職業 Psychiatrist
初診 昭和 37 年 5 月 31 日
1920 Univ. of Berlin, 卒
現住所 62 Los Angeles Calif. USA
祖父系
父系
患者系
子孫系その他
祖母系

FIGURE 2.5 Hospital admission form for Frederick (Fritz) Perls, 1962

(Archives of Sansei Hospital for Morita Therapy, Kyoto, LeVine, 2009)

Included in the hospital archive was a diary written by Perls in German and English. Perls penned the following passage at the time of his hospital admission on 12 July, 1962.

> I do not want to explain too much about myself. I simply want to stop smoking. That is why I am here. And also, Sato talks about Zen and Morita therapy and how they have something to do deeply with each other.
>
> *(Fritz Perls, 1962, Sansei hospital archives)*

I presented this history in 2008 with excerpts from Perls' handwritten diary at the International Congress of Gestalt Therapy in Manchester, United Kingdom: this was discussed during the co-presentation with Professor Jon Frew, Gestalt scholar, trainer, and practitioner. My section of the presentation was called: *Squaring History: Fritz Perls, Japan, and Morita therapy in 1962*.[33]

The following passage is from Perls' 1962 diary:

> Ditran. Morita therapy. Patient must stay in bed. But patient gets up. You bring patient back to bed. How *not* to get tobacco? Have you had a drug addict in treatment? I tried hypnosis and auto-suggestions – no good. When tension comes I don't know that I take a cigarette. Cigarette is suddenly in my mouth and I am smoking.
>
> I am very successful. I am not happy. I have compulsion to smoke. No good for lungs and psyche . . . Is there enough supervision to prevent my getting cigarettes? Strong supervision needed. Can a nurse be employed who speaks English or German fluently?
>
> My power of visualization (inner seeing) is like in a fog (smoke-screen) and my taste is fuzzy (from too much smoking). I hope to clear up the fog – the fuzziness. I am convinced that all this is connected. That the smoking is a compulsive resistance to prevent myself from seeing clear.
>
> *(Sansei hospital archives, Kyoto, permission from S. Usa)*

In his biographical text, *In and Out of the Garbage Pail* (1969), Perls wrote for public eyes about his experience as an inpatient at Sansei hospital in Kyoto, but did not name the therapy or the hospital:

> A doctor had designed a method of treating neuroses. Three days in bed. The patient is only allowed to get up to go to the john. Let's try this! Use it for smoking interruption! Young doctor speaks no English. Non-medical assistant makes all arrangements. I ask for interpreter. Yes, but I have to pay extra. Have a good room by myself . . . I stand it for over two days, then throw a temper tantrum, run out and buy cigarettes.
>
> *(Perls, 1969, p. 106)*

In fairness to Perls, while I am unaware of the full scope of treatment at Sansei hospital in the early 1960s, during my visits to this hospital between 1989 and 2011,

I observed sketchy supervision of patients and inconsistent attention to patients' safety and health by S. Usa. Three inpatients told me directly of their experiences to this effect. Perl's impression of Morita therapy and his abrupt departure may well be related to his experience of neglect. He did indicate that he had requested medication to soften his withdrawal symptoms, and he was denied assistance. Had he experienced Morita therapy in a centre that did not render Zen as a stark, stern treatment, and had his psycho-physiological withdrawal from nicotine been medically and therapeutically attended, he might have experienced the integrating and nurturing nature of Morita therapy and advanced it, clinically. Alternately, if Perls had documented formally the details of his treatment at Usa's hospital, I am certain Kondo and other English-speaking Japanese therapist-scholars would have set the record straight about what is and is not classic Morita therapy.

When referring to Zen in the 1950s, D.T. Suzuki became known for his phrase, 'A rose is not a rose that we call a rose'. Perls is known for his phrase, '. . . a rose is a rose is a rose'. While this reframing by Perls may appear insightfully Zen to his American audience, Perl's passage shaved clean the nuanced edges of Zen intended by Suzuki. Also, this excerpt derives from the poem by Gertrude Stein, *Sacred Emily*, which was written in 1913 and published in 1922 in *Geography and Plays*: 'Rose is a rose is a rose is a rose.'[34]

Suzuki meant that once the mind gives a rose a name, the living form is objectified, which diminishes our access to the essence of rose. Currently, too, some of Morita's terms have been homogenised and taken out of the sequential context of the therapy. For instance, one North American interpretation of *arugamama* has been rendered by a catchy phrase: 'Accept feelings as they are.' Morita never intended acceptance to be interpreted in this way (conversations with Kondo and Kora, 1996). Rather, as discussed throughout this book, *arugamama* is an orientation or perception where upon one *sees into* that which arises. Fujita (1986) uses the term *jujitsu-hon'i* (authentic existence) to explain self-realisation that arises from relinquishing to the nature of one's true nature inside Nature (pp. 74–75). Thus, emotions happen in accordance with how they arise, naturally. *Arugamama* coincides with Zen *suchness* wherein one takes or sees the suchness inside reality – it's isness – and responds accordingly. One responds to emotions and reality without the judging mind or command to accept anything – without naming a rose as a rose.

About the time Perls was leaving Japan in the 1960s, Kondo (1960) and Kora (1965) were active in publishing articles on Morita therapy in ethno-psychiatry journals in the USA. Also, David Reynolds (1969) completed his ethnographic study on traditional Morita therapy in Japan as part of his doctoral dissertation in anthropology. Comparative analyses of religion and East–West approaches to therapy were strong in this era (Kumasaka, Levy, and DeVos, 1965; Ohara and Reynolds, 1968; Iwai and Reynolds, 1970; Ikeda, 1971; Jacobson, 1974; Murase and Johnson, 1974; T. Suzuki and R. Suzuki, 1981). In addition, this was a time when Morita therapy was being reviewed for its experiential therapeutic strengths, as found in the article by Tomonori Suzuki (1969) on 'Noiroze no taiken ryoho' (Experiential Treatment of Neurosis).

Another bridge for Morita therapy in North America comes from Suk Choo Chang, a psychiatrist and psychoanalyst who endorses Morita's experiential-based therapy. During Chang's youth in Korea in the 1940s, he suffered from anxious symptoms and was taken to a psychiatrist by his father. The psychiatrist suggested that he read Takehisa Kora's articles on Morita therapy – from which Chang claims he gained inspiration and relief from the various quotes, including passages on Zen (Chang, 2010). Eventually, following medical school and the events of the Korean War (1950–1953), Chang migrated to the United States and took up analytic training in New York. He resides in Seattle currently (personal correspondence, 2012). Chang published 'Morita Therapy' in the *American Journal of Psychotherapy* in 1974. Overall, Takehisa Kora (disciple of Morita) influenced his orientation. Herein, Chang poses a dynamic question that encourages therapists to reflect on the dimensionality of their practice. 'What is the nature of *person*, and does one relate to each other and the society and the still larger scheme of things – the cosmos and history?' (Chang, 2010, p. 141).

The 1970s: Zen and alternative consciousness revisited

The 1970s was a promising period for Morita's name to benefit from counter-culture movements in Europe and the United States, an era with a strong interest in peace, spirituality, and transcendence. This orientation coincides partially with phenomena under exploration in the 1971 book, *Be Here Now: The Cookbook for a Sacred Life.* This book was on the shelves of many university students and scholars of social science (including my own); it is an illustrative text revealing the transformative spiritual journey of Richard Alpert (born in 1931) who changed his name to Baba Ram Das in India. Even Kondo had a personal first edition copy in his Japanese study room.

Be Here Now was published by the Lama Foundation and sold for $3.33. As brief history, in 1961 while at Harvard, Ram Das co-explored consciousness with Timothy Leary, Ralph Metzner, Aldous Huxley, and Allen Ginsberg. At that time, a variety of psychedelic-based substances were used to assist exploration of 'the source of consciousness' itself. Mind expansion via chemical induction became a catalyst for spiritual seeking at that time. Ram Das (1971, pp. 104–107) describes 'The Hermitage' and the solitude period that community members undergo (alongside Abbot visits) at a spiritual community in the United States. While slightly resembling the seclusion, rest of Morita's first stage, Morita did not advocate placing the mind anywhere, ingesting neuro-altering substances, or meditation.

While Ram Das seems to capture Morita's message by his phrase *Drop into Reality*, I wonder what his message and method of exploration would have been had he entered Morita's four stages of therapy. Again, the path Alpert took represents what he thought was a crossroad in world history. Meanwhile Morita remained inside Asian borders. In fact, Ram Das almost went to Japan, but chose India as his junction instead. I wonder. Had he gone to Japan around the time Perls was exploring Morita and Zen – how might he have interpreted his own quote? 'You can't rip the skin off a snake. The snake must molt the skin. That's the rate it happens' (Ram Das, 1971, p. 57).

Inside and outside Japan, exploration into Zen in Morita therapy surged in psychiatry and psychology journals. Rokuro Ishida (1971) wrote an article on *Dialectic*

Characteristics of Naikansei in which he explored Morita therapy through the philo-sophical lens of Kitarō Nishida (1870–1945), and Nishida's thesis on *The Good* (1950). In particular, Nishida adopted Western terms when attempting to convey for a Western audience the experience of 'Pure Experience' (*junsui keiken*). For Nishida, pure experience precedes individual experience, which stands in contrast to views by William James wherein personal experience precedes pure experience. Had Nishida challenged the human-centric views of Descartes 'I think, therefore I am', he might have asserted 'I think, therefore, according to nature'.

More pointedly, Ishida was intrigued by Nishida's philosophy on pure experi-ence, as was D.T. Suzuki. In fact, Kondo told me that Suzuki was interested in Morita patients' experiences of real self, and that Suzuki thought the supine posi-tion in the seclusion stage could prime a client for enlightenment. The strategic enactment of 'inbetweeness' as a pure experience is essential to the therapeutic process and outcome. In Morita therapy, the between-moments hold significance once anxiety runs a natural course in the first rest stage. I notice often in my prac-tice how a client holds the past and future simultaneously when faced with a life transition phase, as long as anxiety is not given power by the mind to force vacilla-tion. Ishida noted that significant change is related to the 'dialectic transition at the time of deep meditation'. I would hypothesise strongly that this is the therapeutic moment when anxiety drops off – a view consistent with Zen.

From another perspective, Takeo Doi (1920–2009) explored human emotions and how relational dynamics and obligations of Japanese culture shape states of emotions, such as shame (Caudill and Doi, 1963). By contrast, Morita did not label emotional states, per se, and focused on situations, perceptions, and cogni-tions – cultural or otherwise – that interfere with the natural rhythms of emotion. Doi points to *amae*, a term he coined from the verb *amaeru*, which simply put is the dynamic process whereby one person is induced to care for the other (Doi, 1986). Doi wrote *Anatomy of Dependence* as the definitive text in Japanese on *Amae* in 1971. John Bester translated it into English in 1973. As an extension of his 1958 article in *Neurologia Japonica*, 'Psychopathology of *Shinkeishitsu*, especially regard-ing the psychodynamics of *Toraware*', Doi argued that shinkeishitsu (anxiety from over-sensitivity to body function) and *toraware* (obsessive thinking) cannot be cured through any Zen-based practice, such as Morita therapy, since the patient's early developmental dependencies are evidenced in *amae*, and this socio-cultural presen-tation requires therapeutic intervention by an analytic-dynamic method (conversa-tion with Takeo Doi in Kondo's office in Tokyo, 1999).

Despite the fact that Doi was interested in pathways for patients to overcome what he called 'infantile dependencies', he failed to account for the capacity of humans to spread awareness outside the social sphere. I met Dr Doi in 1999. Dr Kondo arranged this meeting in his own office just months before his own death. I was struck by Doi's adherence to psychoanalytic ideas, and linear notions of consciousness, which are threaded through his article on Morita therapy and psychoanalysis (Doi, 1962). That impression aside, within the context of the psy-choanalytic exchange, the therapeutic environment can be a change agent.

Jeffrey Davis (1972, p. 727) wrote a letter to the editor of the *New England Journal of Medicine* in which he highlighted the humane nature of the hospital environment at the Suzuki Morita clinic in Tokyo, as directed formerly by Tomonori Suzuki. Davis became a Morita disciple after being treated by Morita therapy for anxiety. Suzuki (1969) describes his experiences emerging from complete rest in 'Experiential Treatment of Neurosis' (published in Japanese as *Noiroze no taiken ryoho*), as well as the on-going nature of his own recovery. Davis notes that 'realization of cure' can arrive two years after discharge with a success rate of 90% for treatment of severe anxiety and depression. T. Suzuki and R. Suzuki (1981) validated this finding further in 'The effectiveness of inpatient Morita therapy'. Kora and Ohara (1973) and Kiefer (1976) maintained the dialogue on whether Morita required cultural adjustments for Western consumption; this dialogue started more formally in 1968 in the publication by Kenshiro Ohara and David Reynolds on 'Changing methods in Morita psychotherapy'.

Comparisons continued between Morita and Zen. In 1973, Taro Matsubara contrasts the theory and practices of Morita and Freud and shows how Morita therapy relates to Zen. In his article, 'Japanese psychotherapy (Morita therapy) and its relationship to Zen Buddhism', he discusses the use of Morita therapy for dissociation and depressive reactions often found in those exhibiting psychotic features. Similarities between Zen monasteries and Morita hospital settings are discussed by Shoji Nakamura in his 1974 article, 'A study into the similarities between life in Zen monasteries and Morita therapy with special emphasis on human relationships and the experiential process'. Nakamura's article is vital to debates on how much Zen and environmental structure inform Morita theory and practice. Along these lines, the nature and tone of the therapist's home and communal environment is a contributing factor to patients' experiences of safety and vitality.

Interests in Zen and therapy percolated in Europe when research-practitioners explored this theme more formally. In the Netherlands, Hans Rappard (1976) has been an activist for Zen and psychotherapy. He has explored the 'conditions' of Morita therapy that facilitate an outcome of 'selflessness' found in Zen but considered by Western egocentric theorists to be anything but therapeutic. H.B. Gibson (1975) published, 'The Centenary of Shoma Morita' in the *Bulletin of the British Psychological Society*. Known for his research and practice in hypnosis, he describes the residential benefits of Morita therapy. Perhaps over-emphasising the behavioural benefits, he outlines the essential structure of therapy with 'graduated steps' towards health, including complete rest, 'relative' seclusion, and 'deliberate' stimulus deprivation for a short period in the beginning, and increased engagement over time – for increased patient autonomy.

Outpatient Morita therapy was introduced by Hiroshi Iwai in 1974 in his article, 'Brief Morita Therapy in Kyoiku to Igaku' (pp. 807–814). His description is different from the outpatient methods of Morita therapy currently in vogue. In particular, he describes outpatient use for treating obsessive symptoms for those with immature characters and the importance of enhancing authentic self through therapy. This aspect of outpatient Morita therapy has yet to be realised in current guidelines in Japan.

Most essential are matters of Zen and authentic self that were explored fervently by Horney. The Zen notion of authenticity is different from self-actualisation or self-esteem, as often endorsed in humanistic psychology in the West. In Zen, authentic self is reflected by *jun-na-kokoro*, or pure body-mind-spirit – the original self, untainted by the judging mind. Kokoro is likened to 'the essence or heart of things'.

In 1975, a psychiatric textbook edited by Silvano Arieti and Gerard Chrzanowski, *New Dimensions in Psychiatry: A World View*, introduced Morita therapy to medical scientists in English-speaking countries.[35] In this text, Akihisa Kondo (1975, p. 446) provides a pivotal chapter on 'Morita therapy: Its sociohistorical context' and introduces Morita's philosophy of human nature with relevant Zen notations.

Adaptations of classic Morita therapy in the 1980s and 1990s

It is difficult to gauge how far Morita's progressive experiential-based therapy can be stretched – across inpatient and outpatient care – before his sophisticated principles and methods lose validity and reliability. While it seems probable that Fritz Perls could have adapted some of the paradoxical elements of Morita therapy when developing his Gestalt therapy in the United States, he left Morita in Asia.

It was not until the 1980s that written material about Morita therapy reappeared and expanded (T. Suzuki and R. Suzuki, 1981; T. Suzuki, 1989; Hasegawa, 1989). In addition to journal articles, books were being published in English. Chihiro Fujita (1986) produced a foundational book, *Morita Therapy: A Psychotherapeutic System for Neurosis*, which describes the theory and classic practice.

The era of adaptation of Morita therapy hit its first peak in the 1980s and early 1990s. Prior to this time, psychiatrists like Karen Horney and Erich Fromm were curious to simply know more about Morita and his theories and methods. Perhaps most influential in stirring productive tension was anthropologist David Reynolds, who posed arguments against Morita therapy being adopted by Westerners. I recall vividly the heated debate in 1990 at the First International Congress of Morita Therapy in Hamamatsu, Japan. Many opinions were aired about Morita's viability in the West. Some Japanese and North American scholars agreed with Reynolds that foreigners could not endure the first seclusion, rest period of therapy.

Bravely, the late Mr Yozo Hasegawa put sound cases forth from *Seikatsu-no Hakkenkai* (*Discovery of Life* organisation in Tokyo) about Morita's universality.[36] What emerged for me professionally from these unfounded assumptions was the impetus to design a trial for application of the classic therapy outside Japan. I chose an Australian man who was diagnosed with complex trauma and symptoms of *shinkeishitsu*. Dr Kondo travelled to Australia to meet my client, confirm the diagnosis, and provide direct supervision as a way of validating the use of Morita's four stages in Melbourne. Prior to that first case study that proved significant, Reynolds had convinced members of the Japanese Morita Therapy Society that Westerners could not tolerate the residential rest stage – and that the four stages were not practical to administer outside Asia.

The first wave of tension over 'too Japanese for the West' culminated in 1992 in a debate between Reynolds and Christopher Ives (scholar and professor of Japanese and Religious Studies) in the *International Bulletin of Morita Therapy*. Ives raised questions about the maintenance of a traditional training protocol. He discussed the role of the *deshi* and the position assumed by the apprentice. Ives spoke of the distortion to Zen as North American culture penetrated its essence during its adoption. The *deshi* tradition shifted from one of an apprentice under the guidance of a wise master of a craft to *gakusei,* or a student seeking intellectual knowledge; there has been less emphasis on the passing down of traditional, embodied knowledge. In addition, Ives raised the issue preserving the *iemoto* system that assists the protection of the integrity of traditional practice. In such tradition, the master chooses the student. Such custom, however, competes with consumer-oriented values where opportunities for training depend on making applications with the right credentials, with less emphasis on the integral character and teachable-spirit of the student (Ives, 1992b, 1992c).[37]

Not long after this discourse, Reynolds clarified his allegiance to and divergence from Morita's core principles alongside another indigenous Japanese therapy (*Naikan*)[38] from which he developed a lifeway that he branded 'Constructive Living' (Reynolds, 1984a). Reynolds' system promotes the 'practical doing' aspects of Morita therapy and the 'acceptance' orientation of Naikan therapy, without claiming a new formulation of Morita or Naikan therapies.[39]

Adaptations to Morita therapy and preservation of the classic method

When placed side-by-side, key principles underlying Constructive Living's core philosophy and action methods resonate with the 'Guidelines for Practising Outpatient Morita Therapy' as advanced by the Japanese Society for Morita Therapy (2010).[40] By no means am I suggesting plagiarism by Reynolds. Rather, he began his adaptations in the 1960s and eased his contention that Westerners could not tolerate Morita therapy. Following, he tightened these imposed cultural boundaries by designing his own system. Regardless of such intention, he set a bar retrospectively for what Morita therapy is and is not – well before the Society's guidelines were designed and printed for distribution. In 1992, Reynolds (pp. 20–21) modified his point on the development of outpatient approaches to Morita therapy:[41]

> Western counseling psychology offers no such regular live-in training in Morita therapy to my knowledge. And the result of counseling training in the West is an office-based practice that would shun outside the office contact with clients though Morita actually lived alongside them . . . Morita therapy provides a new and radical perspective for rethinking the whole theory and practice of Western psychotherapy.
>
> *(Reynolds, 1992, pp. 20–21)*

In April 1993, I presented an Australian case study at the Second International Congress of Morita therapy in Fukuoka, Japan (*Case Study of an Inpatient Morita Therapy Treatment in Melbourne, Australia*).[42] This was the first time in the history of Morita therapy that a Western client was treated by the four-stage residential therapy in a Western context. That remarkable case began the momentum for a foundational practice by LeVine and Kondo for the Classic Morita Centre, which was known formerly as the LeKond Centre until 2002.

As I reflect upon scholar-practitioners outside Japan who have been curious about Morita therapy, I keep returning to Karen Horney. She began inquiring about Zen, ego, and no-self most intensely after her 1952 excursion to Japan where she visited traditional or classic Morita therapy practice locations. Sadly, she simply did not have enough life time to get fully unstuck from analytic interpretations of 'psychic existence'. In the end, however, she came close to bringing an ecological, cosmological view of self into psychoanalytic theory.

Since the hotbed of Zen dialogue in the 1950s and 1960s, the inquiry into consciousness in the 1970s and 1980s, and adaptations to Morita's methods that began in the 1990s, Morita therapy in English-speaking countries has assumed three tracks. These range from Morita's original progressive method that upholds his theory of consciousness to an adapted version that either channels Morita's pure-rest/pure-mind and ecological-based features into individual and group counselling, or one that relies on a humanistic framework for Western consumption. Global development follows three tracks: (1) classic, original Morita therapy in a home setting; (2) Morita-based counselling that attends to stages two, three and four, and; (3) action-based counselling.

(1)   Morita's classic four-staged residential therapy has been practised in Australia by LeVine and associates since 1997. The therapy duration is usually three to five weeks, therapy begins with the rest stage. Therapists who train at the Classic Morita Centre are required to experience the four stages in the eco-setting as part of their professional supervision.

(2)   Morita-based counselling relies on stages two, three, and four in an outpatient setting. In 2006, Brian Ogawa established a university accredited certificate programme in Morita therapy at Washburn University in the United States. The course includes residential intensives, lectures, experiential workshops, an international seminar and an introduction to *fumon* and silence with roleplay.

(3)   Action-based counselling methods have been designed to reflect the theoretical guidelines set by a Japanese committee inside the Japanese Society for Morita Therapy. Ishu Ishiyama (1986, 1988, 1991, 1996, 2003) led the development of an 'Action-based Counselling' model globally across three stages: (1) 'subjective' (explore and express), (2) 'objective' (confront and reframe), and (3) 'action' (respond and act). The 'Exeter model' of Morita-informed mental health outpatient practice was spearheaded by David Richards and associates at the University of Exeter; they advance Morita's law of emotion and nature engagement (Shugg, Richards, and Frost, 2016).

As stated earlier, the first action-oriented interpretation of Morita therapy appears in works by anthropologist David Reynolds in the 1960s, which culminated in the release of his book *Constructive Living* in 1984. At that time, Reynolds offered a 12-week *Morita Guidance Course* that promoted the motto *accept ourselves and our feelings as they are and focus on doing what we need to do in every moment*. Lacking training and credentials as a counsellor or psychotherapist, he soon abandoned this course to develop the TōDō Institute and a lifeway programme intended to train lay associates. Basically, he merged 'acceptance and gratitude' aspects of Naikan therapy (Krech, 2002) with extractions from Morita's theory, 'act according to reality' and 'accept emotions as-they-are'.[43]

Overall, the portrayal of Morita therapy sits inside a larger international arena of mental health politics, evolution, and revision (Goddard 1991; Kitanishi and Mori, 2008). Most uniquely, Morita therapy emerged out of a rural setting. Herein, Morita therapy is not 'psycho' therapy or counselling. Rather it is a sequenced experiential therapy that begins with complete rest. The four stages promptly change what is perceptual and visceral over cognitive—which is where Zen rumbles.

During the era of mental health revisions globally, written material about Morita therapy began reappearing and expanding in the 1980s (T. Suzuki and R. Suzuki, 1981; T. Suzuki, 1989; Hasegawa, 1989). Bruno Rhyner raised the issue about Zen in his 1988 publication: 'Morita psychotherapy and Zen Buddhism: a comparison of theoretical concepts' in *Psychologia*. In addition to journal articles, books were being published in English. Fujita (1986) produced a foundational book, *Morita Therapy: A Psychotherapeutic System for Neurosis*, which describes the theory and classic practice. The translation of Morita's 1928 thesis took over six years to complete and was published with SUNY Press in 1998 (Kondo, translator and LeVine, editor). Brian Ogawa (1988, 1989) brought Morita's theory into the field of traumatic studies in *Walking on Eggshells, Practical Counseling for Women in or Leaving a Violent Relationship*. His later work, *A River to Live By: The 12 Life Principles of Morita Therapy* (2007) and *Desire for Life: The Practitioner's Introduction to Morita Therapy for the Treatment of Anxiety Disorders* (2013) offers a philosophy for daily living that is different from *Constructive Living*.

Ever since Reynolds published his ethnographic-based doctoral study on Morita therapy, interests in the preservation and dissemination of an untainted Morita therapy have waxed and waned in North America, Russia, and the United Kingdom. Most start with the assumption that non-Japanese clients and mental health national structures are not equipped to offer the therapeutic rest stage and nature setting. This assumption has led to the grafting of Morita therapy onto humanistic models in counsellor education. In Russia, for instance, broadcasting of Morita's 'theoretical' seeds has been advanced by Natalia Semenova, a clinical psychologist in the department of outpatient psychiatry at the Moscow Research Institute. Her audiences are primarily informed of Morita's theory and Ishiyama's action-based model or counselling (Semenova, 2016). Questions, however, are rarely asked about how Morita residential therapy can inform Morita-based counselling reliably.

Meanwhile, clients of various cultures have moved successfully through the classic treatment in Australia since 1997. This outcome seems unrelated to a geo-national hardiness factor, and most connected to case formulation, design and use of space, and the supervision and training of therapists who deliver the methods. Can so-called Westerners invest three to five weeks of their lives to experience this eco-logical approach to therapy? Can a pure form of Morita based counselling uphold Morita's theory of consciousness? Such questions are pertinent to safeguarding classic Morita therapy in this century.

In France, for instance, anthropologists and psychologists have taken an interest in the traditional form of Morita therapy. Rémi Bordes (2011) invited my chapter on 'Morita therapy and the Meaning of Silence' in his edited book on indigenous therapies. Another work that aligns Morita therapy and Zen appears in French and Japanese by Shigeyoshi Okamoto (2007).

While in Japan it is difficult sometimes for people to arrange the time for inpa-tient care, the idea of therapeutic rest and seclusion is not regarded as odd. In other places in Asia where young adults consider a year of monkhood as part of their normal development, Morita therapy's first stage is viewed with interest. Again, assumptions about Morita therapy being 'too Japanese' for transfer across other cultures are interesting to ponder. For instance, practitioners of Euro-American derived therapies such as Cognitive Behavioural Therapy (CBT), Mindfulness, and Acceptance and Commitment Therapy have introduced these systems into mental health settings across Asia, Africa, South America and Indigenous Australia, with little accountability for how related 'cognitive systems' reinforce Western cultural values.

Overall, CBT reflects a worldview that places actions, feelings, thoughts, and symptoms into desirable or undesirable categories. Herein, the therapist assumes the role of change agent, and as one who is there to assist the client to feel better or resolve something.[44] The place of treatment is often an indoor setting, and evi-dence-based research is conducted mostly in urban regions. All too often, urban models of psychiatric care filter into rural regions, and developed country models are usually adopted into underdeveloped regions of the globe.[45] In keeping with comparative analyses on Morita therapy, discussions grow on how cognitive-based therapies overlap and depart from Morita's method and philosophy (Spates, Tateno, Nakamura, Seim, and Sheerin, 2011). Similarly, Kwee and Ellis (1998) discuss narrative-based methods (metaphor, parable, paradox, and analogies) used across Zen and REBT (Rational Emotive Behavioural Therapy). Across these comparative modalities, Nature takes a back seat to therapists and their methods that are pro-moted as the change agents.

The classic Morita therapist relinquishes power to the four-staged progression of treatment. Accordingly, the therapist is trained to observe minute behavioural changes in clients that are idiosyncratic and culturally relevant – without verbal exchange. In most forms of psychotherapy, verbal exchange is encouraged, if not a pre-requisite, and the therapist assesses the content of that exchange. Morita therapists assess the quality and tone of the client's silence and engagement in Nature across the four stages. Careful study is made on clients' stillness (silence by curiosity, or silence by agitation), which are cues to clients' readiness to move from Stage One to Stage Two.

Drawing on paradox, the first stage of therapy is designed to disengage the person from dialogue and decrease sensory stimulation. Oddly enough, by denying stimulation in the first stage, clients get bored with their symptoms and begin to experience the environment with all their senses. Not only does this return them to the natural cycles of their diurnal mammal-hood, boredom paradoxically increases their awareness of their restlessness. Overall, the predictable and safe setting gives clients an experience of a non-chaotic external environment – without the use of mindfulness or meditation methods. The capacity of therapists to facilitate therapeutic environments sets clients on a natural course towards their creative, innate expression through activity. According to Takehisa Kora (1968, p. 318), 'nature is not (hu)man-centered . . . and anxiety is inseparable from human existence'. In line with Karen Horney, 'Since helplessness is an essential part of every anxiety, what accounts for helplessness?' (Horney, 1952b, p.89). Such a therapeutic question sits like a Zen Koan—moving us to engage clients across safe contexts.

Notes

1 Rudyard Kipling (1865–1936), whose years spanned those of Morita's, travelled to Japan in 1889 and 1892 while writing his collection of travel letters and prose, which were published in approximately 1889. See Kipling (1988).
2 Historical descriptions of Whistler's art and politics are found in the biography by Stanley Weintraub (1974).
3 European artists explored Japanese images, such as Vincent van Gogh and his Mount Fuji prints in the 1880s, Paul Gauguin and his fan gouaches, as well as images by Edgar Degas, Edouard Manet, and writings by Gustave Flaubert (see Lionel Lambourne, *Japonisme: Cultural Crossings Between Japan and the West*, 2007). At the same time, Japanese artists imitated European styles and methods, such as the works by offbeat photographer, Sugita (known as *Ei Kyū*) from Miyazaki.
4 An illustrative cultural synopsis is found in *Starcrossed: A Biography of Madam Butterfly* by Brian Burke-Gaffney (2004) who explores Nagasaki where the opera's scenes took place.
5 Just after the Great Kantō Earthquake of 1923, surrealist philosophy, literature and poetry swelled in Japan. The first surrealist anthology was orchestrated by Junzaburo Nishiwaki in 1927. (See the *Poetry and Poetics of Nishiwaki Junzaburo: Modernism in Translation* by Hosea Hirata, 1993). Following, the first Japanese surrealist manifesto appeared in 1928, and included the philosophy of European surrealist journals (*Surrealism: Revolution by Night, National Gallery of Australia*, Canberra, Optus, 1993, pp. 205–209). According to Takehisa Kora (Morita's protégé), Morita appreciated the non-conventional ideas embedded in this period (Kora, personal interview, 1992).
6 Inside the United States, the gap between Japanese and American exchange widened when President Roosevelt signed his Executive Order in 1942, whereby 90% of the

Japanese mainland population in the USA were placed in interment camps in the United States. Of these, two-thirds were Japanese born, USA citizens (Weglyn, 1976).

7 See Appendix for Kondo's autobiographic synopsis of this event.

8 In Japanese Zen practice, the paradoxical question posed to a student by a Zen teacher, or the nonsensical answer given to a student's question by the teacher is known as a koan. The koan recipient is expected to bypass the logical mind; koan practice is one pathway towards enlightenment. See the writings by Steven Heine (1994, 1997, 2008).

9 Suzuki participated in the East–West Philosopher's conference at the University of Hawaii in June 1949. From there, he went to Claremont Graduate School to teach for two semesters, and then to New York City to lecture at Columbia University in 1951 where he met Karen Horney.

10 Paul Tillich (1952, p. 2) reflects on being and courage: 'Courage can show us what being is, and being can show us what courage is.'

11 It is essential to clarify that Zen (while having roots in Buddhism) is not a religion or spiritual practice. There is no transcendent God, idol, or gods, no mantras, objects, and images of the Buddha. In essence, there is no separation between Zen and ordinary life and Nature. Shintoism, which often includes animism, is literally, 'the way of the gods'. Considered the original spirit core in Japan, its animism lies in *Kami*, or the great source of life manifested in mountains, rivers, sky and all of Nature.

12 Richard J. DeMartino (1991) offers a biographical sketch of Horney and her New York entourage of Zen-philosophy scholars who met in New York and Japan in the early 1950s. He comments, too, on Zen (DeMartino, 1983).

13 Kelman gained his MD from Harvard. He was a disciple of Karen Horney and an associate and supervising analyst of the American Institute for Psychoanalysis for more than 50 years. Like Horney he was interested in post-Freudian analysis and fostering the intrinsic nature of his patients. He aligned with the philosophy of Martin Buber, Paul Tillich, Erich Fromm, and Akihisa Kondo, with whom he had personal associations. After Horney's death, he described Morita therapy as untenable for import into Western contexts. Kondo told me that he was 'disheartened' by that assertion (Kondo, audiotaped conversation, 1989).

14 'In Zen, coincidence is a fabricated notion' (Kondo, personal audio taped conversation, 1990).

15 This is a quote from an unpublished account that Kondo entrusted to me. In the published version Kondo 1991, comments about Freud were omitted by the editors at *The American Journal of Psychoanalysis*.

16 In *Developments in Horney Psychoanalysis*, Rubins (1972, p. 38) misdated Horney's excursion to Japan as 1951; it was 1952.

17 While the history of Zen in Japan falls outside the scope of this book, the reader is directed to review the history of Myōan Eisai (1141–1215), a founder of Japanese Zen, and Zenji Dōgen (1200–1253) who founded the Soto school of Zen (Ts'ao-tung) in Japan.

18 It is significant to note that the purpose of my association with Shin-ichi Usa has been solely to document history. I do not endorse his distorted application of Zen at the former Sansei hospital in Kyoto, which compromised the health of Japanese inpatients.

19 As described elsewhere, Koji Sato (1905–1971) was a psychologist and scholar of Zen, and an associate of Genyu Usa and Takehisa Kora (Morita's protégé); he was knowledgeable of Morita therapy. It was Sato who assisted Fritz Perls to experience Morita therapy in Kyoto in 1962.

20 I thank Ann Lammers and her generous correspondence. Through her, I was fortunate to meet Jungian analyst, Thomas Kirsch, MD, who is the son of the late James Kirsch and member of the C.G. Jung Institute in San Francisco (T. Kirsch, 2014). Over a dinner in San Francisco, we meandered in dialogue across psychoanalysis, Carl Jung, James Kirsch, and Akihisa Kondo. For this, I am truly grateful and honoured.

21 Freud wrote *The Interpretation of Dreams* (translated by A.A. Brill in 1913 and first published in 1900). He contemplated consciousness in ways that extend beyond a general theory of cognition in vogue today, and ways consciousness evokes imagery. 'The point is to induce . . . the state of the mind before falling asleep . . . we are accustomed to speak of fatigue as the reason of this slackening, the merging undesired ideas are changed into visual and auditory images . . . in which the condition differs from falling asleep' (p. 14). In his letter to Fredrich Schiller, Freud considered imagination and how 'mindfulness is contrary to this induced necessary "first" state of consciousness' (pp. 14–15). (This 1913 book was in Akihisa Kondo's personal library in Tokyo).

22 This remarkable collection of articles included (in order of presentation) Karen Horney, Akihisa Kondo, Norman Kelman, Alexander Reid Martin, Frederick Weiss, Harold Kelman, Paul Tillich, Charles Hewitt, Benjamin Wassell, Lois DeRosis, and Sidney Rose.

23 As an historical note, Horney and Kondo had discussions with Tillich on Morita's philosophy of life force, alongside dialogue on Tillich's notions of essence (personal taped conversations with Akihisa Kondo, 1992). The progression of Morita stages, use of initial seclusion and rest, and therapeutic use of Nature assist this process of cultivating mind.

24 An abstract of remarks by Karen Horney as moderator of a discussion of Dr Kondo's paper on Morita Therapy at a meeting of the Association for the Advancement of Psychoanalysis held on 9 November 1952 is found in the *American Journal of Psychoanalysis*, 13, 87–88.

25 Horney facilitated the development of social psychiatry, founded and established the American Institute for Psychoanalysis in 1941, and founded *The American Journal of Psychoanalysis*.

26 The temple complex situated in South Kyoto is a National Treasure and listed with UNESCO. Sanbō-in garden contains over 700 stones and is designed for viewing from certain perspectives within a building. The garden was designed as a strolling and sitting garden with stones, ponds, and bridges, and the crane of fortune, the tortoise, and the isle of eternal youth. A noteworthy large stone is called *fujito-no-ishi*. The spirit stone is linked to betrayal and death. (See Berthier, 2000.)

27 I regret that I waited too long before proposing to Kondo that we meet with DeMartino for conversation. By the time we made letter contact in the late 1990s, Richard was in late stages of neurological decline and regretfully lacked the energy for written or verbal dialogue.

28 It is noted that Masao Abe, like Akihisa Kondo, was a proponent of Pure Land Buddhism, and critical of Tillich's Christian-centric views.

29 For a fuller discussion see Abe (1989).

30 Nishida Kitarō, 1870–1945; Shin'ichi Hisamatsu, 1889–1980.

31 In *Religion and Culture: Essays in Honor of Paul Tillich* (1959) editor Walter Leibrecht offers a list of distinguished contributors of that time including Erich Fromm, Karl Jaspers, Reinhold Neibuhr, and Yoshinori Takeuchi who discussed 'awakening' and the mythical elements embedded in religion. Horney was a colleague and friend to Paul Tillich and associated with his entourage of scholars.

32 Erving Polster (1966) links the General Semantics Movement as initiated by Alfred Korzybski (1879–1950) with Gestalt therapy. While Korzybski coined the phrase 'the map is not the territory', his notion of a *time-binding* phenomenon was first coined in 1921. This concept was reformulated by 'here-and-now' theorists and by proponents of Existential psychotherapy who neglected Korzybski's views on ancestral ethics. Morita's theory of consciousness has more in common with *time-binding* than here-now summations. The reader is directed to *Korzybski: A Biography* (Kodish, 2011).

33 At the International Congress of Gestalt Therapy in Manchester, UK (August, 2008), LeVine and Frew presented a seminar: *Squaring History: Fritz Perls, Japan and Morita Therapy – Comparative Analysis of Morita and Gestalt Therapies* (unpublished paper).

34 Stein's first 'Rose' is in reference to a person. Gertrude Stein published *Geography and Plays* in 1922 (Stein, 1993).

35 Arieti (1981) touched on themes embedded in the complex, creative potential of Morita therapy in *Creativity: The Magic Synthesis*.

36 My sincere gratitude is extended to Mr Yozo Hasegawa (1914–1992) from *Seikatsu-no Hakkenkai* (Discovery of Life) in Tokyo; he broke Japanese protocol by publicly endorsing the trans-cultural capacity of Morita therapy. 'Is it not odd that Japanese and Europeans and Americans train in Orthodox Psychoanalysis, while many are hesitant to train in the traditional Morita Therapy?' (Personal conversation between Hasegawa, Kondo, and LeVine, Tokyo, 1991).

37 More personally, I was fortunate to have trained in Morita therapy under the *deshi* and *iemoto* tradition provided by Kondo sensei. This deshi tradition is embedded in upper levels of supervision at the Classic Morita Therapy Centre, known fondly as the Classic Morita Centre or CMC.

38 Naikan therapy was developed by Yoshimoto Ishin, a devotee of Jōdo Shinshū Buddhism. The core practice is one of purposeful and directed self-reflection (sometimes called *mishirabe* or deep meditation). The client discloses intimate details of personal relational history to a Naikan monk or guide who, in turn, becomes a witness to the reflector's history. The long process leads to a perceptual shift in one's capacity to appreciate what others have given. A reliable analysis of this method occurs in Chikako Ozawa-de Silva (2006).

39 Following his publications, *The Quiet Therapies* (1980), and *Playing Ball on Running Water: Living Morita Psychotherapy* (1984b), Reynolds developed his formal guidance framework for daily living and clarified further the elements of Naikan therapy and Morita philosophy. These books are valuable for those wanting to shape constructive behaviours, while gaining an understanding into a philosophy of living day-to-day.

40 The Guidelines for Practising Outpatient Morita Therapy (English edition) was published in 2010 by the Japanese Society for Morita Therapy (translated and edited by Ishu Ishiyama). Key theory and practice components of the outpatient method include the 'Entry Point' where the counsellor (1) promotes an understanding of symptoms, (2) points to the self-defeating mechanism, *toraware*, and (3) explains the *arugamama* attitude. The basic therapeutic components: (1) increase client's awareness and acceptance of symptoms, (2) recognise and mobilise client's desire for life, (3) clarify the vicious cycle, (4) give instructions for constructive action taking, and (5) facilitate client's re-evaluation of their behavioural patterns and lifestyles – all accomplished through therapeutic dialogue with *fumon* positioning by therapist, and diary guidance.

41 To Reynolds' assertion, I would add that Morita's attention to the construction of a therapeutic environment via his sequential use of space, light, and place during rest and activity stages in treatment is unique to mental health considerations in vogue today, including the current Outpatient Guidelines by the Japanese Society for Morita Therapy.

42 Soon after that first Western case study, I had the privilege of being invited as the editor of Kondo's English translation project for Morita's 1928 publication (Morita 1928/1998). The draft took four solid years to complete while Kondo researched the finer distinctions of meaning underlying Morita's terms. Needless to say, we digressed often to discuss the practice of Morita therapy; this process advanced my own scholarship and practitioner capacity. Kondo died the year after SUNY Press launched publication.

43 Under the guidance of Takehisa Kora and consultation with Yozo Hasegawa and David Reynolds, Ishu Ishiyama developed the *International Bulletin of Morita Therapy* and maintained the role as Chief Editor through the University of British Columbia. The inaugural issue arrived in May 1988. David Reynolds held a post as Associate Editor until 1991; I was invited on board in 1989 and maintained a role as Assistant Editor until the close of the journal in 1993.

44 Many of the ideas embedded in USA derived therapies have strong ties to religion of that nation, such as the Christian values for forgiveness, interpretation of feelings as positive or negative, and splitting experiences into good (God, heaven) or evil (devil, hell). Psychotherapies emerging from urban regions often carry developed world views

by assuming basic needs are met in clients, such as access to capital for service, safe and efficient transportation, clean water, nutritious food, immunisation and health care, or protection from political and/or domestic violence. Baseline poverty and generational trauma are rarely considered in case formulation that is symptom driven.

45 Similarly, Dr J. Bhoomikumar (Director of Chey Chumneas Hospital: Center for Child and Adolescent Mental Health, Takhmau, Cambodia) is aware of the impact an environment has on health care; he has assisted the construction of gardens and small animal habitats, open play and outdoor counselling and sitting areas, and traditional Khmer houses in which children and their families can rest together when a child needs on-going assistance in physical therapy, occupational therapy, and speech therapy, and trauma-informed therapy.

3

MORITA AND CONSCIOUSNESS

Man with the Cobalt Tent
This summer morn on the outskirts of Tokyo, I watch a man lift his cobalt tent from the place where he had stayed overnight. With his back to me, he gathers the taut plastic into a small fold, revealing, in no particular order – eight hardcover books, one teacup, one teapot, a felt hat, umbrella, small-filled cloth bag, a short-handled broom, and one black-and-white cat. He places all, except the broom and cat, inside a wooden crate on the back of a bicycle. In a slower pace, he squats and pushes his nose into the face of his cat before placing her in the basket attached to the handlebars. He sweeps the area clean in careful strokes before tucking the broom into the square box, closing the top, and pedalling away.

—(Tokyo field notes, August 10, 2013)

As he moves out of view, a trace of this gentleman's true nature holds the space. I ponder 'consciousnesses' and how he has come to live in this way.

Exploration into consciousness

During Morita's lifetime, scholars wrestled with and reasoned through questions about consciousness. Does consciousness exist without a human mind? Does consciousness reside anywhere? Is consciousness related to human transformation? Is consciousness the same as awareness? How far does it range? Is it a manifestation of the human soul? Is consciousness the manifestation of all of life?

When considering environmental, cultural, and political influences, this matter cannot be reduced easily to an Eastern or Western philosophy. What is clear from chronicling the term is how theories, structures, and functions of consciousness have shifted over time.[1] This chapter brings forward Morita's complex perspective on consciousness. His ideas challenge 'awareness' notions found in contemporary therapies, such as cognitive, behavioural, or mindfulness. By restricting consciousness and placing it inside the human mind, the range of opportunities for human contentment may shrink accordingly. By appealing to cognition while problem solving how to live, we may move further away from our authentic nature.

Discourse on consciousness in Morita's era spanned metaphysical, ontological, phenomenological, and existential domains. His was a time when scholars rarely cast consciousness into a biomedical or cognitive science. It is not my intention to form an alliance with any one configuration of consciousness or to assert that Morita's theory concludes the issue. While this concept, I will emphasise, is just a concept, psychotherapy practices are typically informed by the presence or absence of consciousness terms.

As stated throughout this book, the first phase of Morita therapy sets a paradoxical process in motion by sheltering clients in a secluded, safe place. By withholding human-derived stimulation, clients gradually turn their attention to that which is naturally accessible; the cicada's song is penetratingly heard and ordinary stimuli appear in ways untainted by interpretation or past traumatic experiences. Once the senses are engaged evenly, being curious about the world is more possible. In this way, clients who are usually visual in their experience of the world start to hear and taste with a renewed sense of simple delight. They often slow down when eating and drinking and pause to notice the taste, texture, fragrance, and colour in a vegetable, piece of fruit, or cup of tea. At breakfast, they notice the scent of rice as they lift the lid from the bowl. Some experience the force of life in living things. When pulling weeds, they see how roots cling to dirt and dirt clings to roots. One client wrote in his field diary: 'the roots of the lavender plant did not grip so hard the dirt, but the bamboo held on with all her might'.

From the standpoint of Morita, consciousness exists without humans being awakened to it or aware of it. Kondo rendered Morita's term, *mushojūshin* (無所住心), as peripheral consciousness. Ives translates the literal meaning as 'the mind dwelling in no place'.[2] While such depictions of consciousness resonate with Zen, how does it translate into therapeutic practice? Paradoxically, when therapists refrain from directing the client's cognitive awareness to Nature or their own breath, they advance clients' sensitivity and respect to life through engagement in Nature. Herein, they may begin with simple awareness, like the monk in a temple that directs a novice to count her or his breath to rounds of ten. That is the baby step on the path to *mushojūshin*. But what next; how can this be embodied in ways unattached to structured practice? Morita therapists bring the client inside the pulse of Nature rather than taking them on a cross-sectional nature hike. As stated throughout this book, by living day-to-day in the staged therapy environment under the discerning therapist, sensitivity to the ecological complexity of Nature is fostered. The goal of the stages is to sync the client's mind and body to the rhythms of Nature. Herein, awe and pure imagination (untainted by past trauma or conventional ideas) are re-engaged as the ecological order and chaos of life is realised through the senses. The client becomes matter of fact about the place of 'self' in Nature and lives between promoting and demoting self, simultaneously. Compassionate action and pure imagination require this streamed experience of self.

The sequenced structure of Morita's therapeutic method enhances sensory engagement. When clients undertake Morita's progressive structure of therapy their whole person is primed for sensate experience. Morita's practice was in the countryside – a setting where nature's canvas is wide enough to offer animate diversity. The photos (Figures 3.1–3.4) of Morita's home practice in Kōchi, Japan, feature the aesthetic quality of his practice place; architectural structures are enhanced by access to garden and naturescape.

Consciousness, existence, and Zen

Given the tricky political context of his era, debate continues as to whether or not Morita drew upon Japanese Zen in his philosophy of consciousness, structure of practice, and design of the environment.[3] All too often, non-Japanese scholars who offer commentary on Morita and Zen have sketchy operational knowledge of Morita's practice (Leonhard, 1965; Kasulis, 1977, 1981; Smith, 1981). Another complicating factor stems from the depiction of Zen as a philosophy, a spiritual practice, or a pathway for human development, particularly as depicted in the North American context. Consider Thomas Kasulis (1981), who coined the term 'Zen Humanism' in his book *Zen Person, Zen Action*. Kasulis offers a kindred book for psychotherapists, with guidance for daily living. Morita's theory, however, steers clear of framing Zen in human-centric terms. Zen dwells in no place for nobody. Overall, Morita devised a therapeutic method intended to expand the range of consciousness by casting off the self as the centre of experience. Afterwards, human perception is recalibrated and authentic self is attained once one lives according to Nature. In this way, non-subjective contemplation moves one to action.

By and large, the sequenced method of Morita therapy depends on the natural environment to cradle the self until the self is secure in its own insecurity; it is then that the self is cast into Nature. Krishnamurti describes this process (1970, pp. 157–158):

> seeking out of something beyond the inventions and tricks of the mind, which means having a feeling for that something, living in it, being it – *that* is true religion. But you can do that only when you leave the pool you have dug for yourself and go out into the river of life. Then life has an astonishing way of taking care of you, because then there is no taking care on your part. Life carries you where it will because you are part of itself; then there is no problem of security, of what people say or don't say. . .

In *Zen Skin, Zen Marrow: Will the Real Zen Buddhism Please Stand Up*, Steven Heine (2008) offers a perspective that maintains an equal tension between the

FIGURE 3.1 Front entrance to Morita's practice and home in Kōchi, Japan

(Photo by LeVine, October 2015)

FIGURE 3.2 Side entrance to Morita's practice and home in Kōchi

(Le Vine, October 2015)

FIGURE 3.3   Morita's home landscape in Kōchi, 1926

(With permission from Mishima Morita Hospital Archives, 2016)

idealist-humanist view of Zen and Japanese history, culture, and tradition. Herein, Heine supplements the perspective put forth by Kasulis. Fujita (1986) brings us even closer to Morita's perspective on authentic self, Zen, and Nature:

> This is Oriental philosophy: only if one empties oneself and casts the self into the mu of nature can the authentic subjecthood of self be realized . . . as advocated by Buddhism, particularly Zen...
>
> *(Fujita, 1986, p. 317)*

   In spite of the orientation assumed by psychiatrists practising in his era, 'consciousness' for Morita was not bound by medical science, humanistic philosophy, religion, spiritual practice, and theories of the unconscious. Pressures to reinterpret traditional Japanese thought into Western discourse set a slippery course for scholars and artists during the Meiji era (Marra, 1999).[4] As mentioned earlier, it was expected that traditional principles underlying the aesthetics of Japanese art forms be ignored. Artists were required to discontinue functioning as a conduit for 'manifested spirit' when creating calligraphy, *ikebana* (flower arranging), *haiku* (17-syllable poem steeped in Nature), architectural structures, painting, or sculpture. Reverence for nature, simplicity, restraint, directness, solitude, and emptiness were overridden by the practicality and technology of craft making, akin to the goals encompassed in the ancient Greek term, *techne*.

森田正馬先生宅見取り図

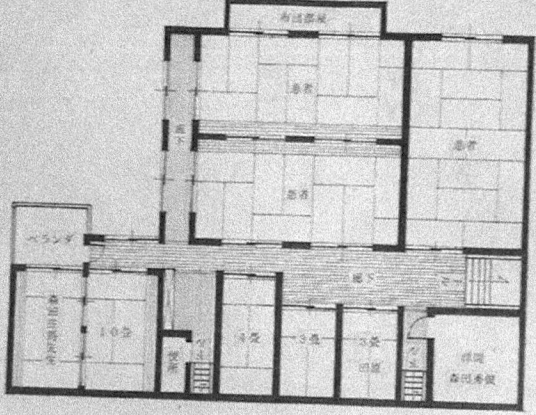

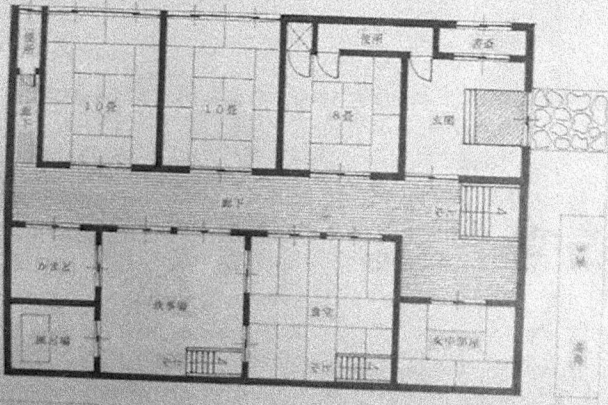

FIGURE 3.4 Floor plan of Morita's home practice (the squares inside each room indicate number of tatami mats)

(With permission from Mishima Morita Hospital Archives, 2016

FIGURE 3.5   Morita and Kora at train station (Morita seated; Kora in black round glasses (R), approx. 1935)

Throughout the early 1900s, Japanese scholars took on the challenge of communicating the essence of Zen and consciousness to foreigners. Influential Kyoto philosophers in Morita's era include Shin'ichi Hisamatsu (1889–1990),[5] Keiji Nishitani (1900–1945), and Kitarō Nishida (1870–1945). Kondo and I had discussions often about overlaps in philosophy between Morita and these Zen specialists of the Kyoto School. While we could not conclude that Morita was aligned with one particular figure, we discussed how Hisamatsu shared Morita's 'down-to-earth' pathways to 'pure self'. Also, the theory that Nishida came to later in life approximated Morita's theory of consciousness.

> Unlike other lay practitioners like D.T. Suzuki, Nishitani Keiji, Ueda Shizuteru, and indeed Nishida himself, all of whom drew inspiration from the Pure Land traditions of their families as well as from Christianity and its mystical tradition, Hisamatsu positioned himself firmly within the Zen tradition. His aim was to carry Zen beyond the monastic walls and into the contemporary world . . . Hisamatsu was not a systematic philosopher in the western vein.
>
> *(Heisig, Kasulis, and Maraldo, 2011, p. 221)*

Hisamatsu's extended thesis on 'Oriental nothingness' explains self-realisation as one's self that returns to the source of nature. At this juncture, his descriptions of pure mind resonate with Morita's ideas.

In his early years, Nishida compared Zen to Western mysticism. His ideas evolved gradually across decades of Zen practice after which he decided that mysticism and Zen are opposed to each other (Shibata, 1981). Like Nishida, Morita advanced Zen throughout his own theoretical discourse without elucidating if or how Zen practice leads someone to an enlightened experience (*kenshō*). Morita was interested in his patients' experience of authentic self as they moved between and within the physical (indoor and outdoor) spaces across the stages of therapy. [6] Nishitani's famous quote stands as illustration: 'From the pine tree, learn of the pine tree. And from the bamboo, learn of the bamboo.' [7] Nishida captures this same sentiment:

> If we see our spirit as the unifying activity of reality, we must say that there is a unity to all things in reality, that there is spirit in it.
>
> *(Nishida, 1990, p. 75)*

Nishida reflected his position in a letter he wrote in 1943 to his disciple, Nishitani:

> For sure, I am not a Zen specialist. But people in general have the wrong ideas about Zen. I believe that the life of Zen consists in grasping Reality.
>
> *(Shibata, 1981, p. 131)*

Notably these Zen scholars and practitioners from the Kyoto School, Nishitani, and Nishida, dwelled in Zen practice; they carved their theories out of their experiences. In effect, this is how Morita developed many of his ideas, and how he came to formulate a method that moves clients into experiences that penetrate their whole being.[8] The level of commitment required in Zen practice matches the level of steadfastness expected of Morita inpatients during their seclusion rest in the first stage of therapy. It is only when clients give in to rest and solitude that they find themselves free from the torment of their own isolation; this can sometimes lead to an experience of consciousness that resembles Zen Awakening.[9]

Nishida put forth his ideas about the contradictory tensions found in Nature in ways that support Morita's contention that we suffer less when we maintain an even tension between 'natural desire for life' and 'natural fear of death'. It is here, in this dynamic tension, that we might realise our 'place' inside Nature and live an ethical life accordingly. 'We are living while struggling with the world' (Nishida, 1958, p. 206).

Nishida wrote about 'the logic of place' (*basho no ronri*) in ways that resemble Morita's discourse on the logic of emotion, which renders nothingness as the ecology of non-existence. By living in the tension of existing yet one day not existing, our capacity for ethical action is enhanced further.[10] Chihiro Fujita qualifies *Mu* when interpreting Morita's formulation:

> Something absolute comes from nothing' (michi or dō). The emphasis is to be placed on 'absolute' rather than 'nothing'.
>
> *(Fujita, 1986, p. 50)*[11]

Over the course of my supervision, Kondo discussed the portrayal of *life force* by Morita and Shinran (1173–1263), the founder of Jōdo Shinshū Buddhism.[12] Intersecting themes merge and diverge across the formulations of consciousness set forth by Morita, Shinran, Nishitani, and Nishida.[13] For instance, in *Intelligibility and the Philosophy of Nothingness,* Nishida (1958) describes consciousness as having a life of its own, much like that proposed by Morita and some of the existential philosophers of his time:

> Let us for a moment, regard the unity of our consciousness, and proceed from there: Each phenomenon of consciousness is [somewhat] independent, and expresses itself. Each pretends [at the same time] to be the Self.
>
> *(Nishida, 1958, p. 188)*

Above all, Nishida and Morita situate human existence inside the rhythm of our cosmos as the constituting boundless consciousness, which I have come to call *shoreless consciousness.*[14] During Morita therapy, clients' natural rhythms of emotion and diurnal movements are reinstated through residence in the therapeutic place. The strategic use of silence in the first stage occurs in a near-empty room with windows and hallway doors that are semi-transparent. The windows and doors act like teasers for clients' imaginations. With such reduced stimuli clients listen to activity outside their room, which coincides with their shift away from preoccupation with symptoms or their past. Gradually, as thoughts and emotions run a natural course, the mind stops dwelling on its own content. Following a mindful state, rest and seclusion propel them into senseful engagement in the world on the cusp of Stage One and Stage Two.

Care needs to be taken by the therapist during the transitions between stages since past traumatic sense memories may arise that unsettle the client; I recall a client who was repelled by the smell of roses; her abusive mother would douse her in rose talcum power after being cruel to her. Of course we cannot know all the sensory triggers that our clients harbour, but one role of the therapist and staff is to contextualise clients' symptoms for them and respond sensitively.

On the phenomenology of consciousness

As addressed previously, Japanese scholars study Western texts, while Westerners seem to study their own texts more exclusively. Accordingly, as one example of this, Inoue cited Georg W.F. Hegel (1770–1831) since he considered Hegel's ideas to bridge Buddhism and the Western philosophy. In particular, he focused attention on Hegel's portrayal of 'organicism'[15] (Blocker and Starling, 2001, p. 133). Hegel inspired philosophers globally through his work on the *Phenomenology of Spirit* (1807/1977), which he originally titled, *Science of the Experience of Consciousness.*

Among European thinkers of his day, I find the work of Henri Bergson, French philosopher and friend of William James, to parallel Morita's ideas more closely than that of Hegel or Heidegger. For Bergson, consciousness is a life force that infuses and kindles all living matter. In *Creative Evolution* (1944; first published in 1907 as *L'évolution Créatrice*), Bergson reveals his philosophy of consciousness in his second chapter in a section titled: 'Life and Consciousness: The Apparent Place of Man in Nature':

> Life, that is to say consciousness launched into matter, fixed its attention either on its own movement or on the matter it was passing through; and it has thus been turned either in the direction of intuition or in that of intellect.
>
> *(Bergson, 1944, p. 199)*

> Consciousness, or supra-consciousness, is the name for the rocket whose extinguished fragments fall back as matter; consciousness, again, is the name for that which subsists of the rocket itself, passing through the fragments and lighting them up into organisms. But this consciousness, which is a need of creation, is made manifest to itself only where creation is possible.
>
> *(Bergson, 1944, pp. 284–285)*[16]

While aligned with various European philosophers and Zen scholars, Morita's portrayal of consciousness in the field of psychological medicine remains incomparable.[17] This is true now and in the past when North American and European scholars were concentrating on expanding the 'unconscious' construct, ego, and self. In *Zen Buddhism, Freud, and Jung*, Thomas Kasulis writes:

> Freudian analysis is primarily aimed at revealing aspects of the unconscious to the conscious; Zen is concerned with the different modes of consciousness, viz., thinking, not-thinking, and non-thinking … pre-reflective non-thinking is a form of experience that has not yet been restructured either by conscious or unconscious forces … Both Freud's psychoanalysis and Zen endeavor to relieve people of their being compelled, but the processes by which they see to achieve results and the rationales behind those processes are radically different.
>
> *(Kasulis, 1977, p. 83)*

As we shall see in Chapter Four, Morita had much in common with existential-based psychotherapists, such as Paul Tillich (1886–1965, German-born American), and Viktor Frankl (1905–1997, Austria). Tillich, in particular, was impacted by his two-month excursion in Japan (Wood, 1961). In his monograph, *Paul Tillich: Journey to Japan in 1960*, Tomoaki Fukai (2013) reviews Tillich's journey, lectures, and conversations with Buddhist scholars and practitioners.

Together they maintain that emotional experience is an aspect of consciousness. Notwithstanding differences, Morita formulated his theory and practice with as much rigour as Sigmund Freud, Jacques Lacan, and Wilfred Bion brought to psychoanalysis, or as Carl Jung generated in his theory of the 'collective unconscious' and related use of mandalas and dream work.[18]

While Morita agreed with the psychoanalytic premise that dynamic tensions in relationships are essential to human existence, his boundless view of consciousness broadens this anthropomorphic framework. Unique in his time, Morita encouraged collaboration between philosophers and scientists in order to safeguard the human spirit. In many ways his ideas were reminiscent of the German philosopher, Christian Wolff (Christian von Wolfius, 1679–1754), who asserted that philosophy is wrought by the nature and structure of the human mind. Wolff contended that metaphysics includes aspects of ontology, cosmology, psychology, and natural theology.

Morita found many contributors to the debate on the boundaries of consciousness, medical science, and philosophy.[19] Amongst these were Franz Anton Mesmer and his disciple the Marquis de Puységur who shared interests in 'natural energetic transfer' and magnetism.[20] Other scholar-practitioners were James Braid, Jean-Martin Charcot, Silas Weir Mitchell, Otto Binswanger, and Sigmund Freud. In fact, letter correspondence was extensive between Freud and Ludwig Binswanger between 1908 and 1938 (Fitchtner, 2003). Pierre Janet identified dissociation and the subconscious, and Karl Jaspers proposed the 'wave' of consciousness in 1913 (Jaspers, 1963). Morita commented on *Does Consciousness Exist?*, published by William James in 1904.[21]

> William James (1890) divides philosophy into the soft-minded and hard-minded schools . . . If a client's emotional base is ignored, any intellectual pursuit (by the therapist) only serves to increase the distance between the experiential mastery and therapeutic resolution.
>
> *(Morita, 1928/1998, pp. 7–8)*

Collectively, these pioneer scholars were noted by their successors who advanced further consciousness theories while holding philosophy and science as complementary. Among those in the generation following Morita were Takehisa Kora, Akihisa Kondo, Karen Horney, Melanie Klein, Jacques Lacan, Carl Jung, Fritz Perls, Alfred Adler, J.P. Sartre, Simone de Beauvoir, and Albert Ellis. Collectively, they could be regarded as our *consciousness explorers*.

Range of consciousness

Conducive to complex dialogue, in the 1930s, 1940s, and 1950s, existential philosophers allowed for 'inconclusive' analyses in their exposés on consciousness and soul. Like Morita, existentialists challenged the ways in which consciousness, ego, and self were being portrayed in psychiatry. This was captured early on by Jean-Paul Sartre in *The Transcendence of Ego* (*La Transcendance de l'ego: Esquisse d'une description phénoménologique*), an essay written in 1934 and published in 1936:

> The ego is not the owner of consciousness; it is the object of consciousness.
>
> *(Sartre, 1957, p. 97)*

In *The Ethics of Ambiguity* (1948), Simone de Beauvoir claimed that a pre-existing *Absolute Consciousness* leaps forward once the intellectual self no longer mediates experience. She insisted that consciousness was ambiguous.

> This 'absolute consciousness' . . . by transcending self, one springs from one's heart . . .
>
> *(de Beauvoir, 1948, p. 156)*

Morita, on the other hand, lived and wrote in an era when philosophers and practitioners contemplated whether consciousness moves humans to action or whether action is a product of a shifting consciousness. Varying metaphors depict consciousness as a moving force. Most notable, perhaps, is William James' *stream of consciousness*, and Karl Jaspers' portrayal of consciousness as a wave, which evokes depth, movement, and expanse differently than a stream:

> Consciousness may be pictured as a wave on its way to the unconscious. Clear consciousness is the crest, the crest becomes lower, the wave flatter, until it completely disappears. We are dealing with a changing manifold . . .
>
> The term 'consciousness' denotes first of all the actual inner awareness of experience . . . Consciousness can shrink (narrowing of consciousness) or . . . grow dense (clouding of consciousness).
>
> *(Jaspers, 1963, pp. 139, 138)*[22]

Morita commented on an undulating consciousness:

> and I am not satisfied by theorists who put 'consciousness' into a fixed grid of categories. Rather, I try to observe and describe the phenomenon as it exists naturally, scientifically, and realistically . . . Changes occur in the human mind=body, night and day, regardless of whether a so-called consciousness or unconsciousness is recognized.
>
> *(Morita, 1928/1998, pp. 117–118)*

Overall, depictions of consciousness range from still to flowing, physical to metaphysical, and altering to transformational. Novelist Virginia Woolf gives consciousness an engulfing quality in her essay, 'Modern Fiction' in *The Common Reader*:

> Life is not a series of gig lamps symmetrically arranged; life is a luminous halo, a semitransparent envelope surrounding us from the beginning of consciousness to the end.
>
> *(Woolf, 1925, p. 150)*

For Russian born Helena Petrovna Blavatsky (1831–1891), consciousness is infinite; it is like a mountain to be climbed, with transformation as the peak experience.[23] If consciousness peaks, it remains unclear whether consciousness is material, insubstantial, moving, or static. Social historian Theodore Roszak comments on the significance of Blavatsky's theory; he coined the terms *ecopsychology, spectrum of consciousness*, and his work has been associated with EcoBuddhism (Roszak, 1975, 1992).[24]

> At the same historical moment that Freud, Pavlov, and James had begun to formulate the secularized and materialist theory of mind that so far dominated Western thought, HPB and her fellow Theosophists were rescuing . . . a forgotten psychology of the superconscious and the extrasensory.
>
> *(Roszak, 1975, pp. 124–124)*

As suggested in various cultures, if consciousness plays a role in human transformation, it remains unclear how or by what mechanisms this happens (Baars, 2003). Indian philosopher Jiddu Krishnamurti (1895–1986) challenged spiritual disciplines, disciples, and communities that endorse pathways to a loftier consciousness. For him, we are transformed by engaging fully in the environment, rather than living according to a spiritual discipline (Krishnamurti, 1970). While Morita and Krishnamurti shared views on the art of practical living, for Morita enlightenment and transformation are grounded in responding to and being moved by nature.[25] As he wrote in 1928:

> My therapy is different from Zen, which prescribes sitting in meditation. It is 'training by experiencing practical events,' as described by O-YO-MEI (MING Wang Yang: 1472–1528). My training does not direct a person to concentrate her or his energy solely on the hypogastric region, as practiced in the art of abdominal breathing. Misdirected people tend to seek mental training in some kind of theory, or they try to force themselves to fit into a certain categorical framework. This process is like making an initial error of an inch and ending up a thousand miles off course.
>
> *(Morita, 1928/1998, p. 96)*

Among the discussants on consciousness in Morita's time is a psychiatrist rarely mentioned in mainstream North American literature, the British born Canadian Richard Maurice Bucke (1837–1902). Bucke (1991) was a psychiatrist who wrote *Cosmic Consciousness: A Study in the Evolution of the Human Mind* in 1901.[26] William James, whom we know Morita read, was interested in the way Bucke translated his own personal mystical experiences into theory. In his chapter on 'Mysticism' in *The Varieties of Religious Experience*, James quotes Bucke:

> The prime characteristic of cosmic consciousness is a consciousness of the cosmos, that is, of the life and order of the universe. Along with the consciousness of the cosmos there occurs an intellectual enlightenment which alone would place the individual on a new plane of existence.
>
> *(Bucke cited by James, 1985, p. 398)*

If Morita and Bucke had been in contact, I imagine they would have discussed Bucke's 'consciousness *OF* the cosmos' and Morita's 'consciousness *AS* the cosmos'. Bucke contrasted the *simple consciousness* of animals to the *consciousness of humans* who access the world through their senses, and harbour an awareness of being aware. He advanced *cosmic consciousness* whereby humans experience the universe as a living presence. In North America, Bucke's notion that 'consciousness extends cosmically' was as unprecedented as Morita's assertion in Japan that 'consciousness extends peripherally'.

In *Morita Therapy: A Psychotherapeutic System for Neurosis*, Chihiro Fujita discusses nonconsciousness of nature:

> The concept of nature (shizen) is integrated in the Japanese sense of life. It has the same meaning in Morita therapy, in the sense of a 'return to nature' (shinzen ni kaere) . . . It is not an artificial construct but, rather, a nature that is nonconscious and inevitable for normal human life . . . In Morita therapy, this means a patient's restoration of trust in his or her human nature. To discard all mental artifice and place absolute trust in one's essential human nature, regardless of consequences, is the goal of Morita therapy. This, again, is the condition that Morita calls arugamama, the condition of casting off the artificial ego and returning to authentic human nature. It is a condition probably equivalent to the jinen hōni concept expounded by Shinran.
>
> *(Fujita, 1986, pp. 50–51)*

As stated at the opening of this book, a distinguishing feature of Morita's theory is that the human mind is not a receptacle for consciousness. For Morita, consciousness is as omnipresent as Nature – the origins of which can never be examined under a microscope.

Nature, therapeutic alliance and indigeneity

As a pragmatist, human rights advocate of mental health, clinician, academic, and philosopher, Morita's unconventional attitudes guided him to observe and design life-enhancing environments that assist the 'gradual' and natural recovery of his patients who were harmed in asylums in the 1920s. He commented on various shock-inducing methods of his era (such as cold water immersion, chaining, and seizure induction) with concerns that any quick neurological fix could lead to other imbalances in the client's bio-psychic system.[27] Too much tampering by artificial means in the long run protracts suffering due to an unnatural recovery pace. Thus, he created a therapy that has its own organic evolution within and between the stages so that the mind can return to its spontaneous function. For Morita, health of the therapeutic milieu is just as essential to a client's progress as the treatment methods and presence of the therapist. As an illustrative passage, Morita critiqued the methods of Otto Binswanger (1852–1929), the Swiss neuro-psychiatrist noted for his work in neurasthenia, epilepsy, and hysteria (Schneider and Wieczorek, 1991):[28]

> Although I tried various therapies, including hypnosis for clients with anxiety disorders, I did not obtain results beyond the temporary relief of symptoms in clients. I also used the life-control method for many years and followed Binswanger's (1911) theory, only to find it manneristic, too theoretical, relatively impractical, and ineffective. Binswanger's methods deprived my clients of spontaneous activity. Initially, I tried to modify and extend these existing systems, but later designed my own method of treatment.
>
> *(Morita, 1928/1998, p. 35)*

No doubt, Morita was influenced by his mentor, Shūzō Kure (1865–1932). Kure had studied in Germany and later prompted humane reforms in Japanese mental hospitals (Fujita, 1986, pp. 82–83). By contrast to Morita, however, Kure was overly influenced by theories of somatic medicine, biochemistry, and electro-physiology related to the theories and research of Emil Kraepelin (1856–1926) in Germany.[29]

Over time, Morita was less influenced by mentors and brought forward his own views on psychiatric medicine and the nature of consciousness. He never dismissed the significance of his intrinsic observant and sensitive nature and how he came experientially to develop his theory on the nature of emotion. In one instance as a young adult, he became dismissive of his parents' lack of university support. Fed up with his own agony, he decided to 'study himself till death' as an 'I'll show you' reaction to his parents. While directing his anger and pouring himself into study, he discovered that once he was absorbed in work, his anguish faded. This realisation became foundational to his theory on the complex nature of anxiety.

Morita's stance resembles that of psychiatrist Thomas Szasz (1920–2012) as both dared to name the dysfunction in the very systems designed to cure mental illness.[30] Szasz wrote about the myths of mental illness and psychiatrists' use of power to apply harming treatments to inpatients in the name of cure or therapy. He is known to quote the English writer G.K. Chesterton illustratively: 'Wisely warned – do not free a camel of the burden of his hump, you may be freeing him from being a camel.' Given that Morita did not situate consciousness in the brain or mind, his therapy is not a 'psycho' therapy, per se, and in Japan is known as Morita *ryoho*. *Ryoho* means literally, remedy or method. Morita comments:

> As a saying in Zen teaches: 'If one tries to eliminate a wave with another wave, one will invite numerous waves.' Similarly, when people strive to remove their pain and agony, they try to eliminate a wave in their minds with yet another wave; their minds inevitably become more confused and disturbed. Any attempt to control the mind can be likened to a person trying to lift her or his body alone by will power without the use of support . . . Through such experiences, I let my clients know that it is impossible

to voluntarily develop the past emotion of fear or anxiety unless proper conditions are provided.

(Morita, 1928/1998, pp. 39–40)

Morita investigated methods and therapeutic places that are health enhancing as well as health eroding.[31] Such an orientation is different from standard mental status exams that assess a client's orientation to time, place and person. Morita was interested routinely in the impact that contexts have on a person's creative capacity. For Arieti (1981) and Williams and Yang (1999), one's creative potential advances and retreats according to the environmental context. In Morita therapy, the emphasis is on engaging all the senses in the 'natural' environment, while assessing the clients innate talents.

Since most psychosocial disorders follow a progressive path, Morita responded by developing a therapy with progressive intent. This design makes clinical sense. Morita wrote at length about the complex relationship between thinking and feeling and responding with action, and how emotions are as logical as thoughts, and a gateway to intuitive action:

A person's fear of death or fear of ghosts is a natural human response. The exaggeration of these fears is due to contradiction by ideas; it is useless to try to eliminate fears by intellectually saying to oneself that, 'One can live one's life fully because of one's fear of death' or 'Ghosts do not exist.' According to 'ordinary logic,' one may objectively criticize emotional reactions by saying that there is no need to fear death. This is the reason I have discussed 'emotional logic' and 'emotional facts'. The fear of death is a subjective fact in human emotional experiences . . . It is, therefore, faulty common sense to try to ignore or reject emotional facts by intellectual means . . . I believe that one can make accurate clinical judgements by assessing emotional facts and by applying proper knowledge to them . . . it is the contradiction by ideas ridden with 'faulty knowledge' that prompts one to first eliminate the uncomfortable feeling and produce a positive feeling in its place before approaching (the feared object) . . . this faulty process creates fertile conditions for the formation of an obsessive disorder.

(Morita, 1928/1998, pp. 5–6)

Despite the constraints imposed during the Meiji period in Japan, Morita's personal history and indigenous, geo-cultural roots could not be severed by the politics of government or medicine. As one would expect, the span that Morita gave to consciousness reflected Japanese cosmological views, as evident in the ways spirits of the dead are experienced and venerated during *Obon* season in Japan.[32] In 1904, Morita published, *Inugami* or 'Dog God of Tosa' in *Neurologia Japonica*, where he distinguished superstition from spirit and cultural phenomena.[33] Superstition, for Morita, is established when there is no systematic tradition, ritual or universal form associated with fears or behaviours (Morita, 1928/1998).

With a wide-angle perspective, Morita and Kokyo Nakamura (1881–1952) formed an alliance, and established together the *Japanese Society for Psychiatry* in June of 1917.[34] They co-founded the journal *Ijoshinrigaku* (Journal of Abnormal Psychology) in October of that same year (Fujita, 1986, pp. 86–87). Morita wrote papers on such topics as the study of dreams, subconsciousness, the imitating nature of children, and superstition and delusion.[35]

As reviewed throughout this book, the arras of Shintoism, Zen, and Jōdo Shinshū Buddhism offer a unique interface between consciousness, life force, and living an ethical life. Foremost, such a rich philosophical complex paves ways for clients to return to original or pure self.

LeVine: I wonder how you might describe *muga?*

Kondo: *Muga* is misunderstood often as someone's true nature. But it is misleading to think that can find true nature by looking inside the self. One's authentic nature is threaded in Nature.

(Kondo, Tokyo, personal conversation, 1993)

Across Asia and Africa, a plethora of indigenous and traditional treatments continue to remind us of the essentiality of the natural, phenomenal world. For instance, if we look towards Ayurveda medicine in India,[36] we find an echo of Morita's concepts. In the Ayurveda system, humans are regarded as a microcosm of nature with basic elements being related to the senses: seeing (fire), hearing (ether), tasting (water), smelling (earth), and touching (air). Ayurveda maintains that the body's sensory system is expressed in these five basic elements that dwell in and spring from pure 'cosmic consciousness' (Lad, 2007). When assessing patients' life pulse, physicians study the condition of the voice, breath, and vital pressure points (*marma*), and assess the texture of the pulse with their fingertips (interview with Rajesh Kotecha, MD, Director of the Chakrapani Ayurveda Clinic and Research Center in Jaipur, India, January 2011).

Morita's philosophy of 'life force' resonates with a range of other indigenous positions on the matter. In the United States, for instance, Lakota Indian activist Russel Means (Brave Eagle, 1939–2012) declared that humankind becomes unwell collectively when neglecting our place in Nature.[37] Lakota people reference *wakan* as the sacred mysterious force that sustains the world (Philip, 2001).[38] In New Zealand, psychiatrist Mason Durie (1999, 2004) contributes models for Mäori Health based on the 'domain of interconnectedness' in which the social domain is one aspect.[39] Even experiences of self and time correspond to the relatedness among wind, stars, the departed, deities, and all forces of nature. This perspective emerged from research by Harris (2017) with African refugee survivors who sought traditional methods of healing for trauma.

Akin to Morita's peripheral consciousness, Durie portrays Mäori consciousness as a centrifugal force that flows away from micro to macro dimensions and broad encounters with ever-evolving forces of life. By experiencing consciousness in these ways, one understands the Lakota way to keep our place in Nature. Aboriginal Australians take this further since individual and collective survival and health depend on 'looking after Country'—as life force that runs through all living matter. Morita's *arugamama* is 'isness', which is to live by Nature – regardless of whether one accepts it or not. Then the body-mind is an active *receptacle* in Nature. Kondo (1962) describes 'acceptance' as 'creative-passive activity'.

In *Ancestral Power: The Dreaming, Consciousness and Aboriginal Australians,* Lynne Hume (2002) writes on 'sub-universes' and 'altered consciousness' inside Aboriginal consciousness in Australia. Putting aside her choice of 'altered' for consciousness (particularly for First Nation Peoples as the term 'altered' may marginalise indigenous experiences of consciousness), she rightfully identifies 'impersonal forces'. In this way, consciousness exists with or without the presence of human existence, which resonates with Morita's persuasion.

In academic psychology, globally, indigenous approaches to therapy are framed often as *alternative*. The following passage in *Redevelopment or Domestication: Indigenous Peoples of Southeast Asia* (McCaskill and Kempe, 1997) discusses how indigenous wisdom on wellbeing and human-ecological reciprocity have been dislodged and disempowered.[40] This passage speaks of Indigeneity.

> Although largely unstated, many government officials and developers view indigenous culture as inferior to that of the dominant society . . . it is the non-material, or metaphysical, aspects of indigenous culture that is the most difficult for outsiders to comprehend and appreciate . . . Traditional indigenous culture is based on the knowledge that all things in life are related in a sacred manner and are governed by natural or cosmic laws. The land, therefore, is held to be sacred . . . In their relationship to the land, people accommodate themselves to it in an attitude of respect and stewardship. To do otherwise would be to violate a fundamental law of the universe ...
> *(McCaskill and Kempe, 1997, pp. 42–44)*

Morita teased out the natural angst associated with living fully in ways that differed from philosophers of his time. Like other indigenous views, his was in keeping with his ancestors. Morita stresses that life has a rhythm that we can trust, which is essential to our existence and extinguished existences. Health is maintained by keeping an even tension between feeling significant and insignificant, simultaneously. Kinship is vast; human well-being is intricately tied to our obligation to safeguard our ecosystem. In this way and in accordance with Lakota tradition – we hold place in Nature. In the context of Morita therapy, Drengson (1990) calls this ecosophy or ecological-derived wisdom.

Again, classic Morita therapy begins with seclusion and rest in a natural setting. The minimisation of sensory stimulation during this retreat in the first stage, paradoxically, is essential to our receptivity to Nature and a primer to forming a therapeutic alliance – with the environment at large not just the therapist. In the subsequent stages, diary writing, outside gardening, art making, readings and observations on soil, herbs, insects, clouds, trees, and birds, with group cooking and work are engineered so that clients spread their relational realm. One Morita client told me that his decision to quit smoking tobacco came from his 'obligation to care for this breathing planet'.

During supervision under Akihisa Kondo, I learned how to study my client's curiosity as it arises – the timing of noticing and reinforcing that first impetus is critical for treatment mapping. That which naturally intrigues a person is what moves them into life-enhancing choices and activities. That is how the client's transitional stages in therapy are charted at CMC. Kind and spontaneous action emerges as the genuine response to Nature – to consciousness(es). In this way, Morita's eco-progressive therapy restores and replaces one's authentic self.

After complete rest of mind and body, clients engage therapeutically with social and natural surroundings in ways that activate their wisdom and curiosity. As a delicate tension between fear and desire is reinstated, spontaneous action emerges in genuine response to the environment. Meanwhile over- or under-attachment to the idea of happiness or misery fade, and one gets freed from approach-avoidance cycles.

Akin to the man with the cobalt tent who opened this chapter, the ways in which he lifted and stroked his cat and handled his books show his responsive, authentic nature. Morita devised a therapeutic method that resituates the self in the environment in relationship to space, light, rest, activity, and other (animal, rock, plant, person) for restorative purposes. The process is gradual, purposive, and pro-gressive – inside an inspired and inspiring therapeutic place.

Notes

1 Parts of this section were presented at the Morita Therapy Congress in Fukushima, Japan in November 2013.
2 Thanks to Professor Christopher Ives for translation and conversation.
3 While the history of Zen in Japan falls outside the scope of this book, consciousness considerations are prevalent. The reader is directed to review the history of Myōan Eisai (1141–1215), a founder of Japanese Zen. Eisai was trained in the Lin-chi (Rinzai) house in China, and returned to Japan to generate the first Rinzai sect (which was adopted by the Shoguns). Zenji Dōgen (1200–1253) founded the Soto school of Zen (Ts'ao-tung) in Japan. He taught sitting meditation or *zazen*. Going back further to Buddhist roots, Dōshō (629–700 CE) was exposed to the ideas of *Bodhidharma*, whose origins remain unclear (Dumoulin, 1989). Dōshō studied for nearly a decade in China under a Buddhist monk who had made a pilgrimage to India, Weishi Xuanzang. Xuanzang developed the 'Consciousness Only' School, which manifested from his interests in Indian Yogācāra wherein consciousness is a manifestation of karma. Dōshō emphasised Hossō, which was the Japanese form of the consciousness-only philosophy. When serving as a priest at Gangō-ji temple in Nara, he developed Japan's first meditation hall.
4 For a fuller understanding of this period, review philosopher Amane Nishi (1829–1897). He translated into Japanese the work of American theologian, Joseph Haven (1816–1874), *Mental Philosophy* (*Shinrigaku, Science of the Mind*). In order to balance cultural con-tradictions, he imported Western ideas while advocating the preservation of indigenous Japanese culture. For an excellent description of this challenging period of history, see Michele Marra (1999), *Modern Japanese Aesthetics: A Reader.*
5 Hisamatsu criticised monastic approaches to Zen practice. He studied Buddhism and philosophy under Kitarō Nishida at Kyoto University, and sought to integrate active, daily living with study and practice until one is awakened to 'formless self'. (For a clear discussion on 'formless self' according to Hisamatsu, see Ives (1992a, pp. 69–84).

6   This was a time in history in Japan when E. Inoue (1905) integrated Buddhism into the first basic book on psychology, *Psychotherapy.*

7   See Nishitani (1990) *The Self-overcoming of Nihilism* and Nishitani (1989) 'Encounter with Emptiness: A Message from Nishitani Keiji' (pp. 3–4).

8   The commitment level essential to Zen practice is required of therapists who train at the Classic Morita Centre.

9   As a private practice note, Morita therapists and attendants require a steady tolerance for client ambiguity, particularly since clients doubt the therapy and the therapist most often in the first stage.

10   For a discussion on this culturally influenced term, see Roger-Pol Droit (2003), *The Cult of Nothingness: The Philosophers and the Buddha.*

11   For a contemporary discussion on this term, see: Alfred Bloom (1992), *Strategies for Modern Living: A Commentary with the Text of the Tannishō.*

12   Shinran (1173–1263) was the founder of the Shin school Jōdo Shinshū Buddhism (Pure Land Buddhism). As follower of Honan (founder of Pure Land Buddhism in 1175), Shinran brought Pure Land to 'ordinary' countryside people, at a time when Buddhism belonged to the nobility. In short, Shinran moved Pure Land from intellectual rationalism to ordinary daily living – a process that resonates with Morita as he took patients out of institutions in order to care for them in his rural home while providing rest and progressive experiences of wisdom by ordinary Nature.

13   For a full discussion, see: Kitarō Nishida (1990), *An Inquiry into the Good.*

14   Within this realm, we can find Nishida's 'logic of place' and Morita's 'logic of emotions' which are realised when the judging, framing mind gives way to pure experience. Naturally, the shore has no boundary.

15   Hegel considered 'vitalism' more seriously than other philosophers of his time, wherein a vital life force runs through living things in ways unattached to the biological elements of life. This resonates with Morita's ideas.

16   When reviewing definitions of consciousness in the 1920s, I found many that contained this phenomenal dimension: 'Consciousness has been considered by philosophers to be: (1) an attribute or condition of soul, or of spiritual substance not necessarily conscious; (2) itself a spiritual substance or self-dependent phenomenon; (3) an epiphenomenon, or dependent accompaniment of physical existence; (4) that of which all phenomena, physical as well as psychical, are forms; the ultimate form of existence' (Webster's New International Dictionary, 1927, p. 477).

17   Morita's analyses are in keeping with contemporary theses on 'the phenomenological mind' (Gallagher and Zahavi, 2008).

18   A thorough review on consciousness and therapy is found in H.F. Ellenberger (1970): *The Discovery of the Unconscious: The History and Evolution of Dynamic Psychiatry.* A pertinent review of Lacan is found in *Lacan and the Political* (Stravrakakis, 1999).

19   Franz Anton Mesmer (1734–1815); Marquis de Puységur (1751–1825); James Braid (1795–1860); Jean-Martin Charcot (1825–1893); Silas Weir Mitchell (1829–1914); Otto Binswanger (1852–1929); Sigmund Freud (1856–1939); Pierre Janet (1859–1947); William James (1842–1910); and Karl Jaspers (1883–1969).

20   Mesmer saw health as the free flow of the process of life through thousands of channels in our body; illness is caused by obstruction to this flow. This description is similar to Ayurveda Consciousness in India. See: Crabtree (1993).

21   *Does Consciousness Exist?* was published by William James in the *Journal of Philosophy, Psychology and Scientific Methods* on September 1, 1904, and republished posthumously in 1912 as *Essays in Radical Empiricism.*

22   Karl Jaspers first published this work in 1913.

23   Blavatsky edited the first theosophical journal, *The Theosophist,* which she helped found in 1879 in Bombay; it remains in existence today.

24   Roszak (1933–2011) is known for his portrayal of 'counter culture', which he coined in *The Nation* in 1968. He also developed the phrase 'spectrum of consciousness' that is often attributed mistakenly to Ken Wilbur. He coined the term 'ecopsychology' in 1992 in *The Voice of the Earth: An Exploration of Ecopsychology.* For him, an ecological approach

to therapy is vital for remedying the alienation between people and their natural environment. (See Coope, 2010.)

25 There are references to Morita's training in Rinzai Zen (as compared to the Soto school) at the Zuirokuzan Engaku Kōshō Zenji (Engaku-ki) Temple in Kamakura (Rhyner, 1988). He trained under Roshi Kōsen, who influenced D.T. Suzuki and Kitarō Nishida. Biographic history is discussed by Michiko Yusa (2002) in *Zen and Philosophy: An Intellectual Biography of Nishida Kitarō*. Kato (2005) gives an historical overview in his article 'Zen and psychology'.

26 Given James' review of Bucke in *Varieties of Religious Experience* (originally published in 1901) and how Morita read and referenced James, it is possible Morita came in contact with Bucke's theory, too, but I could find no confirmation of this.

27 I have no doubt that if Morita were alive in 2014, he would have maintained this view and challenged the use of electro-convulsive therapy still in vogue in some psychiatric hospitals.

28 Otto is not to be confused with his nephew, Ludwig Binswanger (1881–1966). Ludwig is a noted figure in Existential Psychology; he devised the concept *daseinsanalyse* when attempting to define existential analysis. Ludwig met Freud in 1907, and also maintained relations with Jung. Binswanger's renowned work (1963) on *Fundamental Forms and the Recognition of Human Being-in-the-World* (*Grundformen und Erkenntnis menschlichen Daseins*) drew from Edmund Husserl and Martin Heidegger's writings. Morita may well have known that Otto was the analyst to Friedrich Nietzsche and conversant in existential philosophy.

29 Kraepelin set in motion the course that psychiatry is a branch of medical science, and views of mental illness as having a genetic or physical cause. See Richard Noll (2011), *American Madness: The Rise and Fall of Dementia Praecox*.

30 Thomas Szasz, MD was born in Hungary and migrated to the United States in 1938. His most well-known book, *The Myth of Mental Illness* (1960), contends that involuntary psychiatric hospitalisation can resemble imprisonment under the guise of treatment, and that 'mental' illness is not an illness per se, but rather relates to problems in living. For Szasz, psychiatry confuses (mis)behaviour and disease, and labels wrongly certain people with a 'mental disease' while denying their responsibility as moral agents. Control is prioritised often for the 'sake of society'.

31 Questions such as these relate to the phenomenon of demoralisation that was first identified by Jerome Frank in 1974 (Frank, 1993; de Figueiredo, 2007).

32 The equivalent of the *Obon* season in Japan is found in other Buddhist countries, such as *Pchum Ben* in Cambodia.

33 In 1905, Morita wrote a series of five articles for an art magazine that he titled *Appearances of Dolls* where he analysed 'consciousness of beauty' and personality (Fujita, 1986, p. 87).

34 I was in the process of confirming the finer details of this historical note on Morita's role in the development of the Japanese Society for Psychiatry with Chihiro Fujita, but he died in 2014.

35 I note discrepancy in the literature regarding this history. Driscoll (2010) reports that Nakamura was the founder of the Japanese Society for Psychiatry. Joint discussion in 1992 (Tokyo) with Takehisa Kora and Akihisa Kondo support that Morita and Nakamura were co-founders. See: Mark Driscoll (2010), *Absolute Erotic, Absolute Grotesque: The Living, Dead, and Undead in Japan's Imperialism, 1895–1945*.

36 Buddhism and Hinduism have influenced Ayurveda's notion of balance, with emphasis on maintaining balance in one's life-style patterns. Diagnosis of patients is founded on 'essence' and psychic strength, digestive capacity and diet, physical fitness and body form, constitution, age, and reported abnormalities.

37 Ron Kurtz (1934–2011) was the founder of Hakomi Therapy. The name itself is from Hopi language and means, 'How do you stand in these many realms?' Hakomi was influenced by Native American ecological values, as well as Gestalt therapy, Reichian Character Theory, Milton Erikson, Feldenkrais, and Psychodynamic therapy, with principles

strongly rooted in Taoism and Buddhism. 'Ultimately . . . Hakomi form expresses organicity, mind-body holism, and unity' (dialogue with Hakomi therapist, Jim Lehrman, California, 2012).

38 Most eloquently, in *De-colonising Methodologies: Research and Indigenous Peoples,* Linda Tuhiwai Smith (1999) speaks to the timeless consequences of oppression on Indigenous peoples' lived experience.

39 For an indigenous perspective on ecological development, see Mason Durie (2004) and Urie Bronfenbrenner (1979).

40 Indigeneity, a term adopted by The World Bank in 1991, reflects the ways indigenous people identify with geographic regions and natural rhythms and resources, which include their attachment to ancestral bodies and territories. Socio-political reflection of this term points to the collective loss from colonial engagement and the imposition of reconstituted boundaries of self, time, place, and space. This term offers insight into the ways psychotherapists assess and treat the partial or whole person in regard to the environment.

4

EXISTENTIAL REFLEXIONS IN MORITA THERAPY

> Desire does not exist if one returns to the origins of human nature.
> —(Morita, 1928/1998, p. 92)

Morita contemplated the relationship between consciousness and human emotion as vigorously as prominent existential thinkers of his time. His philosophy on 'living according to Nature' is as much existential as it is practical. Moreover, Morita was as intrigued by the 'stream-of-consciousness' proposed by William James as his European contemporaries, Jean-Paul Sartre and Pierre Janet.[1]

While European existentialists considered how one might live authentically while 'being-in-the-world' (*Dasein*), Morita built a system of therapy with steps paradoxical enough to unearth the client's experience of being-in-Nature.[2] In keeping with this perspective, Morita was unconcerned with the existential mantra that *existence precedes essence* – a notion attributed to Sartre (*l'existence précède l'essence*).[3] It was irrelevant to Morita whether existence precedes, overlaps, or trails essence, or is void of essence altogether. For Morita, to simply live in accordance with Nature, without a mantra, arbitrator, or omniscient other, our own authentic nature and innate talents are realised.

Scholars on existence are not exclusive to existentialists, as seen in the work of Lewis Gordon (2000) who dismisses the essentiality of 'essence' in *Existential Africana: Understanding Africana Existential Thought*. The reader is directed to the profound writings of Frantz Fanon (1925–1961), a Martinique-born French-African psychiatrist who is a pioneer of Africana existential philosophy and the psychiatric justice movement. In *Wretched of the Earth* (Fanon, 1966), he demonstrates grippingly how French colonial systems infiltrated psychiatric medicine in Algeria. Psychiatrists (alongside police and soldiers) became 'the official instituted go-betweens, the spokesman of the settler and his rule of oppression' (p. 29). Herein, psychiatric cure of an indigenous person is to 'make him thoroughly a part of a social background of the colonial type', while removing people from their natural and cultural landscapes of 'veiled women, the palm-trees and the camels . . .' (pp. 200–201). While political worlds apart, Morita and Fanon's views of psychiatry converge on the inverse relationship between oppression and authentic existence. For the purpose of this chapter, however, European philosophers who were writing during Morita's era are reviewed since Morita accessed and responded to them.

Morita's theory on 'pure emotion' is tinged broadly with existential and Zen assurance. Emotion that is experienced as it is rising and falling naturally – without interpretation – awakens us to consciousness:

> if a person tries to mould the self to the ideal that one should love everybody and hate no one, conflict between one's natural feelings and one's ideal images occurs as s/he tries to achieve the ideal; this process increases the person's anguish . . .
>
> *(Morita, 1928/1998, p. 53)*

In Morita's era, philosophical threads were shared between Edmund Husserl (1859–1938), Martin Heidegger (1889–1976), and Sartre as they related the essential structure(s) of consciousness to the phenomenology of emotion. Sartre and Morita, in particular, believed that James failed to consider the emotion-of-consciousness. In his text, *On Understanding Emotion,* Denzin (2009, p. xiv) comments that outside the phenomenologists, 'No sociologist or psychologist, to my knowledge, has analysed in detail emotionality as a facet of lived consciousness . . .' This statement is evidence, again, of a leading Eurocentric lens. Had Denzin reviewed Morita's theories, he would have found such an analysis by our Japanese psychiatrist.

Emotions and *consciousnesses*

Sartre brings 'emotional consciousness' forward in *Psychological Phenomenon of Imagination* (1940, 2004) and *Imagination: A Psychological Critique* (1962) when he represents emotional consciousness as a feature of the phenomenal, imaginative realm. As illustration, 'fear of the dark' is interpreted often as an intrapsychic or intrapersonal reaction to an object or event, such as 'I feel afraid of the dark'. From Sartre's unique phenomenological perspective darkness dwells in emotional consciousness where fear manifests naturally in the phenomenon we call darkness. I note that this is different experientially from a cognitive-based fear that manifests as a reaction to darkness.

Morita takes Sartre's theory further by operationalising an experiential therapy that situates emotion inside Nature, as a dimension of *consciousnesses*. Morita's notion of consciousness includes all of life in the biosphere and is different from Carl Jung's *collective unconscious*, which is human-centric in conception (Jung, 1969).[4] For Morita, the nature of night – ever shifting in hue – is as predictable and variable as human emotion.

Taking this further into practice, during the seclusion stage of Morita therapy, a client may feel scared in the dark. While bringing a calm presence to the room, the therapist makes no attempt to eradicate the reactive fear of fear that the client expresses. Human uncertainty rises naturally in the dark; in a secure trustworthy place, fear runs its natural course. In the Morita therapy context, reactive fears recede. Over time, clients experience earthly darkness as darkness from whence they realise fear of the dark to be an ordinary emotional phenomenon. We are wired as diurnal mammals. Most profoundly, *pure fear* can stimulate creative imagination, whereas *reactive fear* can stifle imagination. To drive home this distinction, children are afraid of the dark naturally and innately seek objects, places, and people to soothe them. They might conjure an imaginary animal or cling to a teddy bear to soothe or protect them – which is a natural artefact of this fear. Adults have this option, too, but are often socialised out of this imagining or attaching potential.[5] Being cautious or hesitant initially when in earthly darkness is part of being a diurnal mammal. Morita constructed his first stage of therapy so that a client might experience fully the natural discomforting and comforting aspects of darkness. Herein, the nuanced changes of darkness are as moving a phenomenon as emotion and consciousness.

Clients who endured cruelty in the dark often feel vulnerable in the first stage of Morita therapy when no artificial light is allowed. In this circumstance, a therapist may introduce a nightlight for the first few days until trepidation runs its course and clients develop a relationship to the rest place as a safe place. Gradually during the first stage, clients notice the quality of light that enters the room from outside the window; soon after, their sense of curiosity about the outside world increases. At the end of this stage, fear of darkness is freed from past experiential contaminants, and clients experience moments of natural discomfort. Such perceptual and emotional shifts are noted by the Morita therapist as a criterion for moving the client into Stage Two of therapy.

Sartre and Morita include emotion in their theory of consciousness and diverge from James' dichotomous view that physiological and psychological matter binds emotion. Sartre's 1939 essay, *Sketch for a Theory of the Emotions* (*Esquisse d'une théorie des emotions*) advances a theory on the inclusion of moving emotion in 'consciousnesses' akin to Morita's theory of emotion. Similarly in *La Transcendance de l'ego* (The Transcendence of Ego), Sartre (1936) critiques the phenomenological view put forth by Husserl that the ego is the material of consciousness. For Sartre, humans have the ability to contemplate something in its absence (1939, 1948, 1956, 1957). Immaterial self is known through emotion:

> a problem will arise that the psychologist does not even suspect: can one conceive of consciousnesses which do not include emotion among their potentialities or must we indeed regard it as an indispensable constituent of consciousness? Thus the phenomenologist will interrogate emotion about consciousness … inquire not only what it is, but what it has to tell us about a being, one of whose characteristics is just this, that it is capable of being moved.
>
> *(Sartre, 1939, pp. 10–11)*

Like Sartre, Morita honoured emotion as a core feature of consciousness. From this theory, as stated earlier, he designed a method that leads clients to experience 'pure emotion'. This is another juncture where Zen informs Morita's views on context and emotion, which leaves cognitive methods out of his therapy:

> William James (1890) divides philosophy into the soft-minded and hard-minded schools . . . When compared to beliefs that are acquired through experience, knowledge and ideas that are imposed arbitrarily are rarely effective and worthy . . . If a client's emotional base is ignored, any intellectual pursuit (by the therapist) only serves to increase the distance between the experiential mastery and therapeutic resolution.
>
> *(Morita, 1928/1998, pp. 7–8)*

Morita designed his staged therapy so that clients might experience with their entire being the essentiality of pure emotion. Humans cannot 'choose' to see reality as it is (*arugamama*). They see into reality once they stop interpreting events according to their reactive fears or their desire to be symptom free:

> This inverse relationship is described by a Zen phrase, keroketsu, which is the state of a donkey tied to a post. That is, a donkey that is tied to a post by a rope will keep walking around the post in an attempt to free itself, only to become more immobilized and attached to the post.
>
> *(Morita, 1928/1998, pp. 7–8)*

In *Existential Psychotherapy*, Irving Yalom (1980) contends that therapy is meant to de-repress clients, that is, to move them towards full awareness. 'Pure anxiety' emerges as a natural response to life's uncertainties.[6] For Yalom, one can choose to live in a 'state of forgetfulness of being' by living in denial, or one can dwell in this anxious truth and live fully, regardless. This 'de-repression' to which Yalom speaks is similar to Morita's *akiraka-ni mikiwameru* – living with clear discernment. From the standpoint of Morita, clear awareness and meaning arrive when one just rests, just collects and smells lavender, just peels back the stringed husk on the corn. How else can we experience *consciousnesses* running through living matter?[7]

Along a similar vein, Morita would agree with Jean-Paul Sartre that we are responsible for our interpretations. Morita therapy takes this philosophy further by assisting clients to suspend making interpretations, which is critical to their therapeutic progress. This orientation is counter to cognitive theories. Through sense-full engagement with Nature, the critical mind is interrupted as one sees into the wisdom that comes from pure emotion. Herein, too, imagination is free from a judging mind.

Cosmomorphism: indigenous views on certainty and doubt

To live according to Nature is to live in the tension between uncertainty and certainty, while honouring the continuity of life and finality of living. Existentialists,

like scholars and practitioners of Zen, have established a core philosophy on solitude and doubt without a figure to worship, or guarantee for an afterlife. Relatedly, European existentialists were socialised inside societies that value and endorse
monotheism. In that context, if they questioned life after death publicly, they were
dismissed often as being nihilistic. In *Being and Nothingness: An Essay on Phenomenological Ontology* (1956) Sartre argues that God's existence is not relevant when it
comes to ethical action. In a section titled *Religion and View of Life*, Morita comments:

> People develop overwhelming fears associated with the four inevitable events
> in human life: suffering, aging, becoming ill, and dying. The origins of most
> religions have been based on recognizing and responding to these events.
> When a person transcends her or his ego and refrains from satisfying ego-
> centric desires with religion, s/he can find liberation, peace of mind, and the
> meaning of true religion.
>
> *(Morita, 1928/1998, p. 95)*

As we have seen, Morita was influenced by key Japanese scholars of his time
who expressed Nature's reflection of human nature. As Zen master and founder of
the Soto sect, Zenji Dōgen also known as Kigen Dōgen (1200–1253) advanced pun
in his poetic philosophy. He is noted for taking the Japanese word for sometimes,
uji, formed by combining two Kanji (Chinese characters) for being (u) and time (ji)
(Heine, 1997, p. 2). In many ways, Dōgen is to Japan what Heidegger and Husserl
are to Europe; Dōgen advanced human nature by contending that natural emotions
arise once the mind is cultivated to yield to Nature.

This view is epitomised in Dōgen's passage (translated by Heine, 1997, p. 52):[8]

> Why blame the moon?
> For whether gazing on its beauty
> Summon tears,
> Or whether it brings consolation,
> Depends upon the mind alone.

Akin to Dōgen, Morita was freer from being critiqued by one-God advocates
than his Euro-American philosophers.[9] Thus, Morita could explore the cosmological realm of a philosophy of uncertainty more than his existentialist peers in
Europe.[10] In Japanese culture, despite Meiji era pressures to adopt Western ways and
forgo attachments to Buddhism, exclusive worship to one deity was not coerced,
particularly since Shinto and animistic phenomena stream through Japanese culture. There was no pressure on Morita to polarise the world into good and evil, or
to judge emotions as good and bad; being happy is neither better nor worse than
being sad when context is included. In this way, the symbiosis of doubt and uncertainty provide the perceptual field from which to live life inside all its dimensions.

Morita's theory of peripheral consciousness underscores cosmos-centric views
held by indigenous people globally. His renegade nature mirrored that of French

anthropologist Maurice Leenhardt (1878–1954), who analysed the impact of Christianity on indigenous cosmology.[11] Leehardt devised the term *cosmomorphism* to depict the state of perfect symbiosis with the surrounding natural environment (Clifford, 1982). This orientation is consistent with Morita's view of consciousness.

We see evidence of cosmological sensitivity as far back as Epicurus (341– BC) who published thirty-seven books 'On Nature'. Epicurus attempted to trace 'human unhappiness' to mistaken beliefs about society, nature, gods, destiny of the soul, and objects that are valuable and invaluable.[12] His motto was 'live quietly'. We know that Morita read Epicurus who contemplated the source of life. In *Soul and Body in Stoicism*, Anthony Long (1982) examines the soul philosophy of Epicurus wherein life depends on the union between body and soul; metaphorically, soul provides glue for the human body. Looking back further on phenomenal views of life, Diogenes of Sinope or 'Kyon' (400–325 BC) claimed that human happiness is obtained by living according to nature.[13] Such core views veer from anthropomorphic perspectives, such as those embedded in the 'positive psychology' movement that is in vogue today (Seligman, 2011) or the theory of 'posttraumatic growth' as discussed by Tedeschi and McNally (2011).

Morita maintained a pure phenomenological view by neither justifying or denying the existence or non-existence of soul or God – to do so anthropomorphises consciousness and dismisses the flow of life embedded in emotion. It is at this juncture that cosmomorphism is realised in the theory put forth by Morita:

> Caution is advised when philosophical or religious persuasion appeals to the intellect and is not practical. From the viewpoint of natural science, God is not an actual entity; rather God is a transitional psychological object that is created by different cultural groups. What a person calls God, Buddha, or the Absolute is actually the truth of the universe, that is, the law of nature itself. True religion is not something that exists to gratify human desires, to cure an illness, or obtain peace of mind and a life of ease . . . As humans, we cannot overcome natural law, we can simply obey it and accept the fact that the impossible is impossible. This is true faith. In contrast, when we try to make the impossible possible, when we deceive or make excuses for ourselves, or when we comfort ourselves and assume a false feeling of security at hand, we are participating in superstition.
>
> *(Morita, 1928/1998, p. 90)*

In a similar vein, when self is the observer of self or the observer of nature, one moves further away from realising her or his authentic nature – authentic self:

> When people are fully mindless, absolutely committed, and become one with the present moment, they can no longer be aware of their own states. This is akin to the fact that one can neither see her or his own face directly, nor observe the whole image of a mountain once s/he enters into it. The reason that people do not understand such distinction is because contradiction by

> ideas governs their minds and confuses their ability to distinguish between
> subjectivity and objectivity, purpose and means, and results and conditions.
>
> *(Morita, 1928/1998, p. 15)*

This passage illustrates Morita's persuasion that falls between existential philosophy and Zen. Sartre, for instance, relates intuitive apprehension to the natural
angst associated with being solely and utterly alone. And while this is a human fact,
so too, is a sense of solitude that accompanies this experience if the judging mind
falls away. Reactive fears are quieted, too, when clients realise that other humans
cannot know their feelings or thoughts, totally and completely. And yet, we are
collectively bound by this existential fact. Sartre sees this solo fact, ultimately, as
'being condemned'. Conversely, Morita contends that emotional consciousness
runs through Nature. Therein sits a great liberation. Emotion is not an artifact
of the human species. Consider how the Sherpa (*Shawa*) in Nepal perform *puja*
(a spirit-based ritual) before climbing a mountain, she or he will refrain from
climbing if a mountain's tempestuous nature is felt. Some Shawa women feel
the rage of the mountain, Ama Dablam (personal conversation with three *Shawa*
women, Namche Bazaar, 2002).

Mythology, culture, and creative tension

For those born into Western mythology, resolution and completion to a story's ending is valued. In fact, a hero does not rest until there is a conclusion where goodness
wins against evil. Classic Greek tragedies and myths that Freud read, for instance,
demonstrate ways that characters participate in each other's fate. Such fatalistic or
positivistic conclusions do not exist in Japanese mythology.

Consider the great goddess in Japanese mythology, Izanami, who gave birth to
Japan's landscape; she was the Great Mother who nourished and devoured inhabit-
ants (Kawai, 1998). By contrast, Euro-American characters embody distinct polari-
ties and establish themselves as naive and vulnerable (good), or calculating and
opportunistic (bad). Similarly contrasted, in Japanese folk tales, the one who sets the
taboo has an unhappy ending, rather than the one who breaks the taboo as happens
in European myths). No direct punishment occurs in Japanese myths. Thus, there is
little retribution-based anxiety for the reader of these tales to absorb.

In the renowned tale, a boy named *Momotarō* (Peach Boy) was born of an ordinary peach. As the hero, he walks away and receives no tangible reward, like a prin-
cess or pot of gold. Wisdom is his ultimate gift. Most significantly, in Japanese tales
there is no resolution or completeness to a story's ending, and the main character
disappears without seeking revenge when a taboo is broken. The hero in Greek
mythology, for example, is often born of greatness, akin to the child of Zeus. And
the hero, almost always male, is expected to slay the dragon and get a treasure; he
sometimes gets to marry a beautiful virgin. Such cultural narratives trickle into our
measures for better outcomes in mental health research – where happy feelings and
resolution are gleaned as the positive outcome.

Freud and Morita held ideas that parallel the political tone underlying Stoicism, Skepticism, and Epicureanism as systems that account for social circumstances. Freud was intrigued by Greek allegory and theorised about the unconscious forces at play in *Oedipus Rex* by Sophocles. In this drama, Oedipus acts out a taboo against nature; along the way, a Sphinx poses riddles. Freud was captured by the mythology of Psyche who symbolised the 'longings of the soul'. Her fragile winged form of beauty captured him; Psyche had to 'enter the underworld and retrieve something there before she could attain her apotheosis' (Bettelheim, 1982, pp. 11–15). By contrast to Freud's choice of characters to highlight, if Morita had contemplated such stories, he might have focused on the Sphinx. After all, the Sphinx poses questions that are intended to tripwire the rational mind, akin to paradoxical methods used in Zen. This role assumed by the Sphinx in *Oedipus Rex* is a bit like that of the therapist in Morita therapy.

Morita's philosophy was as much existential as it was naturalistic. Early naturalist philosophy (akin to the one developed by Thoreau) had roots in the writings of Johann Christoph Schiller (1759–1805) who wrote on independence, reason, and nature. He was inspired in turn by Immanuel Kant (1724–1804)[14] and his theory of 'forms of intuition' and acquisition of knowledge from experience (Kant, 1996). Many of Kant's ideas overlap with the sublime that is present in the Morita therapy ecological setting. Clients learn that the more we regard ourselves as not belonging to nature and assume the right to tame nature, the more independent or powerful we might feel. However, the cost of living in this way takes us further away from experiencing the sublime.

French existentialists and Morita, in particular, did not place unconditional trust in a supreme being, regardless of whether such a being exists. Rather, they put faith in the stream-of-existence that manifests even when we no longer exist.

R.H. Blyth (1952; 1964b) explores existential themes through haiku. He remarks.

> Existentialism is, we might suppose, different for every person; even if it is the same, we have no way of experiencing the fact. Its mark is anguish, which is never-ending, for the relative cannot really grasp the absolute, and yet it is somehow 'absolutely' bound to try to do so.
>
> *(Blyth, 1964a, p. 172)*

On the surface, Morita's therapeutic methods seem simple. However, the stages of therapy are fine-tuned by the therapist to reduce the mind's quest for deeper understanding. It is not until the forces of Nature stimulate the client's curiosity about the world that the struggle settles, after which an Awakening can occur.

In a similar way, by rendering Freud's 'psyche' as 'soul' as he originally intended, his analytic methods foster insight that goes deeper than cognitive understanding.[15] However, Austrian-born psychologist/psychoanalyst Otto Rank (1884–1939) developed a theory that parallels Morita's philosophy on life force and weak-willed disposition. With strong interests in art, literature, myth, and religion, Rank held equal 'life instinct, death instinct, and creative enactment' as core themes that emerge in psychotherapy. Akin to Morita, Rank (1989) contends that the human urge to create establishes one's individual uniqueness, while the instinct for death pushes one to engage in community. Morita sought to equal the tension between these two tugs. For Rank, those with a 'productive will' tend to engage in the world with their full imaginative capacity.[16] Morita, too, saw purpose and imagination going hand-in-hand. Although Rank and Morita overlap in theory, I found no historical document where one references the other.

Rather than align with a client's agony over feeling unproductive, Morita therapists engage clients in natural spaces and activities that generate creative action. Morita's theory differs from behavioural therapy by calling on the environment as a key source of stimulation for curiosity and wonder, which stimulates creative tension and engagement:

> Just as Montessori (1909) believes that spontaneous activity is highly effective in fostering education in children, so my therapy is designed to promote the desire for spontaneous activity in my clients . . . One does not become interested in a task unless one actually begins the task.
>
> *(Morita, 1928/1998, pp. 44–45)*

Figure 4.1 shows Morita actively engaged in holding brush and painting ball. The Japanese caption reads, 'Showa sixth year fifth month' or May 1931.

In *Psychotherapy and Existentialism*, Viktor Frankl (1967) wrote on meaningful work and creative activity emerging out of one's experiences and 'encounters with what is true, good, and beautiful in the world . . .' The bountifulness of this philosophy merges with Morita's.

> Life can be meaningful in a three-fold way: first, through what we give to life (in terms of our creative works); second, by what we take from the world (in terms of our experiencing values); and third, through the stand we take towards a fate we no longer can change (an incurable disease, an inoperable cancer, or the like). However, even apart from this, man is not spared facing his human condition which includes what I call the tragic triad of human existence: namely, pain, death, and guilt.
>
> *(Frankl, 1967, p. 25)*

Like existential philosophers and therapists, Morita generated a body of philosophical thought that demotes the centrality of self while holding to the worth of self. Moving clients gradually to live inside the rhythm of Nature during therapy leads them to this paradoxical tension of being. Once there, they experience a deep sense of self-significance rather than importance. This insight manifests in a way that sticks to one's ribs – *taitoku*.

Before Zen became topical in psychological theory, Morita contributed *arugamama* as a construct relevant to his long-term aim in therapy – wherein literally, one comes to reside in and respond to the 'isness of reality'. The staged, eco-based

FIGURE 4.1   Morita engaged in ink brushing in 1931

(With permission from the Mishima Morita hospital archives)

experiences directed by the therapist make this probable. Herein sits Morita's unique philosophy for living according to human nature.[17] Again, the therapist formulates the stages according to a client's developmental age, culture, and readiness for engagement in creative tension.

Suchness and de-acceptance

Regrettably, many English language publications mistakenly define *arugamama* as 'accepting reality as it is'. When the term 'accept' is paired with 'isness' or 'suchness' in the Zen sense, thinking about reality takes precedence over sensing and perceiving reality. As discussed earlier, by piggybacking an acceptance framework on to the 'suchness' of reality, Morita's experiential and ecological orientation gives way to a Western-derived criterion – and the creative force underlying nature of unresolved tension loses its therapeutic traction. In 'Between wonder and doubt: Psychoanalysis in the goal-free zone', Cooper (2002) refreshingly minimises goal setting and accounts for therapeutic advances that emerge out of creative tensions and cites D. T. Suzuki's discourse on Zen and Wilfred Bion's notion of 'O'.

Akin to existential and dynamic therapists, Morita was not invested in whether someone accepts reality or not. What matters is that a client responds to reality as it unfolds – the power of a process-oriented and eco-centric therapy. The process of encountering and responding to reality 'as it is' is likened to mountaineering. While climbers prepare their packs in advance with essentials that account for weather and terrain conditions, they often encounter situations where their senses drive their judgement: they see the movement of cloud build-up, feel the shift of wind direction on their skin, feel and smell the drop in humidity by skin and nose, and hear the sound of leaves rustling high in a tree. They do not think to accept anything. They simply move forward naturally and experientially to seek shelter. All in all, *arugamama* is about being sharply attuned to the moment 'arising' – the emphasis is on *movement inside moments* rather than the moment, here and now. This distinction cannot be stressed enough as it forms a unique difference between being mindful of the moment and sensing and responding to the arising moment when acceptance has no place.

According to Fujita (1986, p. 43), the whole of Morita therapy takes the client 'into essential confrontation with reality' until experience 'harmonizes the contradiction of life and death in human existence'. This passage illustrates the complexity of theory behind the experiential stages of Morita therapy, and how existentialism advances to existential naturalism.

Michael Jackson (2005) highlights the philosophical tensions between 'being-in-the-world' (*Dasein*, by Martin Heidegger) and existential anxiety that accompanies felt isolation as depicted by Sartre. In *Lifeworks: Essays in Existential Anthropology* (2012), Jackson discusses the ways humans across cultures negotiate safety with the forces that surround them. His fieldwork documents how humans anthropomorphise inanimate objects as sources of connection. Jackson's research sheds new light on the theory of 'object relations' as created by a contemporary of Morita, Melanie Klein (1882–1960) (Mitchell, 1986; Klein, 1986; Sayers, 2000).[18] According to Jackson, humans can approach an object 'as if' it has a life force, which bridges isolation and connection via ritual activity, which engages the senses in the world.

Essential to Morita's first stage of therapy is the provision of a safe, contained and supervised place where clients dwell initially in the pureness of aloneness.[19] Maritain (1955, p. 193) writes on intuition and pure experience that inspires poets. 'Poetry does not refer to a material object closed in itself, but to the universality of being and beauty, perceived each time in a single existence . . . in order to keep contact with the universe of intuitivity.' Pure experience occurs when the mind no longer judges or compares experiences. At CMC, a client was given a tea cup with a thumb impression for holding. At first it was odd to have a cup without a handle. Later she wrote, 'I asked to make a tea cup today in the studio. No handle. Just my thumb pushed into clay. I will meet my cup at morning tea.'

Some students have asked me if meditation or a seven-day *sesshin* can lead to this state. Perhaps. If one has a pure encounter with anxiety while in a supporting environment with a mentor who assists full integration of this experience – this is possible. Morita therapy has safety built into the stages; the first stage flows into successive stages where encounters with Nature change the perceptual pathways of awareness. As Fujita writes,

> Morita's technique of absolute, isolated rest and work therapy is a means for a patient to discover the true self by cultivating the basic creativeness, endurance and spirit of service required to reveal oneself in human life, rather than by eliminating the various symptoms one at a time.
>
> *(Fujita, 1986, p. 308)*

By bringing a Shinto lens to Morita therapy, Wataru Kaya (2009, p. 60) reinterprets the meaning of flexible living. Morita's experiential core assists clients in slicing through the 'paradox of thinking'. The progressive stages of engagement and the natural environment move clients to stop directing their minds to direct their actions. The therapist is non-directive so the client learns to live responsively. In the presence of danger, one moves out of harm's way; in the presence of gentle touch one responds accordingly – naturally.

By working and living alongside others we respond to the needs of animals, plants, and take on healthful tasks such as cooking. In so doing, we move away from preoccupation with uncomfortable symptoms. As clients move from seclusion to engagement across the four stages of therapy, they maximise ecological connections and learn to live with existential tensions: aloneness and solitude, the responsibility underlying freedom, the fact of being and someday not being, and the never-ending search for meaning (Yalom, 1980).[20] Morita therapy offers a way of doing this.

Most importantly, while going through the rest stage, clients stop translating experience into language. Consider existential-psychologist Rollo May:

> How can we know whether we are seeing the patient in his real world, the world in which he 'lives and moves and has his being,' and which is for him a unique, concrete, and different from our general theories of culture? In all probability we have never participated in his world and do not know it directly: yet we must know it and to some extent must be able to exist in it if we are to have any chance of knowing him.
>
> *(May, 1958, p. 4)*

This orientation to therapy is shared between Morita and Yalom.[21] For Yalom, the notion of 'de-pressing' the inquiry into the puzzles of existence is akin to Morita's notion of living in the certainty of uncertainty. In the suchness of this natural dilemma, one no longer dwells in the denial of its existence. May writes on context and therapy:

> Our Western tendency has been to believe that understanding follows technique; if we get the right technique, then we can penetrate the riddle of the patient . . . The existential approach holds the exact opposite; namely that technique follows understanding . . . what distinguishes existential therapy is not what the therapist would specifically do, say, in meeting anxiety or confronting resistance or getting the life history and so forth, but rather the context of his (her) therapy . . . the context is dynamic, immediately real, and present.
>
> *(May, 1958, p. 77).*[22]

Morita expresses the same:

> it is not until a person experiences complete solitude that s/he realizes that others cannot be relied upon for sympathy or assistance . . . regardless of whether it is a sensation, mood, reaction, or behavior; understanding occurs in one's intuition or self-awareness itself, apart from objective appraisal.
>
> *(Morita, 1928/1998, pp. 23–24)*

Morita therapy assists clients to minimise their reliance on caustic people and places, and to form therapeutic alliances with a safe therapist, therapeutic environment, and Nature. People subjected to prolonged cruelty are primed for experiencing dread often. As illustrated in the next chapter, Morita's sequenced therapy provides a unique place with elongated time where clients can catch up with and live their own lives.

Notes

1 Existential philosopher Jean-Paul Sartre (1905–1980), psychologist-philosopher Pierre Janet (1859–1947), and American psychologist William James (1842–1910) wrote during Morita's lifetime.
2 Heidegger (1971) clarified *Dasein* or 'being-in-the-world' in ways that link one's past, present, and future, while bridging one's sense of aloneness through reciprocity. For a cautionary note on Heidegger's political leanings, see Elizabeth Bellamy (1997) *Affective Genealogies: Psychoanalysis, Postmodernism, and the 'Jewish Question' after Auschwitz*.
3 This three-word concept was realised in Sartre's Paris lecture in 1945 on *Existential is a Humanism (L'existentialisme est un humanism)*.
4 Carl Jung (1875–1961) built his dream analysis around the belief that symbols and experiences are shared across and within human culture and stored in the subconscious human mind as the repository for human collective experiences. Morita, by contrast, did not place 'peripheral consciousness' inside a human unconscious structure as consciousness spreads across all of life.
5 Those steeped in spirit-based cultures where mountain, stone, water, tree are perceived to be emotionally available validate a wider realm of consciousness (LeVine, 2010).

6 Wholesome or uncontaminated anxiety is experienced when the mind does not lead one to become worried about being anxious.
7 Another existential psychotherapist that resonates with Morita is Heinz Lichtenstein (1904–1990) who was a student of Martin Heidegger, and Rollo May. In fact, Morita has much in common with the existential revolutionaries (my term) such as Frantz Fanon (1925–1961 from Martinique/Algiers), Anita Desai (1937–, India), and existential naturalists, Henry David Thoreau (1817–1862, USA), and Annie Dillard (1945–, USA).
8 This process of cultivating the mind is embedded in Dōgen's notion of *gūjin* – translated more literally as total exertion; religious and Buddhist scholar Christopher Ives renders this as 'the pouring of oneself into what one is doing' (2011, personal correspondence with Ives).
9 Friedrich Nietzsche (1872) points to the political tensions impacting philosophy in his well-known passage: 'All things are subject to interpretation. Whichever prevails at a given time is a function of power and not truth.'
10 *Inquisition* by Edward Peters (1989) offers a most insightful, revised history of the Inquisitions, inclusive of the impact from religious persecution on philosophers' religious intolerance across time and place.
11 Maurice Leenhardt (1878–1954) was a French missionary anthropologist who did research in New Caledonia from 1902 to 1926 and recorded ways Europeans introduced 'spirituality' to indigenous people. James Clifford (1982) reviewed unpublished letters and journals about Leenhardt's life from New Caledonia through to his return to Paris to take the role as academic anthropologist at the École Pratique des Hautes Études. Leenhardt influenced his predecessor, Marcel Mauss, who contended that the human body is both a tool for shaping the world and the foundation in which the world is shaped and perceived. He was succeeded by Claude Lévi-Strauss in 1951.
12 While Epicurus regarded sensation as evidence of effluence – flowing out of energy – he distinguished between sense-impression itself and the judgment of impressions. Morita, too, was interested in fostering practical experiences so that intellect no longer overrides sensation.
13 Diogenes' philosophy is less quoted when compared to others from the pre-Christian era. At that time, 'Kyon' was the Greek term for 'Cynic.' This Greek term was later referenced as 'The Dog' and became identified with Diogenes' raucous lifestyle; such association shifted the original meaning of 'nature' as signifying a libidinous form of passion. All that said, 'to live according to nature' as the 'Cynic' resonates with Morita's ideas.
14 Immanuel Kant had a great influence on the course of phenomenology and Gestalt psychology. He developed three 'Critiques' on reason and judgement: *The Critique of Pure Reason* (1781), *The Critique of Practical Reason* (1788), and *The Critique of Judgement* (1790). It is this third critique that is less popular but holds ideas about purpose and aesthetics upon which Schiller expanded.
15 See Bruno Bettelheim's *Freud and Man's Soul* (1982) and *The Uses of Enchantment: The Meaning and Importance of Fairy Tales* (1975) for discussion on psyche, soul, and imagination. Bettelheim's utilisation of a 'therapeutic environment' in education echoes that of Morita's sensitive construction of an ecological environment in therapy.
16 For Otto Rank, the weakest will is the 'adapted type,' which obeys moral codes of society and is passive and bound to duty. An overly strong will leads one to oppose the status quo in ways that are counter-productive; such fierceness feeds a 'neurotic type' character. Such people are over-engaged in ousting dominance at the cost of their own creative capacity for whole expression. Thirdly, there is the 'productive type' where the will is strong enough but not armed to battle the power holders at the risk of losing resilience.
17 As stated elsewhere, this orientation resonates with Japanese Shinto culture.
18 Melanie Klein (1882–1960) was an Austrian psychoanalyst who studied under Freud before migrating to London to develop her own practice and theory. She developed methods of play therapy for children by which to understand their content and style of play during psychotherapy, and from her observations developed object relations theory, which informed the attachment theory devised by British psychiatrist, John Bowlby

(1907–1990) on infant-caregiver relationships. It is noted that these theories are based on human-to-human relations, symbolically or otherwise.

19 Viktor Frankl (1967, p. 14) defines phenomenology of pure experience as the 'experience of pre-reflective self-understanding rather than interpreting a given phenomenon after preconceived patterns'.

20 Earlier influential philosophers and anthropologists include Ernst Cassirer (1874–1945, German; 'humans are symbolic animals and symbols shape the perception of their reality'), and Oswald Spengler (1880–1936, German; 'culture has developmental cycles, and cultural souls can be observed').

21 Nishida's notion of *koi-teki chokkan* or 'active intuition' is relevant to a discussion on Morita therapy outcomes for those suffering from traumatic experiences, particularly cruelty-based trauma. As Morita stages progress, intuition increases as intellectual knowledge and body knowledge (taitoku) are brought into balance.

22 May was not content with the term, 'existential analyst' and coined 'phenomenological analyst' (May, 1958, footnote p. 77).

5

TREATING CRUELTY-BASED TRAUMA IN AN ECOLOGICAL CONTEXT

This chapter concentrates on a specific spectrum of trauma derived from human cruelty or that which I name, *cruelty-based trauma*. As we have seen, Morita advanced his ecological therapy after seeing psychiatric inpatients suffer from degrading environments and systematic trial and error treatments. Morita therapy offers counterbalancing experiences for clients who live in places where they are disempowered, criticised, ridiculed, kept under surveillance, or shamed – and where they have no enduring advocates to verify their experiences or others to protect them. In the aftermath of such cruelty, a deep sense of futility creeps into one's core existence; life is tentative; life is hard.[1] By contrast to human induced trauma, in the case of a natural disaster, Nature has no malicious intent.

Throughout this chapter case illustrations demonstrate the dynamic use of therapeutic space, the sequence of therapy methods that evolve from seclusion to engagement, and the attentive presence and stride of a therapist's engagement that enhance healthy enduring outcomes. Morita's engaging therapy environment offers complex time and space needed for clients to catch up with their lived history.[2] Foremost for restoration, clients gain the experience of living without intimidation in a safe and experiential context.

As established in earlier chapters, Morita therapists create a safe and simple room for the first stage. In conventional hospital settings, relief of symptoms is targeted and induced by medication or other mind-slowing methods. By contrast, in Morita therapy a period of agitation is expected during the first few days of seclusion until the body and mind ease gradually into the new surrounds. Essential to this process is the understated (*fumon*) presence, predictability, and familiarity of the therapist and team in the natural setting.

Akin to Morita, Arthur Kleinman (1980) challenges the notion that uncertainty and danger are mere glitches in our predictable world. In *What Really Matters: Living a Moral Life Amidst Uncertainty and Danger*, Kleinman (2006) encourages us to take the danger and unpredictability of our worlds as norms to be addressed formally, rather than as categorical anomalies in mental health. Morita therapy is complex and savvy enough to offer this reality-based approach to health practice, and to give clients a chance to experience life with less danger and responsive support – and know the difference when navigating time with others. Throughout therapy stages, the therapist's ethical obligations are underscored to ensure client safety. During the first rest stage, in particular, Morita therapists assess risk regularly for dissociation and adjust the environment and increase contact with the client accordingly, or they discontinue this stage to ensure safety.

The politics of cruelty

Clients who endure cruelty often hold little to no power in family, education, medical, or military systems where harm and neglect occur, or where they may be scared or intimidated into silence. Their functionality depends on the power dynamics or politics between those who govern and those who are governed, and how alliances are formed around harming forces. Within family systems, children have no formal and just avenues to support disclosure or rectify violating dynamics, which is a factor that exacerbates their isolation and compromises their playful imaginations.

To date, formal diagnostic benchmarks for Posttraumatic Stress Disorder (PTSD) have been based on quantifiable events that are injurious to the human psyche. The event-bound categories of PTSD include war and combat, abduction, physical torture, terrorist acts, natural disasters, man-made disasters, transport crashes, sexual violence, witnessing murder, a sudden unexpected death of a loved one, and diagnosis of a life threatening illness. Regardless of context, symptoms are assembled into three categories in the Diagnostic and Statistical Manual Fifth Edition (DSM-5): (1) re-experiencing symptoms, (2) avoidance-based symptoms, and (3) hyper arousal symptoms. The International Classification of Diseases, (ICD-10) provides five categories for 'complex trauma', which increase cultural reliability.

While this diagnostic paradigm clarifies post-trauma responses, it fails to denote symptoms related specifically to human cruelty. Under current criteria, mania, depression, aggression, oppositional defiance, or borderline personality features, for example, are identified often before any trauma-related dissociation syndrome is considered (Baird, 2008; Kaehler and Freyd, 2009). For example, the diagnostic category borderline personality disorder neglects the functional role that dissociative features play in psychic survival. Once classified, clients are treated most often by instructional-based therapies intended to 'manage' their symptoms, with little scope for naming and challenging colluding systems of harm. Rarely considered are relational triggers for fear, anger, or dread that awful things will happen again. By advancing a distinct category for cruelty-based trauma, patterns and sequences of symptoms that include borderline features can be understood in ways that offer complex therapy rather than management models of care.[3]

The noted psychiatrist and Holocaust survivor Bruno Bettelheim (1903–1990) challenges the sole existence of a moral good and examines justification of harm by institutions in the name of moral order:[4]

Violence exists, surely, and each of us is born with (his) potential for it. But we are also born with opposite tendencies, and these must be carefully nurtured if they are to counterbalance those that push us to act violently. To nurture such countervailing forces, however, one must know the nature of the enemy, and this is not achieved by denying its existence.

(Bettelheim, 1980, p. 189)

Morita therapists nurture constructive forces but are uninterested in assisting clients to gain an intellectual conclusion about a perpetrator's motive. Insight happens gradually as they move through the stages and experience the forces of Nature. All too often, clients become mentally exhausted by trying to make sense of cruelty and by using energy to deflect emotions. Overall, clients are most confused by harm from people and those who are supposed to protect them, such as a teacher, relative, neighbour, or sibling. Paradoxically, the therapist invites them to experience more fully the onset and undulation of their anger, fear, confusion, or pity – without reacting. In this way, emotions become visceral evidence of trickery they have endured.

This section presents six institutional domains in which members are rarely held accountable for complicity in harm: (1) domestic sphere where guardians hurt, neglect, confuse, and demoralise vulnerable people (2) education systems where students are hurt physically, psychologically, or emotionally by fellow students, teachers, or administrators, including faith-based schools, and home schooled contexts where punishment, fear and humiliation tactics are used for social control; (3) religious institutions and spiritual cults, where those in empowered roles knowingly or with 'good intention' manipulate scriptures or rituals for harming purposes, as found in cases of gay youth who have been exorcised by Catholic priests; (4) youth detention and prison systems, which operate under sentencing orders by a court of law; (5) medical systems where a person is subjected to treatment without consent such as being administered shocking, confining or medicating treatments in psychiatric units; and (6) government systems and the armed forces where people are conscripted into service, confined and interrogated in detention, or deployed into a war without protective mechanisms in place.[5]

At the macro level, a complexion of examples can be cited internationally where institutional cover-up has been a colluding factor. Consider information withheld by a government during fallout from the Bikini Atoll atomic bomb testing in 1946 (Bradley, 1949), the 1979 'Three Mile Island' nuclear disaster, the Chernobyl meltdown in 1986, the nuclear material leak in Erwin, Tennessee in 2006, and the March 2011 Fukushima earthquake and tsunami that surrounded the nuclear disaster. In the recent case of Fukushima, radiation continues to penetrate the ocean's ecosystem and those in makeshift camps in Japan cannot claim the status and rights of an environmental refugee.[6] Similarly, human cruelty is justified and maintained in the name of national security, such as the torture used at Guantanamo Bay for interrogation, with a chosen location that falls outside safeguarded international jurisdiction. Another example is found in detention centres for Aboriginal youth or refugees seeking asylum in Australia. When refugees arrive by boat they are labelled as illegal immigrants. Children are detained in confined areas for years of their developmental lives; many have limited or no access to healthcare, work, or formal study. By justifying inhumane policies and actions in the name of national security, a nation's integrity is obscured and legal avenues for reconciliation are narrowed.

Morita therapists assist clients to find metaphors in the natural environment that express their double binds. One of my clients told me this:

> I don't want to leave my partner because he has had a life of misery. Yet, I want to leave him because I feel scared for myself everyday I live like a frog with a bubble on my nose. But I am not a frog. My bubble can pop at any time. Then what?

While dread and mixed loyalties exhaust the imagination, resting into Morita therapy gives clients a chance to live another way, while priming them to imagine pathways for sustainable safekeeping – even if it means daring oneself to go solo while expanding a support base. As a related cultural note, a genus for post trauma in Cambodian psychiatry is *Baksbat*; the literal meaning of this term is *broken courage* (Chhim, 2013). Relatedly, Morita therapy provides openings for clients to engage in the broader ecology in ways that buoy their courage and sense of belonging to place.

On dissociation and imagination

For those who endure cruelty, confusion is usual and a sense of feeling integrated and whole is compromised. Some lose access to the memory of their lived history. It is as if one becomes unstuck or frozen in time and place. How this happens is unclear.[7] All in all, related dissociative features are difficult to study consistently before adulthood – often after cruelty has occurred (Macfie, Cichetti, and Toth, 2001; Ford and Courtois, 2003).

My intentioned focus is on the interrelationship of cruelty, trauma, and dissociation. In the literal sense, dissociation is a state of separation or disjunction. In psychiatry, its essential features relate to a disruption in integration and function of consciousness, memory, identity, and perception. These disruptions can be sudden, gradual, transient, or chronic. The phenomenon manifests in a continuum across depersonalisation, derealisation, amnesia, psychic fugue, dissociative, and identity disorder (Perry, Pollard, Blakley, and Vigilante 1995; Putnam, 1997; Wright, 1997; Edge, 2001; Perry, 2006).

Historically, clinical discussions on dissociation include theories of consciousness and ego integrity. In the early 1900s, the French therapist Pierre Janet (1859–1947) coined the terms *dissociation* and *subconscious*. He saw the subconscious as the site where obsessive thoughts are activated, and agreed with Freud that dissociation is a defence mechanism by which a person (consciously or unconsciously) separates the self from the psychic memory of traumatic shock (Ellenberger, 1958, 1970). This view supports those who describe dissociation as an unexpected, partial, or complete disruption of normal integration of one's personhood (Briere, Scott, and Weathers, 2005).[8] With the continued focus on theories of the unconscious in the

Western trauma literature, Morita's phenomenal representation of 'peripheral consciousness' has been left out of discussions on dissociation.

In Morita's era, for instance, Janet suggested that patients' external awareness of the environment narrows as they become depressed. This phenomenal view overlaps with Morita's ideas on anxiety. However, for Morita an increase in anxiety can be a function of a constricted or expansive awareness of the environment; responsiveness to the environment requires peripheral awareness (Morita, 1928/1998). Janet assumed that pre-existing deficits 'in the individual' worsen after experiencing a traumatic event.[9] By contrast, Morita did not fasten pathology to an individual's ego or defence system; rather, he considered the role of a hypersensitive predisposition to body changes alongside environmental conditions:[10]

> regardless of whether it is a sensation, mood, reaction, or behavior; understanding occurs in one's intuition or self-awareness itself, apart from objective appraisal.
> *(Morita, 1928/1998, p. 24)*

Given the way Morita's method is structured around the environment, case formulation requires descriptions of contexts where cruelty occurs; this is essential before admitting a client into the seclusion stage. If a client has been sexually violated in a bedroom as a young child, for example, he or she could become seriously disoriented while in a prone position. Therapists make adjustments for psychological safety accordingly.[11] Since Morita therapy is context dependent, therapists are trained to be sensitive to places that could trigger sensory memories that might unsettle the client. In keeping with this duty of care, therapists inquire about perpetrators' roles in the client's developmental history, the roles of those in the environment who may have colluded by silence, inaction, or action, and places where harm has occurred – including season and time of day.[12] During the seclusion stage, a client needs careful supervision if she or he has endured experiences of cruelty in a dark, enclosed room; similarly, assessing outdoor and open spaces is essential. Intake information is necessary for evaluating the client's risk potential for dissociation and/or suicide. More research is needed to determine the constellation of contextual factors that increase the risk for dissociation across the following five interacting factors: *cruel situations, colluding agents of harm, places of harm and places of refuge and safety, ages and developmental time span,* and *heightened experiences of dread.*

Much research on trauma recovery accounts for therapeutic changes across the behavioural, emotional, cognitive, physical, and spiritual or spirit-based domains. In order to assist the cultural reliability of criteria, I advocate an additional formal domain, *imagination.* Outside of the creative art therapies (art, dance, music), imagination and creative processing are rarely considered formally by clinicians as a domain impacted by trauma. Also, one's experience of dread may relate to a restricted or overly expanded range of imagination, which can put one at risk for dissociation. Relatedly, the theory of consciousness that therapists adopt has bearing on their inclusion/exclusion of the imagination, therapeutic engagement style, and the sequence and methods of therapy.

During Morita therapy, clients activate their practical imaginations in Stage Two when they go outdoors into the garden. This is a time when they no longer ruminate over the past as they did in the resting room. In fact, by moving to another room in Stage Two, they leave behind their history in the former contained space. Once grounding clients in practical activity in the second stage, Stage Three rekindles their fanciful imagination through art making and engagement in Nature. Any flight into the fantasy is tempered by practical imaginings that are reinforced by the therapist across the stages of therapy. One benefit of the progressive stages is to advance the range of imagination so that the lofty and practical co-exist. In Morita consciousness terms, I describe this as assisting the development of a client's *peripheral imagination*.

Morita therapists advance art making and practical construction projects, such as sketching a changing sky, building a chicken hut, or boxing a compost area. The purpose of art in this therapy is to make something aesthetically interesting that involves earthly elements, such as carving wood or sculpting earthen clay. Art making engages the senses; it is not used to tell a story or for art therapy. During Morita therapy, the therapist observes moments when clients pause to look or listen to something that interests them. We stay alert to noticing what engages a client's curiosity. For instance, I noticed a client as she was watching ants. The ants travelled around a small puddle of water. I watched her as she sat quietly in the shade. She moved evenly to gather some tall grass and measured with her hands the width of sticks. She then made a tiny, intricate bridge for the insects by weaving blades of grass around long sticks. In her diary, she drew ants crossing the bridge and she designed tiny hats and shoes for them in her drawing. In Morita therapy, the environment is there to rekindle clients' imaginations and spontaneous playful spirits as they experience trustworthy 'others' in natural places.[13]

Within the realm of imagination, spirit-based cultural factors are essential to consider. This category accounts for the influence by cosmological and animist phenomena on human health across cultures and indigenous communities (Ang, 1980, 1988; Durie, 2004). This term has cultural validity, for example, when accounting for trauma aftermath affecting war and genocide survivors from Cambodia, Rwanda, Guatemala or other cultures when spirit sources instigate harm or protection (LeVine, 2010). As cultural duty of care, spirit phenomena are taken into account by therapists at CMC during clients' assessments.

Most challenging to treat in the dissociative spectrum are disruptions in sentience that occur with no apparent trigger or biological basis, as seen in somatoform dissociation or conversion disorder. Conversions are usually manifested in the motor and sensory systems (Nijenhuis, 2009). At this juncture, one might display frightening, awful experiences symbolically as physical symptoms, or one might generate a distracting life crisis. I recall the case of a young boy in Laos who lost his vision after witnessing his twin brother blown to pieces in a landmine blast; through rest, time, support by community and safe land, art making, and sand play therapy – he made a recovery to full sight.

Similarly, at a far end of the spectrum of dissociation, pseudo-seizures, or psychogenic nonepileptic seizures are known to emerge following severe trauma. Atypical seizure activity may be part of a hyper-hypo arousal circuitry, or associated with conversion and numbing of senses, although more research is needed on arousal switching by the sympathetic and parasympathetic nervous systems (Ozecetin et al., 2009). An example of this numbing effect appears in children who soil their pants but are genuinely unaware of having done so. In fact, some children have bouts of not experiencing certain sensations – and may not feel temperature changes on their skin, or smell their own excrement. Some may not experience early sensations that precede pseudo-seizures.[14]

Theorists are mixed in opinions about whether self-hypnotic states are at the core of dissociative states, but researchers tend to agree that dissociative processes are sequenced in complex ways (Braun, 1988; van der Hart and Nijenhuis, 1999; van der Hart, Nijenhuis, Steele, and Brown, 2004; Rosen, Spitzer, and McHugh, 2008).[15] In the *Handbook of Dissociation*, Watkins and Watkins (1996) discuss the relationship between ego states, regression, and hyperamnesia: 'This distinction between subject experiences and object experiences within the psychological life of an individual has profound significance for treatment' (p. 436). The work on time distortion in Dissociate Identity Disorder by van der Hart and Steele (1997) resonates with the ideas of Pierre Janet. Again, the theory of consciousness that a clinician adopts may be at the root of differences on how one interprets and treats dissociation.

Dissociation has been described as a 'phenomenon of self-fragmentation', occurring from unshakeable fright experienced often in one's early childhood. In part, children are at risk by living in contexts that offer no dependable support for processing their contradictory feelings (Liotti, 1999, 2009). Freyd (1996) discusses how betrayal and double binds manifest into physical symptoms, particularly when someone, often a child, is confused about loyalties. These children are denied a carefree childhood, and the chance for an integrative development across perception, memory, body sensation, imagination, and self-identity (Freyd, 1994; Van der Kolk, 1996; Ogawa, Sroufe, Weinfield, Carlson, and Egeland, 1997; DePrince and Freyd, 2001; van der Hart, Nijenhuis, Steele, and Brown, 2004; DePrince and Freyd, 2004; Dorahy and van der Hart, 2007). They are often void of the experience of unfettered love, an artefact voiced by one of my adult clients:

> Society expects us to love and accept our parents. I do not want to fake my feelings; they still scare me. All in the cult scare me, young and old. I am a lucky one because my auntie and uncle rescued me and gave me back part my mind.

Children are easily conflicted about disclosing harm. Disturbingly, non-disclosure may be the only way to maintain the dependent relationships they have with a perpetrator-carer (McNally, 2007). Children can feel lost without family, village, or cult members in their lives despite enduring cruelty. Confusion runs right through their adulthood. Disclosure takes developmental time, particularly when clients recount harmful histories retrospectively and feel as if they are violating a secret code or person. This conflict can explain a client's incapacity to provide concrete evidence in a judicial or coroner's inquiry.

Clients are at risk for dissociation if as children they had primary carers whose attaching style was overly chaotic or rigid (Main and Hesse, 1990; Mann and Sanders, 1994; Liotti, 1992). Children may not be able to acknowledge abuse if other adults make excuses for their ineffective carers, such as 'she is tired' or 'he is under a lot of pressure'. Many children are expected to make adjustments to a guardian's inconsistencies; some take on the role of carer for their parents. In such contexts, children may develop that which I call a *sporadic attachment style* that accompanies them in adulthood. There may be a tendency to overly please or to be overly dismissive or critical to those in authority. This is another reason that Morita therapists refrain from verbally challenging a client's distress. By taking a *fumon* stance, the therapist gives the client an experience of a reliable contact; what you see as safe is what you get as safe. The dynamic intersection between a client's developmental history, traumatic experiences, and the therapist's interaction is illustrated in the next case.

Traumatic implosion of a peace keeper

Consider a veteran of the United Nations Peacekeeping Forces whom I'll call Kevin. He was in the field at the end of the second Sudanese civil war (1983–2005). Following this experience, he vacillated between trying to comprehend the sinister nature of human beings and wanting to 'escape from society altogether'. He said he joined the forces knowing that 'bad stuff came with the job', but he never expected members of his own unit to become the enemy within. He said he witnessed two men in his unit bully and brutally bash a field colleague. He made a verbal report to his superior who told him the situation was being handled. Later, his colleague was transferred. Kevin never heard what happened to that man. Accounting for the sequence of experiences is important for understanding Kevin's profound sense of rage, disconnection, and dissociation (Paulson, 2004; Paulson and Krippner, 2007). A week later, he was on reconnaissance some distance from his camp. Kevin watched a child being disfigured and tortured to death by rebels. He believed the child was from an indigenous ethnic group and this fact gripped him deeply as he imagined the boy to be far from home. At that time, Kevin and troop members watched from a hidden location and were under orders not to respond.[16] 'I wanted to look away but could not.' Most seriously, Kevin's inaction and his prolonged focus seemed to have 'frozen' the image of the child's exploded face within his visual, olfactory, and auditory memory.

Upon finishing his tour, he had a one-hour group debriefing session as his exit protocol before returning to Australia. Once home, he had insight into his felt sense of 'not fitting in'. 'No one wants to hear the fine details of torture that I witnessed. Besides, my friends have the right to be naive. They did not sign up, I did.' On weekends, Kevin would meet his male friends and binge on alcohol. During the week he would run for two hours each morning, sometimes hung-over, but running was his normal routine while in the forces, and he was at a loss of what to do with his free time.

When I met him, he was confused, socially withdrawn, and experiencing dissociative fugues. 'I am scared of living with my past and I'm scared of living without it. I do not know where I belong anymore.' With this contemplative quandary in mind, one night during a drinking episode with friends, he spoke of the boy who haunts him and told a friend he did not want to live in his own mind. His friend became scared that Kevin may be suicidal, and convinced him to go to an emergency room at a public hospital. Upon evaluation, Kevin was admitted to a psychiatric unit for suicide watch in urban Australia. He had no prior experience in the mental health system. After five days, he was released. He was referred to me by a social worker at discharge. The attending psychiatrist told me that he was unclear about his diagnosis, yet put him on medication for suspected 'traumatic psychosis' as a protective measure. At the time of my interview, I saw evidence of dissociation without psychotic features; complex posttraumatic stress and existential anxiety with a heightened his sense of feeling displaced.

I saw Kevin two days after his release from hospital. He was afraid to sleep for fear he would see images of the child being tortured; mostly he was gripped by his powerlessness to prevent it. He said that he wanted to talk to someone who would let him be scared when he talked about scary things. He worried that he would be put on more medication if he told physicians about his deep rage since leaving Africa. He had some insight into the hospital staff's incapacity to understand his particular range of anger and lived history. I interpreted his decision to withhold disclosure as sound judgement on his part. While in hospital, no clinician or staff member had explored the range of his fear, justifiable anger, existential angst, or the meaning of the boy's torture as related to his own childhood, or the sequence of traumatic events and agents of betrayal.

I invited Kevin to see me two days a week for the first month. Together we came to understand the contexts that triggered and exacerbated his symptoms, which assisted a therapy plan and the development of a therapeutic relationship. I made arrangements for Kevin to be reviewed by a consulting psychiatrist who works with war veterans; the specialist adjusted the medication and gradually discontinued the major tranquiliser and revised the trauma-based diagnosis to exclude psychosis. In the session with the psychiatrist, we discussed together the concrete and symbolic triggers of Kevin's dread, and addressed his fear about his lingering image of the boy.[17]

When I inquired about love relationships, he told me about a letter he received from his fiancée at the end of his tour of duty. She told him that she was interested in another man, and had decided it was best to call off their engagement. He said that things were distant between them on their last time together and that he half expected her departure. He did not write to her or contact her after receiving the letter, which he folded up and put between the pages of a book. He told me that he did not know how to respond to her so he decided to not do anything. In our session that day, he composed a simple reply to post to her.

After six weeks, I set a course for a modified form of Morita therapy with Kevin. He required extended supervision in the rest stage because he could easily spiral into bouts of existential meaninglessness or into a dissociative episode. In particular, I described the meaning and purpose of therapeutic rest in the Morita therapy context and detailed the stages of the therapy and my role throughout the treatment. I asked Kevin to simply rest in the first stage, and to just let images come and go without judging them it to be anything other than an image. After three days, Kevin no longer struggled to dissolve the image of the murdered, mutilated child or to make peace with the boy, or to apologise to the boy in his mind. As the images became less visible, he told me that he missed the boy's presence. 'What if this boy is forgotten, forever?' While interpreting this to be an existential quandary, my response was to say, 'I think you might recall this boy in a different way, one day.' He was eased by my reply. On the fifth day of rest, he recalled a visceral childhood feeling of being on the run. He had lived in chaotic family circumstances as a child. Without soliciting discussion, he told me later that he realised suddenly his personal connection to the boy from this dream. He said it was then that he became less ambivalent about wanting the boy's presence to stay or to go away. He decided to settle into the possibility of any possibility: 'while coming to grips with civilian life, I live in exile in a place that was once home. If this is how it is, I may as well ride into this unusual episode of my life with my head held high.'

Kevin's depiction of his exile existence coincides with the sensitivities assumed by the existential *outsider archetype*, posed in *The Outsider* by Colin Wilson in 1956. Wilson (2001) states that 'perception is intentional' and that one's freedom to exercise imagination is key to dwelling inside one's sensitivities while expanding the human perceptual capacity to witness the beautiful mystery of the first star that rises – and to feel this with all of one's human being.

During the first stage of Morita therapy, the experience of being in the rest room involves a range of psycho-emotional experiences across time – a kind of sliding between past and present. How that happens is unknown – yet it is a frequent comment by my clients. Some of these men and women want to tell the therapist about their vivid dreams because they are surprised about the details of familiar houses and rooms and outdoor landscapes. The Morita therapist encourages them 'to leave the dream in the dream' and notice the details of sounds or light that pours or trickles into their room. The meaning of a dream becomes clear when one does not dwell in finding it; like an illusive word that pops to mind when least expected.

By simply remaining in the rest environment with a therapist nearby, the client's awareness of the surrounding physical world increases. For instance, on Kevin's fifth night, he woke from a dream with details that were unclear. He requested my presence. As I came into the room he began to cry deeply. (It is noted here that Morita therapists do not make interpretations about transference; we simply let a possible relational trigger run its course.) He sobbed for forty minutes. I sat quietly nearby. At one point he tried to apologise for his emotional intrusion. As a paradoxical response, I suggested that he continue to cry as long as it takes to even his breathing, rather than directing him to breathe a certain way. 'We cannot cry forever.' I continued to sit silently near. As he settled, I said I was going to get him some water and would return in a few minutes. In that time, the anticipation of my return settled him more. What was different for him was his experience of 'just crying' without explanation, without thinking. Resting in one place was new for him, as was being free to emote without overanalysing or intellectualising – while experiencing a grounded place with a therapist's grounded presence.

The images of the murdered child subsided but did not disappear until six months after Morita therapy had finished. During that interim period, the major change for Kevin was that he did not struggle to make sense of the image, or ruminate about what he could have done differently. He adopted a pet parrot during this time and told me he never expected to love a bird. He made regular visits to his local plant nursery and gathered potted plants on his veranda; he began a new friendship with the owner of the nursery and they began to take day hikes together.

Formative to this progress was the therapeutic experience of residing in a calm and predictable room with nutritious meals, natural light, and absence of conversation or mental inquiry. An overriding goal was to relocate Kevin inside the rhythm of time, place, and essential Nature. Through Morita therapy, without analysis, meditation, cognitive reframing, eye movement exercises, or other instructional methods, clients are re-placed in their own history and dropped into the rhythm of ecological time.

As therapy progressed, Kevin was able to engage in responsive activities, such as sketching insects, planting fruit trees, collecting and smelling mint leaves and rosemary, and planning and cooking meals. Seeing, hearing, and smelling the burnt flesh from the tortured child did not go away entirely, but other sense associations became available and shared the forefront. The goal of Morita therapy is not to eradicate the memory of traumatic experience (through shocking or numbing methods) since the sensory markers linger even when the cognitive recollection does not. Rather therapeutic activity assists a client in experiencing with all the senses that which I call *the elegance of the mundane*. Bit by bit, Kevin was able to comprehend the absence of normality that existed during his tour of duty. Such 'seeing' is 'obtained by experientially knowing the pulse of daily life that is right before one's eyes' (Morita, 1928/1998, p. 78).

Sensory engagement and collective therapeutic alliance

From a phenomenological perspective, I contend that dissociation is a *sensory detachment phenomenon*. As illustrated in the case of Kevin, the sensory system is assaulted during and/or after seeing, hearing, smelling, tasting, and touching that which is dreadful. It is as if one's experience of self in place and time implodes viscerally once that which is repulsive assaults the senses. By denying cognitive interventions, the Morita therapist gradually brings paradoxical experiences forward through use of the therapy setting. The overriding goal in treating dissociation is to recalibrate the client's sensory network, while providing a natural, safe environment.

Kevin felt estranged from self, others, time, and place. His capacity to live day-to-day in all his senses – evenly and with pleasure – had been harmed. Had this shortfall gone on without building a dependable and collective therapeutic alliance to counteract his sensory detachment, he would have been at risk for suicide. When treating those with complex trauma histories, the therapist needs to foster a thera-peutic alliance that is powerful enough to counteract dissociative responses in their clients. In Morita therapy, therapeutic agency sits in the collective alliance between *client-therapist-place-Nature*. This alliance builds between and across the stages. Those training in classic Morita therapy are expected to fully comprehend and drive this dynamic force for the client's advantage. For Kevin, during Morita's first stage he wanted to align solely with the therapist, but the therapist remained steady in her *fumon* stance; gradually the safe containment of the physical place of the therapy centre grounded him. From there, the therapist strategically assisted his engagement with Nature, which brought him into the daily cycle of day and night. The rooster woke him just as the sun appeared in his window each morning; then the song of the magpie followed naturally. He came to foretell a hot day based on the call of the kookaburra and got excited by this new knowledge. In fact he realised that he had lost the capacity to read warning signs of danger when he had been in the Peacekeeping Forces.

Over time living in the therapy centre, environmental forecasters were help-ful for Kevin's sense of a predictable world in the face of unpredictability. Some-thing about his free-spirited experience of roaming in the woods as a young boy bubbled to the surface and he commented that he felt 'amused' by life around him – the toad's back was a work of art. As benign experiences accumulated in therapy and the therapist maintained a silent strength in presence, he perceived Nature as omnipresent. Here, he gained insight into the *kind-to-sinister continuum* of human potential that sits inside a wider landscape. The therapist used the nat-ural setting in Morita therapy to decrease the dissociative risk for Kevin who had endured so much complicated cruelty. By the end of the third stage of therapy, Kevin's preoccupation with the African boy no longer consumed his sensory field. He could see senseless-cruelty for what it was/is, while his preoccupation with sinister-ism receded.

Following Morita therapy, Kevin re-contextualised his peace keeping experi-ences as incomparable:

> I had been taught by the UN that those in other nations were the enemy. I was supposed to be one of the good guys – someone who stands for peace and democracy. But when I see this child's face in my memory, I am reminded of a deep sickness many do not see. And I do not want to *not* see that. I some-how feel more human. I have gathered myself so that I can live my own life again. I am as spikey and smooth as a cactus.[18]

When I first met Kevin, the image of the murdered child was haunting for him. He knew that no one else saw the child, and his descriptions did not meet criteria for hallucinations. However, induced dissociation through alcohol participated in his decline in self-care, his rejection of people, his increased numbness to the natural world, disruption of his sleep-wake patterns, and increased dread. Therapy could only be gradual and gentle in this case. For Kevin, as the stages of therapy progressed, the appearance of a child roaming outside himself waned. How that actually happened remains unknown.

Admittedly, Morita therapy is not a 'be all and end all' for clients who live through this level of devastating trauma, cruelty, and collusion. Kevin responded therapeutically to the sequenced nature of Morita therapy across the complete rest and seclusion, engagement in nature, art making, social, and food activities. Gradually, he developed a therapeutic relationship to me and life in the setting – ducks, frogs, sheep, and a cat. The four stages provided extended time in a natural setting, which calmed his body-mind. I saw Kevin in my outpatient practice fortnightly for three months after Morita therapy. He contacted me a year later to say that he was not binge drinking in social settings, and that he was dating a woman he met in a non-alcohol setting. Most significantly, he no longer gave testimony to his friends once he realised his own history was 'his' history. His tendency to question intensely the violence in the world became more reflective in scope and less reactionary.

Morita therapists do not problem-solve or philosophise about living in a complex, contradictory, and sometimes vicious social world. Therapists employ their clinical judgement to progress the client through the four stages. It is through those experiences that symptoms are decentralised and one is replaced in time and place. More often than not, clients see collusive dynamics with more clarity during the progressive course of Morita therapy – as was the case for Kevin. It is via the movement through the stages that imagination is recalibrated and the body's neuro-ecological system is revitalised. Kevin remarked, 'My past is about my future; it is not my future.'

Imagination, trauma, and 'empty ideation'

Thoughts on how the human imagination is affected by trauma span centuries. For instance, an existentialist from Morita's era, Friedrich Nietzsche (1844–1900), pondered the 'pessimism of strength' that follows from tragic experience in *The Birth of Tragedy: Out of the Spirit of Music* that was first published in 1872. His thesis is supported by biographic reviews of artists, Frieda Kahlo (1907–1954), Chaïm Soutine (1893–1943), sculptor Amedeo C. Modigliani (1884–1920), writers Franz Kafka (1883–1924) and Beatrix Potter (1866–1943), and music composer Tōru Takemitsu (1930–1996), who all endured war, oppression, physical agony, emotional anguish, and/or debilitating illnesses. 'Not all creative people are notably disturbed; not all solitary people are unhappy' (Storr, 1988, p. x).

Morita held no romantic notions about the role of trauma in creative advancement. For Morita, a genius is a genius, and a creative artist is a creative artist. However, traumatic experiences can depress the energy and natural talents available in a client's body and mind for creative activity, including one's natural thirst for life, *sei no yokubō*. Fujita explains,

> Morita has an appreciative understanding of the conflict and suffering that can occur in the minds of human beings, in line with their living conditions, and accepts these phenomena as natural reactions of the mind. He also takes the position that the true mental nature of human beings is for the self to act and overcome any such suffering. Morita also believes that a human being discovers, by himself or herself, the presence of sei no yokubō, which arise naturally, by following its motivation. He or she will, as a matter of course, reveal his or her true human character and be restored to his or her authentic self . . . Both body and mind turn the self toward an infinite process of development through activities governed by the best method and by continuous effort. And this process is expressed as a manifestation of the whole of life among human beings.
>
> *(Fujita 1986, pp. 178–179)*

Alice Miller (1981, 1984, 1990) reflects on the years it can take severely traumatised people to buoy their imaginations and generate art spontaneously. Her thesis supports use of therapeutic modalities that can rekindle the creative and imaginative capacities of survivors.[19] In Morita therapy, the client's body and mind rest and diurnal rhythms return. In this state, someone is more able to move from fanciful to non-fanciful imaginative states.

The successive stages of Morita therapy gradually bolster the client's readiness for experiencing imagination untainted by trauma. It is during the second stage of therapy into the third that a client sketches, forms clay, and interacts with birds, plants, rain, and animals. The hand's movements, over time, illustrate the movement of an insect, a leaf, a cloud – which is very much the way a calligrapher uses a brush and ink to capture the essence of life in the form. Over time, consistent contact with the natural environment assists the physical and mental suppleness of clients. Their capacity to adapt to current life conditions increases.

Morita maintained an interest in Maria Montessori's ideas about creative education. It is noted that Morita never intended art to be therapy or to be used to 'work through' past trauma. Rather, art in Morita therapy is a method that is introduced only after the clients emerge from complete rest and after they engage in gardening and tasks responsive to the environment.[20] This sequence is essential to one's readiness for creative activity. The goal of art making is mostly about forming a relationship to various medium and textures; the purpose is to build curiosity and stimulate healthy imagination. In the process of making art, the practical and fantastic sides of imagination are mutually stimulated.

Ives clarifies the dimensionality of imagination through the Japanese term kūsōuryoku (空想力), which can connote an 'excursion into imagination'. Overall, *kūsō* carries a main connotation of fanciful thought, idle fancy, or reverie; a literal translation of the whole compound is *empty ideation*. For the purpose of this discussion, the terms that coincide most with Morita's inference to imagination are sōzō (想像) and sōzōryoku (想像力). These terms neutralise the whimsical or less grounded dimensions of imagination (Ives, 2012, personal correspondence). The full notion of 'empty ideation' corresponds with the goal of returning to 'authentic or pure self' via Morita therapy – to the origins of innate creativity – even when challenged by existential despair.

Existential therapy offers a perspective on meaninglessness that encourages creative expression without despair. Therapists work artfully with clients to 'pierce below surfaces to grasp a new relation to the reality of nature' (May, Angel, and Ellenberger, 1958, p. 17). Existential and Zen-based approaches to therapy diminish a therapist and client's dependence on external dogma or conventional ideas about emotions. Once free from others' expectations (that have been adopted as one's own), clients imagine alternative pathways for a sensible future. Morita therapists do not challenge clients' thoughts or emotions directly. Rather, therapists listen to how a client speaks about the past – the hesitation, rush of breath, and posture. Then the therapist orchestrates the therapeutic milieu to facilitate the ebb and flow of complex emotions and to foster authentic curiosity by bringing clients into their senses, literally.

More research is needed on the relationship between cruelty-based trauma, imagination, the creative process, and therapy. It is plausible that Morita's four-staged therapeutic methods engage the right and left hemispheres of the brain strategically, which assists clients to indulge in fantasy without dread. Thus, Morita's sequence of complete rest of mind-body-spirit, followed by light gardening, sketching, diary writing, art making, heavy gardening, animal care, cooking, and play has the potential to stimulate a robust, practical imagination.

Some theories on trauma highlight 'resilience' as an intrapersonal, protective mechanism, wherein one has the capacity to maintain relatively healthy levels of psycho-emotional and social functioning in the face of great adversity (Masten, 2001). Harvey (1996) offers a complex theory of resilience that allows for our human ability to suffer and recover simultaneously.[21] Morita's theory of emotion allows for these presumed inconsistencies in human experience alongside the existential sense of feeling secure and insecure, simultaneously. Classic Morita therapists are neutral when it comes to resilience theories in mental health. Rather, they strive to 're-place' clients inside environments that neutralise eroding social forces. For example, Kevin was perplexed by his own unanswerable questions about humans who use their imaginations to torture and massacre others – and was more sensitive for asking them. His capacity to over-endure sinister external systems was extremely complex; in the end, his courageousness depleted him. As Kevin moved into Stage Two of therapy, he told me the following.

> This is the first time since I was about ten years old that I feel released from fighting for another's peace at the expense of my own. Some kind of deep quiet that is around me has come inside me. Is that weird? I know the world is tricky but perhaps what I need is more straightforwardness around me.

'That weird experience is not so weird once you get used to it,' I replied.

Silence and poise in therapy

Least understood about Morita therapy is the role of silence across the four stages. Silence often sits outside the modern discourse on 'Zen and Psychotherapy'. Hogan Bay (2008), for instance, writes on inner silence from a Buddhist perspective. 'Inner silence is not reactive. Inner silence allows us to hear things clearly and deeply, to hear things as they really are. When we know things as they really are then we can respond effectively without reactivity and burnout' (Bay, 2008, p. 5). While this is so, Morita therapy offers the experience of outer silence and inner silence – like the sound of silence that lingers at the end of the crow's lowest pitched call. In Kevin's case, the silent presence of the therapist offered secure freedom in which to emote genuinely.

First and foremost, the Morita therapist requires training in silence with as much rigour as paradoxical and verbal interventions. All too often in traditional counselling sessions, the room fills with words; silence is considered often to be a therapeutic strategy that facilitates disclosure – more words. In this regard, the role of silence in Morita therapy is unusual to other modalities, but usual to Morita therapy. Silence requires poise and a non-intrusive presence on the part of the therapist. Silence is silence. Silence is not a pause or strategic intervention. Silence is a placeholder for safety so the client experiences a secure place in secure time. Secure silence carries no expectations for verbal exchange between therapist and client; in this way, clients can experience the therapist's presence. Ultimately, silence is a vehicle for extending attachments beyond the therapist-client relationship. Given its ecological orientation, Morita is designed to increase clients' trust in the *enveloping nature of Nature*. Zen is essential to this aim.

In *Buddhism and the Art of Psychotherapy,* Hayao Kawai (1996) writes from a Jungian-informed Buddhist perspective and links the power of silence to relational psychology; herein, the therapist-client exchange is enhanced when they 'just sit together'. Similarly, Melvin Miller (2002) maintains that therapeutic silence is central to the engagement between therapist and client. While Morita might agree, his Zen over Buddhism perspective regards silence as a relational enhancer between clients and Nature. In this context, silence is never deceptive. Suzuki (1971, pp. 179–180) quotes haiku poets who access the natural world through their senses, not their minds, such as hearing with one's eyes and seeing with one's ears in order to grasp how rain falls naturally (Bashō, 1966).

As stated earlier, during the silent first stage, clients' thoughts and feelings rise and fall without a need to make sense of anything – and it is after this period that pure imagination is experienced without dread. Some clients report that they appreciate having nowhere to go when their mind rumbles. Such an attitude is a prelude to curious mindedness. Time and place press on. By the fifth day of rest, boredom leads to curiosity about the natural environment and overtakes them. Dread and ego recede. I cannot stress enough how complete rest and silence are necessary for re-embodiment, and this sequence comes before outdoor engagement is pre-scribed. Without this sequence, curiosity is fleeting rather than embodied. This is the reason that Morita therapists do not instruct mindfulness exercises (McCown, Reibel, and Micozzi, 2010). We pace when and how to bring our clients smack into the middle of life force so they are ripe for perceptual change. Again, Zen.

In the course of Morita therapy, clients move from silence and seclusion to environmental contact where they are to refrain from self-referencing. They learn to pause inside the silence offered by Nature. The therapist might ask them to study the flight pattern of a particular bird; to hear the difference in frog song; or to run their fingers over textured tree bark with their eyes closed. Resting in silence is different from resting while talking, or resting while using an electronic device, or resting while instructing the mind to focus on breath. Silence inside art making, gardening, and cooking provides new moments in perceiving and sensing. One can touch and build that which the senses have not yet experienced – moist porcelain sticks to the hand differently than earthenware.[22] In this way, one is a pioneer of new experiences in a small radius of space and time.

Art making in the second and third stages in Morita therapy is a process by which the whole person becomes engaged. Clients notice that it is incompatible to worry when they are just making art with their own hands – without the judging mind interfering. The therapist looks for signs of a judging mind and intervenes by pointing, perhaps, to the cracking clay that calls out for moisture. Creative move-ments – across art, music, dance, poetry and haiku – engage human imagination in ways that therapeutic dialogue alone cannot do. Kondo would tell his patients to 'Feel deeply without the mind.' At CMC, clinicians select art medium specific to each client. They observe a client's fine motor capacity, natural orientation to the world (visual, auditory, kinesthetic), limitations, and innate talents. Such care is taken since art making has the capacity to reconfigure sensory capacity that has been impacted by war and trauma (Al-Krenawi and Slater, 2007).

At certain times, the aftermath of cruelty-based trauma and confusion sur-faces strongly in a client's awareness and she or he sometimes wants to reflect on the intent of a perpetrator. While Morita therapists acknowledge the agony that accompanies this determination, they bring the client repeatedly into contact with the benign nature of Nature. On one occasion, a client was in the garden weed-ing without wearing gloves. Rather than reinstruct her about safe keeping in the garden, I gave her an insect and spider identification book. I invited her to identify three poisonous and three benign specimens in the garden and to observe and record their movements. Of course, poisonous creatures will not attack a person intentionally but may instil venom if surprised. Once her awareness increased, she wore her gloves responsively without instruction. Later she wrote in her field diary:

> I was surprised by all the tiny aliveness in the soil, I had been paying attention to the goal of removing the weeds. I guess I do that a lot. Pushing to get my degree in economics and to find the right partner and feeling alone because I do not really feel life around me.

Again, the quality of the therapist's silence and presence across the stages gives the client a wordless experience of reassurance. This is significant for clients who have endured broken promises in the past and had previously considered words to be more essential than their intuition and lived experience. They build their capacity to determine trustworthiness through multiple interactive experiences, including the therapist, other clients, the natural environment, and their own body sensations. Morita designed his therapy to increase a client's kinaesthetic awareness. Several contemporaries of Morita have recognised body positioning and visceral awareness, such as Moshé Feldenkrais (1904–1984) who devised the Feldenkrais Method, a somatic educational system, and Frederick Alexander (1869–1955) who developed the Alexander Technique. In particular, Alexander developed his technique in the 1940s via an extensive self-study when he could no longer use his voice as an actor; he fine-tuned his method following a stroke. For Alexander, therapeutic technique should simulate nature (Alexander, 1942). Fascinatingly, Aldous Huxley (1894–1963), a student and long-term friend to Alexander, writes about the technique in *Ends and Means: An Inquiry into the Nature of Ideals and into the Methods Employed for their Realization* (Huxley, 1937). He claimed that the Alexander Technique is less about posture, and more about correct position or balanced, intentional poise.

Sensation awareness occurs naturally for a client during Morita therapy, particularly as the client moves (literally) to feel each body movement while in seclusion with minimal distraction from self-talk. In fact, the client moves out of Stage One with mild body atrophy. During Stage Two, body awareness increases and a re-embodying process occurs. The client experiences the therapist's movements as even paced and deliberate. Again, the quality of silence adopted by the therapist imparts a new experience of stillness for and within the client through association. In Stage Four of the therapy when clients prepare meals and eat together, they are encouraged to notice how they approach food and to develop even-paced movements at the table. Clients who come from traumatic backgrounds often experience their bodies and minds as anything but still and poised, and for many meal times were anything but calm or creatively engaging.

During the few days of secluded rest, past associations run a natural course, and over-thinking and related emoting over one's past subside. The therapist remains aware of the traumatic history of the client, of course, since this free-associating phase can ignite frightening images and feelings that require therapeutic care. However, most of my clients have reported that their experience of 'total' rest in a home-like environment without clocks, phones, or artificial light does not match their anticipatory fear (LeVine, 2000). One woman told me:

> I thought bad demons would overcome me during seclusion so I was hesitant about this method. Now I see how my imagination has protected me, but I did not need to be protected in that room. I felt recharged. It was like tasting lemon glacé on a hot day.

In my clinical practice, I hear often from clients that they discover their body as a source of knowledge. This is referenced most during Stages Two and Three as they are engaged by the garden. By attending to body, place, and process, the therapist provides the chance for the authentic self to be realised, expressed naturally, and savoured.

In psychoanalysis, the analyst utilises the material verbally to facilitate insight in the client. Again, a free association-like process does occur in Morita therapy most often when the client is in a supine position and silent. The difference is that rumination eases as it runs a natural course without a therapist's interpretation. According to Kondo, 'Some psychoanalysts believe that their patients' resistance is at the core of their troubles, but such thinking on the part of the therapist puts too much responsibility on the patient' (1990, personal conversation).

The client's experience of enduring silence and minimal stimulation can lead to insight. According to Martin (1972, p. 120) 'sudden insight, while still a rein-tegration, should not be seen so much as a process of restoring a formerly experi-enced whole. But more a process of becoming part of a still larger pre-existing whole.' In Morita therapy, clients experience the difference between a resting body and a restless body, as well as the fullness of their emotional repertoire. The therapist's *fumon* positioning is vital, too, for holding interpretations at bay and creating a sense of reassurance for the client. This stance is one of cool-warmness which is important when a client feels overwhelmed by feelings, and is particu-larly strategic when a client is in a dissociated state. Akihisa Kondo coined the term *elastic mind* (1953, p. 34). The more lively your hands, the less active your mind, and the more lively your healthy imagination. In Kevin's case we saw how analysing the cruelty he witnessed in Africa while enduring the agonising image of the tortured boy restricted his range of imagination. Above all, he feared his own mind. The elongation of time and space during Morita therapy was neces-sary for him. In that context he could think and cry until he was exhausted from thinking and crying. Then, he could finally rest his mind and body. All along, when clients experience the therapist's solidarity and the holding ground mani-fested in the natural therapeutic setting, their personal integrity is re-established; this advance is vital to those who have endured cruelty.

As discussed throughout this book, consciousness and awareness are not inter-changeable concepts for Morita. Consciousness does not reside exclusively inside the human mind. Rather, *peripheral consciousness* is a mysterious, omnipresent, phe-nomenal life force that exists outside human awareness – the essence that runs through all of life. Most often, clients enter the rest stage of therapy with the goal of feeling better or detoxing from cruelty endured. They have a judging mind that analyses their own symptoms, circumstances, the therapist, and other humans. They sulk over objects denied in therapy, such as telephones, books, pens, or computers, and fretting consumes their experiential awareness. By Stage Two, however, clients spread their awareness outside the self and rekindle relations within and across the animate world – they discover the way a caterpillar moves, how a leaf catches the wind, or how an ant transports a bug bigger than itself. This is the therapeutic experience that brings innocence to the foreground finally, in spite of pain and robbed childhoods. Through the experience of kindness and clear boundaries by the therapist and staff alongside their engagement in nature after rest, they become curious about possibilities. This instils a new-found respect for their bodies and minds, which motivates their self-care.

In *Unformulated Experience: From Dissociation to Imagination in Psychoanalysis*, Stern (2003, p. 31) writes that sometimes in therapy 'we feel safe enough to know ourselves in ways that set us on the edge of danger'. Stern's eloquent phrase nicely fits with Morita's philosophy. When clients experience genuine safety – viscerally and existentially – a safety net is cast for their imaginations, which frees them to roam and explore what was, is, and what can be. In the Morita context, clients are primed to experience their secure place in Nature. The sequenced stages across environments contain and open out clients' imaginations so they may hold dangerous pitfalls and kindness in their peripheral field of vision.

Notes

1 While a subtle distinction, when compared to Mindfulness therapy, Morita therapists do not direct the client to 'observe' nature in a single frame of time and place. Rather, the client experiences the self in a natural and safe place for an extended period of time. Through experience, insight is fostered and the client sees into past dynamics. They experience the elegance of living day-to-day in an ecological setting with purposeful activity – carrying stone, trimming bonsai, feeding chickens, harvesting tomatoes.

2 In *Wounded by Reality: Understanding and Treating Adult Onset Trauma*, Ghislane Boulanger (2007, p. 5) invites us to reformulate analytic interpretations about our clients and to design therapeutic systems that account for a client's 'encounter with the Real'. Herein, Morita therapy depends on the design of therapeutic place.

3 All too often, clinicians who over-focus on symptomology fail to record formally the place(s) where trauma occurs, and the past colluding agents. A layer of neglect is added for clients when therapists fail to inquire about colluding agents in their past trauma.

4 Bruno Bettelheim was an Austrian-born American citizen and child psychiatrist, psychoanalyst, and educator-philosopher. Foremost was his claim that children with traumatic histories are compromised in their capacity to sustain a sense of self. He initiated the Orthogenic School (University of Chicago's Laboratory School); he acknowledged the universality of violence and called on educators to counterbalance this syndrome.

5 One review of epidemiological literature on institutionalised violence, neglect, and abuse reveals that socio-cultural statuses are less randomly distributed than we might want to believe (Tummala-Narra, 2001).

6 Greenpeace has monitored the accident since March 11, 2011. Teams test soil, vegetables, seafood, and land sediment. Early information was released on February 22, 2012 with Greenpeace and the *Asahi Shimbun* Newspaper in Tokyo. Japan's Nuclear Safety Commission (NSC) disclosed that the government concealed radiation impact studies on children's thyroid glands (March 2011). For current updates, see Greenpeace site: www.greenpeace. org/international/en/campaigns/nuclear/safety/accidents/Fukushima-nuclear-disaster/ Radiation-field-team/.

7 Increasingly, research is emerging on the physiology of trauma, including neurophysiological indicators of quick shifts between one's hyper-arousal (sympathetic) nervous system and hypo-arousal (parasympathetic) system (Scaer, 2005).

8 Phenomenological-based questions and analyses are increasing in the literature on trauma-based dissociation (Briere and Spinazzola, 2005; Briere, Weathers, and Runtz, 2005).

9 A most useful discussion is offered by Onno van der Hart and Barbara Friedman (1989) in *A Reader's Guide to Pierre Janet on Dissociation: A Neglected Intellectual Heritage*.

10 Theories from the turn of the last century on dissociation are fleshed out by Kolb (1987). Other articles on the neurophysiology of dissociation and treatment can be found in Schore (2009) and Shapiro (2001).

11 A contextual, descriptive inquiry into trauma history is standard practice at the Classic Morita Centre before one is considered for residential treatment.

12 As duty of care, Morita therapists gather contextual histories about the geo-physical and seasonal environments, and social and family contexts that surround clients' trauma experiences. In addition, it is advised that therapists assess colluding agents who have turned a blind eye to harm. This depth of assessment is critical before admitting a client into the seclusion stage of residential Morita therapy. In particular, dissociative symptoms could manifest during the rest-seclusion period if the triggers of past contexts are not duly considered and adjustments made.

13 Although 'habitat' is recognised as a dimension for trauma intervention in *The New H5 Model of Trauma and Recovery* (Mollica, Brooks, Ekblad, and McDonald, 2015) 'habitat and housing' centres on humancentric space and community.

14 Pseudo-seizure activity, in particular, might be more prevalent when neuro-physical overload intersects with confusion and dread.

15 The BASK model of dissociation allows for a phenomenological view of memory and identity disruption across an individual's lifespan and includes 'sensations' that the body remembers. Bennett Braun (1988) relates dissociation to a hypnotic state.

16 The video *Eyes and Ears of God* (2012) was created by Slovenian peace activist Tomo Kriznar (1954–) through video surveillance. His documentary film involves ethnic civilians and highlights Northern Sudan's military war crimes against local populations.

17 I am grateful to Dr Rob Peterson, a psychiatrist in Victoria, Australia, and for his ongoing assistance in trauma cases such as this.

18 Perhaps Kevin's statement aligns with a quote by Bettelheim (1980, p. 185), 'born of both violence and gentle cooperation; to neglect either in our efforts to better human relations would be fruitless'.

19 Alice Miller (1981) touched on the topic of creativity, imagination, and trauma in *The Drama of the Gifted Child*. Following, she brings this thesis into *The Untouched Key: Tracing Childhood Trauma in Creativity and Destructiveness* (1990).

20 'The guiding principle of the Montessori method is one that encourages children's spontaneous activities, while allowing them to be free and self-reliant; conventional instilling or molding methods are discouraged' (Morita, 1928/1998, p. 98). Morita became interested in Maria Montessori's essays on her educational, experiential method, which were translated into Japanese in 1914; he also favoured the environmental theory by Mitsuzo Shimoda (1942) who highlighted the environmental impact on mental health and the role of education in recovery (Fujita, 1986).

21 Resilience is presented in the literature as an intra-personal quality or intrinsic capacity within an individual. Community psychology contributes an understanding of how contexts influence one's sense of empowerment and wellbeing. These contexts sit within a social, community frame but could be extended to the geo-ecological environment.

22 The following resources discuss how creative arts recoup a client's imagination after trauma: Cathy Malchiodi's *Breaking the Silence: Art Therapy with Children from Violent Homes* (1990) and *The Art Therapy Sourcebook* (2007); David Read Johnson's, 'The role of the creative arts therapies in the diagnosis and treatment of psychological trauma' in *The Arts of Psychotherapy* (1988), and *Essays on the Creative Arts Therapies* (1999).

EPILOGUE

Morita therapy is informed by the science of psychiatry, alongside a theory of consciousness drawn, in part, from Zen and Shinto, with its essence rooted in the Japanese cultural landscape. That is not to say that Morita developed a Zen treatment. Overall, Morita is the first and perhaps most reliable ecotherapy in existence.

The four stages of treatment are progressive. Clients move from total silence and secluded rest indoors, to partial silence and physical movement out of doors, with a contrast that brings the natural environment to the forefront of their experience. Fujita (1986, p. 7) regards the seclusion stage as a 'complete relaxation of body and soul', with a quality of rest that is essential to clients' wellness. Once mind, body and imagination are rested, clients are receptive to Nature's permeating life force.

Morita therapists are not invested in inflating or deflating the client's sense of self. Rather, they orchestrate the therapeutic environment so the client can experience the vitality of each life form. Therapy decentralises the human being in the broader ecosystem, and this creates a new meaning of intimacy. It is in this realm that ego is irrelevant. In fact, Morita did not use this term in his theory or aim to strengthen anything akin to an ego. Over time as the paradoxical structure progresses across the stages, one's experience and expression of self become less guarded and defended. Above all, clients' symbiotic relationship with Nature – originating from the Greek meaning of 'living with' (sýn 'with' and biosis 'living') – is essential to their realisation of authentic self. It is at this juncture that Zen is relevant to Morita therapy.

Morita therapy is designed to assist a client to engage in the 'mystery of the ordinary'. That which one thought was boring or non-essential suddenly unleashes amusement or delight. Nature contains many metaphors for daily living. Consider snails that trail slime during the night. Their routes crisscross and dry to a fine, glistening crust in the morning sun – evidence of paths they will never travel again. What beauty might we leave behind? Herein, Morita therapy holds tremendous

FIGURE 6.1   Illustration by Morita from his personal diaries archived at Mishima Morita
Hospital Archive Library

capacity to be applied across cultures and places; geography may change from place
to place but ecological properties are the same globally.

Throughout therapy, Morita therapists are responsible for maintaining a silent
presence, since the progress of the client is enhanced by the *uncluttered stillness* of
the therapist. Clients with traumatic histories, in particular, get confused about safe
and unsafe situations and places. Their progress is strengthened when the therapist's
presence is secure and responsive. By contrast to the past, a secure silence becomes
the context from which clients experience the natural rise and fall of uncomfortable symptoms and emotions. Eventually, they ascertain safe from unsafe people,
situations, and places. Silence is a shift in the patient's former response patterns that
becomes a shift in future relational exchanges.

I recently corresponded with a psychiatrist in Germany who asked if prescrib-
ing secluded rest alone might assist his patients. I replied that Morita therapy is not
an isolated treatment of rest, and the full rest stage requires a therapist's supervision
and guidance. With regard to duty of care, it is ill advised to prescribe rest alone.
The classic Morita therapist is trained to use the environment to enhance a client's
experience of 'authentic' self.[1] Clients are to experience an unfettered safe place
with a therapist who is present but not imposing. Movement through all the four
stages is what Morita intended.

Overall, I adopted the term *classic* as a way of differentiating the original treatment from outpatient methods since reliable use of ecological spaces and the evolution of the stages form the methodological core of therapy. I find that a classic
Morita therapist's training requires the rigour of a classical dancer or concert musi-
cian. One trains to fine-tune one's observational and intuitive skills, as well as body
movements and attention to space and silence – essential elements for orchestrating

the progression of therapy. In the classic form of Morita therapy, stages do not sit alone, nor do the stages progress without the wisdom of a meticulously trained therapist. From a research perspective, too, consistent stage processes are essential for reliable practice outcomes. I return again to the classical metaphor. A dancer who trains to perform moves differently from a dancer who trains to train; similarly, a martial artist who focuses on winning in combat sacrifices the integrity of presence in the art.

Many of my colleagues have told me that Western clients do not have the capacity to endure Morita therapy. I find this statement to be misinformed and condescending.[2] The capacity of the client to move through the stages is not related to the country where the therapy occurs or the ethnicity of the client but is related to the therapist's training, practice, and design of the therapeutic-enhancing environment. Morita therapists watch for any hint of curiosity in their clients, regardless of culture, nationality, or age, and they reinforce the slightest hint of such. Over the past twenty years, I have treated clients fruitfully from Australia, Canada, Japan, Iran, the United States, and Germany. After all, curiosity is evidence of life force. Also, depression and anxiety do not co-exist in curious moments. Fujita would describe a therapist's role as assisting clients to 'live in accordance with the desire to live' (1986, p. 77).

I recall the few days before Akihisa Kondo's death from cancer nearly twenty years ago. I was in Tokyo with him during the final weeks of his life, sitting with him daily in his home and in hospital. On one of these days, he asked me to arrange to express post a book, *Transformations* by Wilfred Bion (1984). He wondered whether Bion's theory of the 'State 0' had resonance with Morita's theory. After finding the book, I read aloud passages to him for an entire afternoon.

'Ah,' said Kondo, 'Bion speaks about listening to the client without desire, without memory, and without understanding. At first, I thought this might have something to do with Zen. Now I see that Bion was caught by his own ideas on empathy.'

We moved from this discussion to the question of whether Morita therapy could exist without the four stages.

Kondo sensei paused in silence.

Suddenly he paraphrased Dōgen (Zen poet, 1200–1253)[3]:

> Water is clear and the sky is vast.
> Fish swim just like fish; birds fly just like birds.

Notes

1 S. Weir Mitchell (1829–1914) is credited with the rest cure. He entered correspondence with novelist, poet, and women's rights activist Elizabeth Stuart Phelps (1844–1911), she was critical of Mitchell's beliefs that women remove themselves from intellectual and creative pursuit (Bassuk, 1986).

2 Kora (1968) notes that 'nature is not (hu)man-centered . . . and anxiety is inseparable from human existence.' (p. 318).

3. Heine (1997, p. 145) provides the complete passage from Dōgen, which 'stresses the dynamism and spontaneity, rather than the quietude and calm, of meditation experience.'

GLOSSARY OF MORITA TERMS

This glossary is revised and expanded from the 'Glossary of Morita Concepts' in *Morita Therapy and the True Nature of Anxiety-based Disorders: Shinkeishitsu* (Morita, S. (1998). Kondo, A. (trans.); LeVine, P (ed.)).

This author constructed the first glossary with consultation from the late Akihisa Kondo. Most of Morita's concepts were rendered in Chinese characters (Kanji) that contained multiple meanings. Such nuance in terms led to long discussions about the Zen influence on Morita's terminology.

Arugamama (あるがまま) Realising or seeing into phenomena or reality 'as it is', Experiencing the 'suchness of reality' and responding accordingly. By suspending the judging mind and conventional values, realization is primed.

Acceptance without expectations From a Morita perspective, 'acceptance' is unrelated to accession, acquiescence, contemporary principles of mindfulness, or religious scriptures. Morita was sceptical about dogmatic ideas for the resolution of internal conflict. By transcending expectations, one can see reality as it is, regardless of whether one accepts it.

Akirame (諦め) The literal meaning is *resignation*, which coincides with losing one's momentum to endure discomfort when life is tough. The tendency to give up can be related to an underdeveloped will or an innate weak will. However, this is not to be confused by a healthy willpower that is beaten down by traumatic experience. Through resignation, one enters a cycle of choosing to take a path of least resistance, or to give up prematurely. Over time, this cycle decreases life force, and derails one's creative potential. Morita therapy increases one's capacity to discern when to exert a strong will and when it is futile to do so; in this way an enduring will is rekindled. It is noted that too much emphasis on cognitive confrontation early on in treatment by a therapist could increase a client's resignation tendencies. Since exhaustion accompanies *akirame*, rest is useful at the onset of therapy.

Body=Mind   Morita therapy is designed so that the human body aligns with the human mind. Once aligned, people experience more fully the life force in Nature that surrounds them. In this way, they function according to an innate wisdom and intuition that is reinforced by the ecological system they re-contact. If a person gives too much power to mind over matter, then the first port of call for treatment options is often a cognitive intervention. From the Morita perspective, however, when mind rests, body rests. This is a key reason that the first stage of Morita therapy includes seclusion with silence as the restful starting point, usually without medication, meditation instruction, or cognitive restructuring. A client is not instructed to place the mind anywhere in the first stage of treatment. Herein body=mind returns to a state as natural as the surrounding ecology.

Dissociation (Sensory Detachment)   Dissociation is a sensory detachment phenomenon that is linked to complex trauma. The sensory system is assaulted during and/or after seeing, hearing, smelling, tasting, touching, that which is dreadful. Morita therapy recalibrates the client's sensory system gradually across the four stages in a safe, natural environment.

Ego-centred or *jiga*   The concept *jiga* became popular in the 1920s among Japanese academics and adherents of psychoanalysis. The term 'ego' was translated into Japanese as *jiga* in relation to Freud's writing. The Chinese *ji* is the self when it is not stained by its own reflection; *ga* indicates the resultant ego-centredness. The progressive stages of Morita therapy are meant to free the 'self' from self-analysis, so that self realises its natural place in the scheme of purposeful existence within the ecological scape.

Emotional facts or emotional logic   One's true emotional state stands alone as its own fact before one's intellect forms interpretations about what is being felt. It is through the process of emotional logic that emotions run their natural course and the 'contradiction between ideas and reality' (*shisō-no-mujun*) is reconciled. Morita (1928/1998, p. 31) writes of emotional facts:

> pain and suffering gradually subside if one endures them and lets them follow a natural course. Ponder the old lesson . . . when one is angry and wishes to fight, think it over for three days before taking action. Emotion follows its natural course, it assumes a parabolic course, flares initially, reaches a climax, then lessens and/or disappears.

Extroversion   To be extroverted is to engage in relationships outside the self – people, animals, insects, plants, trees, rock, Nature. Extroversion is not exclusive to the social domain.

Fatalism   People who endure oppression and human cruelty naturally develop a fatalistic attitude towards life. This is a natural response to suffering. The ecological connectedness that Morita therapy fosters evens out the tension between optimism and pessimism so that clients are less polarised in worldview. Following, their capacity to respond to the environment is enhanced; their creative potential increases as they are less laden in anxious tension or dread.

Feeling-centred attitude Emphasis is placed on the word *attitude*. Morita developed methods that break down clients' attitudes about their feelings. Morita did not advocate the dismissal of feelings. Rather, he encouraged clients to fully experience the spontaneous rising, falling, and overlapping of feelings. It is the 'attitude' people have about a feeling that interferes with their capacity to feel freely their contradictory emotions with a sense of wonder. Once feelings are judged to be rational or irrational, or good or bad, the wisdom that emotions offer is disrupted.

Fumon (不問) *Fumon* is part of the 'experiential core' of Morita therapy and integral to the sequenced method and related outcomes. This can be translated as 'not questioning' or 'non-questioning' (translation by Chris Ives, 2016). This unquestioning position is assumed in the therapist's body stance. Paradoxically, the therapist assumes a warm, aloof presence. As clients experience the '*fumon* stance' taken by the therapist, their protests, inquiries, and interpretations about their own symptoms recede. Prolongation by the therapist of a *fumon* position assists clients to experience the ways they entrap themselves, which increases their insight and adjustment to their own suffering. A *fumon* stance requires a particular 'demotion of self' on the part of the therapist so that she or he can step aside and let therapy function according to Morita's design. The therapist's initial presence in the first stage resembles that of the *kuroko*, which is a masked puppeteer artist in Japanese '*bunraku*' (puppet theatre). Herein, the artist wears black attire and blends into the background so that spontaneous life movements arise and a story unfolds. During the course of Morita therapy, the therapist remains in the background directing another's narrative without a strong presence. Overall, the unpretentious, paradoxical pose of *fumon* provides 'presence with distance' (as a paradoxical stance) and containment for the client as well as the therapist when the client is agitated or disengaged.

Hakarai (計らい) The literal meaning is *handling a matter or disposing of a matter with discretion or judgement with a strong, directed will*. 'It is sometimes used in Buddhist writings to refer to thinking about things in a calculating way, such as thinking about what is best for oneself' (C. Ives, correspondence). This is the other side of the *akirame* coin, and leads one to exhaustively persevere against the grain of reality, to control outcomes, or to make the impossible possible, which is related to a strong will or self-righteousness. Again, therapists need to consider the role of trauma in the development of this orientation. The cycle of pushing uphill increases frustration and anger, and decreases one's creative capacity. Since exhaustion accompanies *hakarai* (and *akirame*), strategic rest is useful at the onset of therapy.

Hypochondriasis An anxiety-related disorder that occurs when one is oversensitive to fears of disease and death. Restricting day-to-day activities (loss of spontaneity) is one response to such fear. To Morita, fear of death and disability is an indicator of our natural desire for life as humans. Thus, inklings of hypochondriasis are in all people. The degree to which fear is present determines the degree of self-absorption. According to Morita (1998), there are two forms of hypochondriasis: (1) an 'hypochondriacal tendency' that is an emotional base that originates during the course of one's development; and (2) a 'hypochondriacal temperament' that is a sensitive congenital trait that predisposes one to hypochondriasis. One with hypochondriac tendencies is prone to anxiety and obsessive disorders. Morita therapy is more effective for treating those with hypochondriac tendencies than those with hypochondriac temperaments.

Jinja (神社)   This is the Shinto shrine or the dwelling place for *kami*. Unique features that usually distinguish a Shinto from a Buddhist shrine include: the *torii* (gate), shimenawa (plaited straw rope that protects the shrine), *hakuhei* (paper cut, folded and hung in a particular form), and the sacred mirror (kagami).

Jiriki (自力) and *tariki* (他力)   The literal meaning of *jiriki* is *self-power* or reliance on self. This is in direct contrast to *other-power* or *tariki* (他力). For Shin Buddhists, the power of other is deemed to come from Amida. Zen Buddhists would refer more often to *jiriki*. From the perspective of Morita, *tariki* would come from life force that flows through Nature. Morita therapists aim for developing a client's balance between *jiriki* and *tariki*.

Kojiki (古事記)   Ancient chronicles of Japan from 712 CE.

***Mushojūshin* (無所住心)**   Literally, *mushojūshin* means *the mind that does not dwell anywhere*. In other words, mind does not get attached to anything. This is a Zen-based term used by Morita to describe healthy attention that occurs when one extends the mind=body in all directions without attachment to a single focus. This does not imply a scattered mind, but rather a state of complete alertness, aliveness, and fluidity. Morita therapists attempt to remove the narrow focus of attention one places on symptoms, which occurs in those with *shinkeishitsu*; a goal is to increase responsive-spontaneous activity in the client's mind=body. Morita therapists are required personally to maintain this orientation in their therapeutic practice. *Mushojūshin* can be rendered as 'peripheral consciousness' and associated with the life force that runs in all directions.

Neurasthenia   Morita formulated his staged practice with an eye towards assisting clients to recover from neurasthenia. This category was coined in 1869 by George Miller Beard to denote a cluster of symptoms related to exhaustion of the central nervous system: anxiety, fatigue, headache, sexual disinterest, depressed mood, and neuralgia. When William James was diagnosed with neurasthenia, he called it *Americanitis* or a psycho-neurological disorder associated with 'modernisation'. Neurasthenia is currently diagnosed in Japan and other parts of the world, and is part of the International Classification of Diseases by the World Health Organization. After World War II, the term neurosis replaced neurasthenia in the literature. Currently, 'undifferentiated somatoform disorder' and trauma-based syndromes resonate strongly with neurasthenia. The seclusion, rest stage of Morita therapy gives the client a chance to recover neurologically.

Obsessive orientation   Obsessive thinking is evidence of a cluttered mind. Rather than focusing treatment on clients' thought content and process,

Morita therapy decreases mental stimulation in the first stage as over-thinking or over-imagining exhausts the mind=body. Following rest, purposive activity in nature and art making modifies their thought pace and content naturally as anxiety decreases. Clients shift their orientation to ponder day-to-day living with increased clarity of mind.

Paradox in therapy   Therapists select purposive actions, words, or silence that contradict logic. They point to the health-eroding habits in thinking or doing by clients. (Paradox informed the construction of the *13 Pathways to Misery* listed in the Appendix). Paradoxical intention breaks down defensive remarks or postures of a client. Paradox is used to challenge conventional thinking that might interfere with a client living according to Nature and authentic self.

Paroxysmal neurosis   This is an anxiety-related syndrome that manifests symptoms that mimic cardiac distress. According to Morita, those who are over-sensitive to body sensation are more inclined to this syndrome. They focus their attention on their heart rate, which fuels fear about death. This, in turn, increases their heart rate and they convince themselves that they are having a heart attack. The processes that manifest paroxysmal neurosis are similar to processes that perpetuate Acute Stress Disorder.

Rest cure   In 1876, S. Weir Mitchell in Scotland designed a 'rest cure' for those diagnosed with neurasthenia. Mitchell's isolation rest, however, is unrelated to Morita's first stage of treatment. As an historical note, Mitchell was influenced by Beard (1869) and included Beard's controversial 'electrotherapy' in his practice. As Morita read German, he followed the work of German neurologist Paul Julius Möebius (1853–1907), who challenged the use of electrotherapy and client self-reported research. Morita criticised electrical methods of treatment for being abrupt and for altering further clients' natural rhythms and neurological balance of the human body and mind (personal interview with Kora and Kondo, 1994).

Sei no yokubō (生の欲望)   The literal meaning is 'desire for life'. The emphasis, however, is on the *natural* desire for life, which is linked to our natural fear of death. Anxiety occurs when we focus our attention on avoiding death. Morita's staged therapy brings one's desire-for-life to its natural state. This is a keystone concept that directs the four stages of treatment, which increases the life-desire potential for expression.

Seishin kōgo sayō (精神交互作用)   This term denotes an over-sensitive focus of attention or narrow field of attention. The Morita therapist does not want to change someone's natural temperament. Rather, an aim of therapy is to assist clients to spread awareness or field of attention so they are ready to respond to circumstances. Morita gives the example of a mother who is sensitive to the sound her child makes; naturally, a cough in the night by the child wakes the mother. If the mother, however, remains 'over' sensitive, she will not return to sleep and will concentrate on her fear that her child may die. If, however, the mother notices that the cough is weak and then notices that the child has resumed rest with even breathing, she will return to sleep until the next cough wakes her. In the same light, an under-sensitive focus of attention is equally non-responsive to circumstances at hand.

Sensefulness   The term 'sensefulness' describes the process of Morita therapy more accurately than 'mindfulness'. According to Kondo (1990, supervision), Morita's consciousness means awareness extended with all the senses; through therapy, one returns the mind=body to engage with the environment with all the senses.

Shinkeishitsu (神経質)   This is an anxiety-based syndrome that emerges in those who are prone to hypochondriasis and who are timid in character, yet gentle and often sensitive. Those with *shinkeishitsu* are over-sensitive to any subtle change in body sensation; they over-engage in self-analysis by contemplating the origins and catalysts of their symptoms. Morita classified *shinkeishitsu*: (1) ordinary *shinkeishitsu*; (2) *shinkeishitsu* with paroxysmal anxiety; and (3) *shinkeishitsu* with obsessive ideas.

Shinto (神道) **and** *kami* (神)   Shinto means 'the way of the gods'. Shintoism honours the original spirit core of Japan that runs through all of life; there is no founder or sacred text like the Bible, Koran, or Sutras. It is pure polytheism. Sacred spirits animate rock, rain, rice, river, tree, mountain, wind, and so on. Shintoism is a neutral and sometimes optimistic system as there is no inherent evil that polarises man from nature. After death, humans return to *kami* sacred spirit source that runs through living nature. Shinto rituals are performed to call on *kami* for protection. With roots in Confucianism and Buddhism, Shintoism gained status as the national religion in 1868, and lost this status in 1946. Morita's life spanned the formal Shinto era. While the relationship between Morita therapy and Zen has been debated since the 1950s, Morita's theory of consciousness and his sequential methods appear to incorporate Shinto's reliance on *kami* as much as Zen.

Shisō–no–mujun (思想の矛盾)   This refers to the contradiction that exists between ideas and reality. Mental conflict arises when a person attempts to intellectually manipulate, modify, or deny what is real or actual according to her or his desire of how things 'ought' to be. By contrast to cognitive theory in psychology, Morita highlights the contradiction that exists between intellectual logic and emotional logic. When the intellect depresses emotional experience as a source of knowledge, then 'up side down illusory thought' is activated. In Zen, this is called *akuchi*. It is the intention of Morita therapy to dismantle this contradiction by ideas and foster acceptance of facts as facts.

Shoichinen (初一念)   This is a Zen term that indicates 'original thought'. Morita therapy decreases a client's critical judgement of self and comparison to others. One goal of therapy is to return the person to the state of experience before the moment of evaluation or criticism. This is akin to the Zen phrase *know your original face before you were born*. The therapeutic process rekindles experiential-based insight, which follows from complete rest of mind and body. For Morita, insight is not cognitive-based, and occurs once a person stops thinking in words about her or his experiences so that pure emotion arises.

Suffering   Though suffering is a fact of existence, it increases artificially when one compares oneself to others and adopts the attitude that the world is either good or bad. Suffering can increase when intellectual understanding overrides experiential-embodied understanding. According to Kondo (conversation, 1990), 'The greater the ego, the greater the suffering'.

Taitoku (体得)   The literal meaning is *realise with one's entire being*. Such knowledge comes through full body experience. This is often compared to intellectual understanding. When one is in a state of contradiction between ideas and reality (*shisō-no-mujun*), the gap between body knowing (intuition) and intellectual understanding is great. It is this gap that increases suffering, and it is this gap that Morita therapy closes.

Toraware (捕われ)   *Toraware* occurs when one is trapped in a loop of worry and fretfulness, which in turn, diminishes one's capacity to even the tension between the natural desire for life and innate fear of death.

Weak-willed disposition   This term was developed by Morita to classify a particular character structure that is prone to the following symptoms: flat affect, lethargy, low motivation, infrequently feels delight, low drive for self-preservation, tendency to under or over-idealise; and reckless or impulsive behaviours during under or over-idealised states. A weak-willed disposition is found often in those with *shinkeishitsu*. According to Morita, those with this character structure respond to his sequenced therapy in the ecological environment.

Zen (禅)   While Zen has been in existence in East Asia well over 1400 years, its sacred texts are simultaneously theistic and non-theistic and offer ritualistic provisions for individual and community daily living. Regarding Morita's system of practice, Zen provides the phenomenological underpinning that brings Nature forward in psychological medicine.

Zen is realised – paradoxically – through movement in stillness. A passage by Suzuki illustrates natural living, 'the way the flying wild geese cast their shadow on the water below without any idea of doing so, while the water reflects the geese just as naturally and unintentionally' (Suzuki, 1959, p. 17).

APPENDIX

13 Ways to Stay Miserable★
(Circle those that apply.)

1. Have an unhealthy life style.
2. Maintain a substance-loop | incl. caffeine-alcohol-tobacco.
3. Live without safe, kind touch. Stay in harm's way.
4. Live in economic chaos and uncertainty.
5. Live in over cluttered places | incl. polluted air, water, noise.
6. Compare yourself to others.
7. Tell personal things to those who judge you or gossip.
8. Override body knowledge (*taitoku*) by your intellect.
9. Live without 'care' balance.

   Over-care for others (incl. pets), and under-care for self (or vice versa).

10. Worry about worrying.
11. Ignore Ecology.

    (i) Ignore surrounding *Nature*: tree, bird, rain, cicada, turtle, cloud, moon, tides.
    (ii) Ignore 'diurnal' *Human Nature*: hydrate, breathe, rest, move, relate, see, hear, smell, taste, touch, sense.

12. Live without humour, play, music, or dance.
13. Live without curiosity or a practical imagination.

★ Checklist for health-eroding contexts (LeVine, Classic Morita Centre).

BIBLIOGRAPHY

Abe, M. (1989). *Zen and Western Thought*. W. LaFleur (Ed.). Hawaii: University of Hawaii Press.

Adams, H.B. (1964). Therapeutic potentialities of sensory deprivation procedures. *International Mental Health Research Newspaper,* 6(4), 7–9.

Al-Krenawi, A. and Slater, N. (2007). Bedouin-Arab children use visual art as a response to the destruction of their homes in unrecognized villages. *Journal of Humanistic Psychology*, 47(3), 235–305.

Alexander, F. (1942). *The Universal Constant in Living*. New York: Dutton.

American Psychiatric Association (2013). *Diagnostic and Statistical Manual of Mental Disorders* (5th ed.). Washington, DC: American Psychiatric Publishing.

Annerstedt, M. (2009). Health promotion, environmental psychology and sustainable development: A successful 'ménage-à-trois'. *Global Health Promotion*, 16(1), 49–52.

Annerstedt, M. and Währborg, P. (2011). Nature-assisted therapy: Systematic review of controlled and observational studies. *Scandinavian Journal of Public Health*, 39(4), 371–388.

Ang, C. (1980). Les apparitions de fantômes au Cambodge. *ASEMI,* 11(1–4). Paris: Cedrasemi, 437–443.

Ang, C. (1988). The place of animism within popular Buddhism in Cambodia: The example of the monastery. *Asian Folklore Studies*, 47, 35–41.

Arieti, S. (1981). *Creativity: The Magic Synthesis*. New York: Basic Books.

Arieti, S. and Chrzanowski, G. (Eds) (1975). *New Dimensions in Psychiatry: A Worldview*. New York: John Wiley and Sons.

Baars, B. (2003). The double life of B.F. Skinner: Inner conflict, dissociation and the scientific taboo against consciousness. *Journal of Consciousness Studies*, 10, 1, 5–25.

Baird, L. (2008). Childhood trauma in the etiology of borderline personality disorders: Theoretical considerations and therapeutic interventions. *Hakomi Forum, Summer Issue,* 19–21.

Bashō, Matsuo. (2005). *The Narrow Road to the Deep North and Other Travel Sketches*. Yuasa Nobuyuki (trans). Harmondsworth, UK: Penguin.

Bassuk, E. (1986). The rest cure: Repetition or resolution of Victorian women's conflicts. In S.R. Suleiman (Ed.), *The Female Body in Western Culture* (pp. 139–151). Cambridge, MA: Harvard University Press.

Bay, H. (2008). On silence. *Pacific World: Journal of the Institute of Buddhist Studies*. Third Series, 10, Fall, 3–8.

Beard, G.M. (1869). Neurasthenia or nervous exhaustion. *Boston Medical and Surgical Journal*, 80, 217–221.

Bellamy, E. (1997). *Affective Genealogies: Psychoanalysis, Postmodernism, and the 'Jewish Question' after Auschwitz*. Lincoln, Nebraska: University of Nebraska Press.

Bergson, H. (1944). *Creative Evolution*. New York: Random House.

Berman, M., Jonides, J., and Kaplan, S. (2008). The cognitive benefits of interacting with nature. *Psychological Science*, 19, 1207–1212.

Berthier, F. (2000). *Reading Zen in the Rocks*. Chicago: University of Chicago Press.

Berto, R. (2005). Exposure to restorative environments helps restore attentional capacity. *Journal of Environmental Psychology*, 25, 249–259.

Bettelheim, B. (1975) *The Uses of Enchantment: The Meaning and Importance of Fairy Tales*. New York: Knopf.

Bettelheim, B. (1980). *Surviving and Other Essays*. New York: Vintage Books.

Bettelheim, B. (1982). *Freud and Man's Soul*. New York: Knopf.

Binswanger, L. (1963). *Being-in-the-world: Selected Papers of Ludwig Binswanger*. (J. Needleman, Trans.) New York: Basic Books.

Bion, W.R. (1984). *Transformations*. London: Karnac Classics, H. Karnac Ltd.

Blocker, G. and Starling, C. (2001). *Japanese Philosophy*. New York: State University of New York Press.

Bloom, A. (1992). *Strategies for Modern Living: A Commentary with the Text of the Tannishō*. Berkeley, California: Numata Center for Buddhist Translation and Research.

Blyth, R.H. (1952). *Haiku*. Tokyo: Hokuseido Press.

Blyth, R.H. (1964a). *Zen and Zen Classics: History of Zen, Volume Two*. Tokyo: Hokuseido Press.

Blyth, R.H. (1964b). *The History of Haiku, Volume Two*. Tokyo: Hokuseido Press.

Bordes, R. (2011). *Dire les Maux. Anthropologie de la Parole dans les Médecines du Monde*. Collection: Ethique et Pratique Médicales. Paris: L'Harmattan.

Boucher, S.H. (2000) Cognitive performance, fitness and ageing. In S. Biddle, K.R. Fox, and S.H. Boutcher (Eds), *Physical Activity and Psychological Well-Being: An Evidence Based Approach* (pp. 118–129). London: Routledge Press.

Boulanger, G. (2007). *Wounded by Reality: Understanding and Treating Adult Onset Trauma*. Mahwah, NJ: The Analytic.

Bradley, D. (1949). *No Place to Hide*. London: Hodder and Stoughton.

Braun, B. (1988). The BASK Model of Dissociation. *Dissociation* 1(1), March, 4–23.

Briere, J. and Spinazzola, J. (2005). Phenomenology and psychological assessment of complex posttraumatic states. *Journal of Traumatic Stress*, 18, 401–412.

Briere, J., Scott, C., and Weathers, F.W. (2005). Peritraumatic and persistent dissociation in the presumed etiology of PTSD. *American Journal of Psychiatry*, 162, 2295–2301.

Briere, J., Weathers, F.W., and Runtz, M. (2005). Is dissociation a multidimensional construct? Data from the Multiscale Dissociation Inventory. *Journal of Traumatic Stress*, *18*, 221–231.

Bronfenbrenner, U. (1979). *The Ecology of Human Development: Experiments of Nature and Design*. Cambridge, MA: Harvard University Press.

Broocks, A., Bandelow, B., Pekrun, G., George, A., Meyer, T., Bartmann, U., Hillmer-Vogel, U., and Ruther, E. (1998). Comparison of aerobic exercise, clomipramine, and placebo in the treatment of panic disorder. *American Journal of Psychiatry*, 155(5), 603–609.

Bucke, R.M. (1991). *Cosmic Consciousness: A Study in the Evolution of the Human Mind*. New York, NY: Penguin Books. (Original work published 1901).

Burls, A. (2005) New landscapes for mental health. *Mental Health Review*, 10, 26–29.

Burls, A. (2007). Promoting public health and mental well-being through ecotherapy. *Journal of Public Mental Health*, 6(3), 24–39.

Burls, A. and Caan, A.W. (2004) Social exclusion and embracement: A helpful concept? *Primary Health Care Research and Development*, 5, 191–192.

Burke-Gaffney, B. (2004). *Starcrossed: A Biography of Madam Butterfly*. Utah: Signature Books.

Calhoun, C. (2004). *Accidental Wisdom: Robert Merton's Serendipidous Findings*. New Jersey: Bookforum (summer edition).

Caudill, W. and Doi, T. (1963). Interrelations of psychiatry, culture, and emotion in Japan. In I. Galdston (Ed.), *Man's Image in Medicine and Anthropology* (pp. 374–415). New York: International Universities Press.

Chalquist, C. (2009). A look at the ecotherapy research evidence. *Ecopsychology*, 1(2), 64–74.

Chang, S.C. (1974). Morita therapy. *American Journal of Psychotherapy*, 28, 208–221.

Chang, S.C. (2010). Psychotherapy and culture. Morita therapy: An illustration. *World Cultural Psychiatry Research Review*. December, 135–145.

Charcot, J. (1877). *Lectures on the Diseases of the Nervous System*. London: The New Sydenham Society.

Chhim, S. (2013) A place for baksbat (broken courage) in forensic psychiatry at the Extraordinary Chambers in the Courts of Cambodia (ECCC). *Psychiatry, Psychology and Law*. 21(2), 286–296.

Clifford, J. (1982). *Person and Myth: Maurice Leenhardt in the Melanesian World*. Berkeley, CA: University of California Press.

Coope, J. (2010). Ecopsychology and the historian: Some notes on the work of Theodore Rosnak. *European Journal of Psychology*, 1, 4–18.

Cooper, P.C. (2002). Between wonder and doubt: Psychoanalysis in the goal-free zone. *The American Journal of Psychoanalysis*, 62, 95–118.

Crabtree, A. (1993). *From Mesmer to Freud: Magnetic Sleep and the Roots of Psychological Healing*. New Haven and London: Yale University Press.

Culver, C.M., Cohen, S.I., Silverman, A.J., and Shmavonian, B.M. (1964). Cognitive structuring, field dependence-independence, and the psychophysiological response to perceptual isolation. In J. Wortis (Ed.), *Recent Advances in Biological Psychiatry* (pp. 119–128). New York: Plenum Press

Davis, J. (1972). Letter to the Editor. *New England Journal of Medicine*, 286(3), 727.

de Beauvoir, S. (1948). *The Ethics of Ambiguity*. (B. Frechtman, Trans.) New York: Philosophical Library.

de Figueiredo, J.M. (2007). Demoralization and psychotherapy: A tribute to Jerome D. Frank, MD, PhD (1909–2005). *Psychotherapy and Psychosomatics*, 76, 129–133.

DeMartino, R. (1983). On Zen communication. *Communication*, 8. 13–28.

DeMartino, R. (1991). Karen Horney, Daisetz T. Suzuki, and Zen Buddhism. *The American Journal of Psychoanalysis*, September, 51(3), 267–283.

DMoch, W. (2010). *Dropping the Ego: One Shot – One Life*. Conference presentation and visual Kyūdō demonstration at the International Congress of Morita Therapy, March 2010, Melbourne, Australia.

Denzin, N. (2009). *On Understanding Emotion*. Brunswick, New Jersey: Transaction Publishers.

DePrince, A.P. and Freyd, J.J. (2001). Memory and dissociative tendencies: The roles of attentional context and word meaning in a directed forgetting task. *Journal of Trauma & Dissociation*, 2, 67–82.

DePrince, A.P. and Freyd, J.J. (2004). Forgetting trauma stimuli. *Psychological Science*, 15, 488–492.

Doi, T. (1958). Psychopathology of *Shinkeishitsu*, especially regarding the psychodynamics of *Toraware*. *Neurologia Japonica*, 60, 733–744.

Doi, T. (1962). Morita therapy and psychoanalysis. *Psychologia*, 5, 117–123.

Doi, T. (1973). *The Anatomy of Dependence*. (J. Bester, Trans.) Tokyo: Kodansha International.

Doi T. (1986). *The Anatomy of Self*. (M. Harbison, Trans.) Tokyo: Kodansha International.

Dorahy, M.J. and van der Hart, O. (2007). Relationship between trauma and dissociation: A historical analysis. In E. Vermetten, M. Dorahy, and D. Spiegel (Eds), *Traumatic*

Dissociation: Neurobiology and Treatment (pp. 3–30). Washington, DC: American Psychiatric Press.

Drengson, A. (1990). Being with and learning from animals: Morita therapy and natural harmony. *International Bulletin of Morita Therapy* 3(2), 92–97.

Driscoll, M. (2010). *Absolute Erotic, Absolute Grotesque: The Living, Dead, and Undead in Japan's Imperialism, 1895–1945*. Durham, NC: Duke University Press.

Droit, R-P. (2003). *The Cult of Nothingness: The Philosophers and the Buddha*. (D. Streight and P. Vohnson, Trans.) Chapel Hill: University of North Carolina Press.

Dumoulin, H. (1989). *Zen Buddhism: A History, Volume 2*. (J. Heisig and P. Knitter, Trans.) New York: Macmillan Publishing Company.

Durie, M. (1999). Te Pae Mahutonga: A model for Māori health promotion. *Health Promotion Forum of New Zealand Newsletter*, 49, 2–5 December.

Durie, M. (2004) Understanding health and illness: Research at the interface between science and indigenous knowledge. *International Journal of Epidemiology*, 33, 1138–1143.

Edge, L. (2001). The spectrum of dissociation: From pathology to self-realization. *Journal of Transpersonal Psychology*, 33(1), 53–63.

Ellenberger, H. (1958). A clinical introduction to psychiatric phenomenology and existential analysis. In R. May, E. Angel, and H. Ellenberger (Eds). *Existence: A New Dimension in Psychiatry and Psychology* (pp. 92–127). New York, NY: Simon and Schuster.

Ellenberger, H. (1970). *The Discovery of the Unconscious: The History and Evolution of Dynamic Psychiatry*. New York: Basic Books.

Fanon, F. (1966). *Wretched of the Earth*. (C. Farrington, Trans.) New York: Grove Weidenfeld.

Fitchtner, G. (2003). *The Sigmund Freud-Ludwig Binswanger Correspondence 1908–1938*. (A. Pomerans and T. Roberts, Trans.) London: Open Gate.

Ford, J. and Courtois, C. (2003). *Treating Complex Traumatic Stress Disorders in Children and Adolescents*. New York, NY: Guilford Press.

Franck, F. (1978). *Zen and Zen Classics: Selections from R.H. Blyth*. New York: Vintage Press.

Franck, F. (1988). *The Zen of Seeing: Seeing Drawing as Meditation*. New York: Random House.

Frank, J.D. (1993). *Persuasion and Healing: A Comparative Study of Psychotherapy*. Baltimore: John Hopkins University Press.

Frankl, V. (1967). *Psychotherapy and Existentialism: Selected Papers on Logotherapy*. New York, NY: Simon & Schuster.

Freud, S. (1913). *The Interpretation of Dreams*. (A.A. Brill, Trans.) New York: Macmillan Company.

Freyd, J.J. (1994). Betrayal-trauma: Traumatic amnesia as an adaptive response to childhood abuse. *Ethics & Behavior,* 4(4), 307–329.

Freyd, J.J. (1996). *Betrayal Trauma: The Logic of Forgetting Childhood Abuse*. Cambridge, MA: Harvard University Press.

Freyd, J. J. (1997). Violations of power, adaptive blindness, and betrayal trauma theory. *Feminism and Psychology*. 7, 22–32.

Freyd, J.J. (2013). Preventing betrayal [Editorial]. *Journal of Trauma & Dissociation*, 14, 495–500.

Fromm, E. (1951). *The Forgotten Language: An Introduction to the Understanding of Dreams, Fairytales and Myths*. New York: Rinehart & Co.

Fromm, E. (1959). Foreword. In D.T. Suzuki, *Zen and Psychoanalysis.* New York: Grove Press.

Fromm, E., Suzuki, D.T., and DeMartino, R. (1960). *Zen Buddhism and Psychoanalysis*. New York: Harper & Row.

Frumkin, H. (2001). Beyond toxicity: Human health and the natural environment. *American Journal of Preventative Medicine*, 20, 234–240.

Fujita, C. (1967). On self-transcendence in therapeutic change. *Seishin Igaku, Japanese Journal of Psychiatry*, 9(4), 255–259.

Fujita, C. (1986). *Morita Therapy: A Psychotherapeutic System for Neurosis.* Tokyo: Igaku-Shoin.

Fujita, C. (1992). On the possibility of standardizing 'ambulatory' Morita therapy. *Journal of Morita Therapy*, 3, 17–27.

Fukai, T. (2013). *Paul Tillich: Journey to Japan in 1960.* Tillich Research Series 4 Tillich-Forschungen. Berlin: Walter de Gruyter.

Gaines, J. (1979). *Fritz Perls Here and Now.* California: Celestial Arts.

Gaines, L. and Vetter, H. (1968). Sensory deprivation and psychotherapy. *Theory, Research and Practice*, 5(1) 7–12.

Gallagher, G. and Zahavi, D. (2008). *The Phenomenological Mind: An Introduction to Philosophy of Mind and Cognitive Science.* New York, NY: Routledge.

Gausset, Q., Kenrick, J., and Gibb, R. (2011). Indigenous and authcothŏnous with regard to human rights law and anthropology. *Anthropologie Sociale*, 19(2), 135–142.

Gibson, H.B. (1975). The centenary of Shoma Morita. *Bulletin of the British Psychological Society*, 28, 346–348.

Gladwell, V., Brown, D., Barton, J., Tarvainen, M., Kuoppa, P., Pretty, J., Suddaby, J., and Sandercock, G. (2012). The effects of views of nature on autonomic control. *European Journal of Applied Physiology*, 112(9), 3379–3386.

Godart, G. (2004). Tracing the circle of truth: Inoue Enryō on the history of philosophy and Buddhism. *The Eastern Buddhist*, 36, 106–133.

Goddard, K. (1991). Morita therapy: A literature review. *Transcultural Psychiatric Review*, 28, 93–115. Gordon, L. (2000). *Existentia Africana: Understanding Africana Existential Thought.* New York, NY: Routledge.

Hakeda, Y. (Trans). (1967). *The Awakening of Faith Attributed to Asvaghosha.* New York: Columbia University Press.

Harris, A. (2017). A phenomenological study into African refugee men's wellness seeking behaviours, inclusive of community, spirit and ancestral connections. PhD Thesis. University of Melbourne, School of Global and Population Health.

Harvey, M. (1996). An ecological view of psychological trauma and trauma recovery. *Journal of Traumatic Stress*, 9(1), 3–23.

Hasegawa, Y. (1989). A group learning approach to overcoming neurosis: The Seikatsu-no Hakkenkai's method of studying Morita theory. *Rinsho Seishin Igaku*, 17, 1155–1159.

Hashi, H. (2011). Dr. Morita's Psychophysical Therapy and its relation to the way of thinking in Zen Buddhism (English translation). In F. Wallner and H. Hashi, *Globalisierung des Denkens in Ost und West (Global Thinking East and West).* Nordhausen: T. Bautz.

Hashi, H. (2013). Morita therapy as a 'conceptus cosmicus' for psychosis influenced by Zen Buddhism – A comparison of the principles of Mahayana Buddhist philosophy (East Asia) and the cognitive thinking of M. Schlick (Vienna circle). *Biocosmology - Neo - Aristotelism*, 3(4).

Hayes, S., Strosahl, K., and Wilson, K. (1999). *Acceptance and Commitment Therapy: An Experiential Approach to Behavior Change.* New York: Guilford Press.

Heerwagen, J. and Orians, G. (1993). Humans, habitats, and aesthetics. In Kellert, R. and Wilson, O. (Ed.) *The Biophilia Hypothesis* (pp. 138–172). Washington, DC: Shearwater Books.

Hegel, G. (1807/1977). *Phenomenology of Spirit.* (A.V. Miller, Trans.) Oxford: Oxford University Press.

Heidegger, M. (1971). A dialogue on language between a Japanese and an inquirer. *On the Way to Language.* New York: Harper & Row.

Heine, S. (1994). *Dōgen and the Koan Tradition: A Tale of Two Shobogenzo Texts.* Albany, NY: SUNY Press.

Heine, S. (1997). *The Zen Poetry of Dōgan: Verses from the Mountain of Eternal Peace.* Boston, MA: Tuttle Press.

Heine, S. (2008) *Zen Skin, Zen Marrow: Will the Real Zen Buddhism Please Stand Up*. New York, NY: Oxford University Press.

Heisig, J., Kasulis, T., and Maraldo, J. (2011). *Japanese Philosophy: A Sourcebook*. Hawaii: University of Hawaii Press.

Hirata, H. (1993). *Poetry and Poetics of Nishiwaki Junzaburo: Modernism in Translation*. Princeton, NJ: Princeton University Press

Hogan, S. (2001). *Healing Arts: The History of Art Therapy*. London and Philadelphia: Kingsley Publishers Ltd.

Horney, K. (1949). Finding the real self (A letter with a forward by Karen Horney). *American Journal of Psychoanalysis*, 9, 3–7.

Horney, K. (1950). *Neurosis and Human Growth: The Struggle Toward Self-Realization*. New York: Norton Press.

Horney, K. (1952). The paucity of inner experiences. *The American Journal of Psychoanalysis*, 12(1), 3–10.

Horney, K. (1952b). Scientific Meetings: Karen Horney. *The American Journal of Psychoanalysis*, Vol. XII.

Hume, L. (2002). *Ancestral Power: The Dreaming, Consciousness and Aboriginal Australians*. Melbourne: Australia, University of Melbourne Press.

Huxley, A. (1937). *Ends and Means: An Inquiry into the Nature of Ideals and into the Methods Employed for their Realization*. London: Chatto and Windus.

Ikeda, K. (1971). Morita's theory of neurosis and its application in Japanese psychotherapy. In J.G. Howell (Ed.), *Modern Perspectives in World Psychiatry* (pp. 519–530). New York, NY: Brunner/Mazel.

Inagaki, H. (1992). *A Dictionary of Japanese Buddhist Terms*. Kyoto: Nagata Bunshodo.

Ingram, D. (1987). *Karen Horney: Final Lectures*. New York: Norton Press.

Inoue, E. (1905). *Psychotherapy*. Tokyo: Nankodon Shoten Press.

Ishida, R. (1971). Dialectic characteristics of Naikansei (as cited in Ishida R., 1972). *Clinical Medicine of Naikan Therapy* (in Japanese). Tokyo: Bunkodo.

Ishiyama, I. (1986). Morita therapy: Its basic features and cognitive intervention for anxiety treatment. *Psychotherapy*, 23(3), 375–381.

Ishiyama, I. (1988). Current status of Morita therapy research: An overview of research methods, instruments, and results. *International Bulletin of Morita Therapy*. 1(2), November, 58–83.

Ishiyama, I. (1990a). Japanese perspective on client inaction and procrastination: Morita therapy. *International Journal for the Advancement of Counselling*, 13, 119–128.

Ishiyama, I. (1990b). Practice of brief Morita intervention: An interview model with a session illustration. *International Bulletin of Morita Therapy*, 3, 35–60.

Ishiyama, I. (1991). Limitations and problems of directive outpatient Morita therapy: Necessity for modifications and process-related sensitivities. *International Bulletin of Morita Therapy*, 4, 15–31.

Ishiyama, I. (1996). Culturality of psychotherapy: A discussion on introducing Morita therapy into the North American therapeutic cultural context. *Culture and Mind: Japanese Journal of Transcultural Psychiatry Research (Japanese)*, 1, 37–49.

Ishiyama, I. (2003). Bending Willow Tree: A Japanese (Morita therapy) model of human nature and client change. *Canadian Journal of Counselling*, 37(3), 216–231.

Itami, J. (1986). *Psychosomatic Approaches to Cancer Patients by Morita Therapy*. Paper presented at the 4th Morita Therapy Congress, Fukuoka, Japan.

Ives, C. (1992a). *Zen Awakening and Society*. Hawaii: University of Hawaii Press.

Ives, C. (1992b). The teacher-student relationship in Japanese culture and Morita therapy. *International Bulletin of Morita Therapy*, 5, 10–18.

Ives, C. (1992c). Response to David Reynolds. *International Bulletin of Morita Therapy*, 5, 22–25.

Iwai, H. (1974). Brief Morita therapy. *Kyoiku to Igaku*, 807–814.

Iwai, H. and Reynolds, D. (1970). Morita psychotherapy: The views from the West. *American Journal of Psychiatry*, 126, 1031–1036.

Jackson, M. (2005). *Existential Anthropology: Events, Exigencies, and Effects*. Oxford, UK: Berghahn.

Jackson, M. (2012). *Lifeworlds: Essays in Existential Anthropology*. Chicago: University of Chicago Press.

Jacobson, A. and Berenberg, A. (1952). Japanese psychiatry and psychotherapy. *American Journal of Psychiatry*, 109(5), 321–329.

Jacobson, G.R. (1966). Effect of brief sensory deprivation on field dependence. *American Journal of Medical Science*, 243, 558–563.

Jacobson, N. P. (1974). *Buddhism: The Religion of Analysis*. Carbondale, IL: Southern Illinois University Press.

James, W. (1985). *Varieties of Religious Experience*. Cambridge, MA: Harvard University Press. (Published originally in 1902).

Jaspers, K. (1963). *General Psychopathology*. [Translated from the German 7th edition, Jaspers (1913), *Allgemeine Psychopathologie*.] J. Hoenig and M. W. Hamilton (Eds). Manchester, UK: Manchester University Press.

Johnson, D.R. (1988). The role of the creative arts therapies in the diagnosis and treatment of psychological trauma. *The Arts in Psychotherapy*, 14, 269–270. [Reprint of this article in 1999 in *Essays on the Creative Arts Therapies*, (pp. 102–112). Springfield, IL.]

Johnson, D.R. (1999). *Essays on the Creative Arts Therapies: Imagining the Birth of a Profession*. Springfield, Illinois: Charles Thomas.

Josephson, J.A. (2006). When Buddhism became a 'religion': Religion and superstition in the writings of Inoue Enryō. *Japanese Journal of Religious Studies,* Nanzan University, 33 (1), 143–168.

Jones, A. (1964). Drive and incentive variables associated with the statistical properties of sequences of stimuli. *Journal of Experimental Psychology*, 67, 423–431.

Jung, C. (1950). *Psychology and Religion, West and East: Collected Works, Vol. 11*. London: Routledge and Kegan Paul.

Jung, C. (1964). Foreword in Suzuki, D.T. *An Introduction to Zen Buddhism*. New York: Grove Press.

Jung, C. (1969). Archetypes and the collective unconscious. *Collected Works of C.G. Jung, Volume 9 (Part 1)*. New Jersey: Princeton University Press.

Kaehler, L.A. and Freyd, J.J. (2009). Borderline personality characteristics: A betrayal trauma approach. *Psychological Trauma: Theory, Research, Practice, and Policy*, 1, 261–268.

Kant, I. (1996). *The Metaphysics of Morals*. (Mary Gregor, Trans.) New York: Cambridge University Press.

Kaplan, R. and Kaplan, S. (1989). *The Experience of Nature: A Psychological Perspective*. Cambridge: Cambridge University Press.

Kaplan, R., Kaplan, S., and Ryan, R. (1998). *With People in Mind: Design and Management of Everyday Nature*. Washington, DC: Island Press.

Kasulis, T.P. (1977). Zen Buddhism, Freud, and Jung. *The Eastern Buddhist*, X(1), May, 68–91.

Kasulis, T.P. (1981). *Zen Action, Zen Person*. Hawaii: The University Press of Hawaii.

Kato, H. (2005). Zen and psychology. *Japanese Psychological Research*, 47(2), 125–136.

Kawai, H. (1960). Discussions on Morita therapy: A psychotherapy in the line of Zen. *Psychologia,* 3, 92–99.

Kawai, H. (1996). *Buddhism and the Art of Psychotherapy*. College Station, TX: Texas A & M University Press.

Kawai, H. (1998). *The Japanese Psyche: Major Motifs in the Fairy Tales of Japan*. Dallas, TX: Spring Publication.

Kaya, W. (2009). On the Relationship between Arugamama and Kannagaru: A Shinto Perspective on Morita Therapy (abstract on page 60). Paper presented at the 27th Annual Meeting of the Japanese Society for Morita Therapy. Fukuoka: Japan.

Kiefer, C. (1976). Morita psychotherapy. *Medical Anthropology Newsletter*, 7(4), 11–12.

Kirsch, J. (1960). Affinities between Zen and analytical psychology. *Psychologia*, 3(2), 85–91.

Kelman, H. (1958). Communing and relating. Past and current perspectives. *American Journal of Psychoanalysis*, 18, 77–98.

Kelman, H. (1959a). Eastern influences on psychoanalytic thinking. *Psychologia* 2(2), 73–75.

Kelman, H. (1959b). Psychotherapy in the Far East. *Progress in Psychotherapy*, 4, 296–305.

Kelman, H. (1963). Oriental psychological processes and creativity. *The American Journal of Psychoanalysis*, March, 23(1), 67–84.

King, W. (1968). Time transcendence-acceptance in Zen Buddhism. *Journal of the American Academy of Religion*, 36(3), 217–228.

Kipling, R. (1988). *Kipling's Japan: Collected Writings*. (H. Cortazzi and G. Webb, Eds.) London: Athlone Press.

Kirsch, T. (2014). *A Jungian Life*. Carmel, CA: Fisher King Press.

Kitanishi, K. (1987). Expanded application of Morita therapy: A Moritist approach to depressed patients. In Kenshiro Ohara (Ed.), Seishinka Mook No. 19: *Morita Therapy: Theory and Practice* (pp. 109–115). Tokyo: Kanehara Shuppan.

Kitanishi, K. (2005). The philosophical background of Morita therapy: Its application to therapy. In *Asian Culture and Psychotherapy: Implications for East and West* (pp. 169–185). Hawai'i: University of Hawai'i Press.

Kitanishi, K. (2015). *Culture, Nature, and Psychotherapy*. International Symposium (October 15), The 33rd Annual Meeting of the Japanese Society for Morita Therapy. Kurashiki, Japan.

Kitanishi, K. and Kondo, K. (1994). The rise and fall of neurasthenia in Japanese psychiatry. *Transcultural Psychiatry*, 31, 137–152

Kitanishi, K. and Mori, A. (2008). Morita therapy: 1919 to 1995. *Psychiatry and Clinical Neurosciences* 49(5 & 6), 245–254.

Klein, Melanie (1986). *The Selected Melanie Klein*. J. Mitchell (Ed.). NY: Free Press.

Kleinman, A. (1980). *Patients and Healers in the Context of Culture: And Exploration of the Borderland Between Anthropology, Medicine, and Psychiatry*. Berkeley, CA: University of California Press.

Kleinman, A. (2006). *What Really Matters: Living a Moral Life Amidst Uncertainty and Danger*. New York, NY: Oxford University Press.

Kodish, B. (2011). *Korzbybski: A Biography*. Pasadena, CA: Extensional Publishing.

Koga, Y. (1967). On Morita therapy. *Jikei Medical Journal*, 14, 73–99.

Koga, Y. (1973). Zen and Morita therapy. *Practice and Theory of Psychotherapy*, Tokyo, 4(2), 2–11.

Kolb, L. (1987). Neurophysiological hypothesis explaining posttraumatic stress disorder. *American Journal of Psychiatry*, 144, 474–478.

Komatsu, J. (1982). Psychophysiological studies on absolute bedrest stage in Morita therapy (in Japanese). Tokyo *Jikeikai Ika Daigaku Zasshi*, 97, 505–521.

Kondo, A. (1952). Intuition in Zen Buddhism. *The American Journal of Psychoanalysis*, (12), 10–14.

Kondo, A. (1953). Morita therapy: A Japanese therapy for neurosis. *The American Journal of Psychoanalysis*, 13(1), 31–37.

Kondo, A. (1958a). The theory of neurosis according to Morita and comparison to the psychoanalytic theories of Freud and Horney (in Japanese). Tokyo *Jikeikai Ika Daigaku Zasshi*, 73, 2077–2123.

Kondo, A. (1958b). Zen in psychotherapy: The virtue of sitting. *Chicago Review*, Summer, 12(2), USA.

Kondo, A. (1960). Morita therapy and its development in relation to contemporary psychiatry in Japan. In J.H. Masserman and J.D. Moreno (Eds), *Progress in Psychotherapy* (pp. 221–224). Vol. V. New York: Grune & Stratton.

Kondo, A. (1961). The therapist-patient relationship in psychotherapy: On Horney's school and Morita therapy. *Seishin Bunseki Kenyu* (Japanese Journal of Psychoanalytic Research), 7, 30–35.

Kondo, A. (1962). Acceptance: Its meaning in psychotherapy (in Japanese). *Shinkeitshitsu*. 3 (1). 13–18.

Kondo, A. (1963). *Recollections of Dr. Horney*. Unpublished typewritten paper. (Kondo archives gifted to LeVine.)

Kondo, A. (1975). Morita therapy: Its sociohistorical context. In S. Arieti and G. Chrzanowski. *New Directions in Psychiatry: A Worldview.* New York: J. Wiley & Sons.

Kondo, A. (1983). Illusion and human suffering: A brief comparison of Horney's ideas with Buddhistic understanding of mind. In N. Katz (Ed.), *Buddhist and Western Psychology*. Boulder: Prajna Press.

Kondo, A. (1991). Recollections of Dr. Horney. *The American Journal of Psychoanalysis*, 51(3). Human Science Press.

Kondo, A. (1992). A Zen perspective on the concept of self and human nature. *International Bulletin of Morita Therapy*, 5, 46–49.

Kondo, K. (1976). The origin of Morita therapy. In W.P. Lebra, *Culture-Bound Syndromes, Ethnopsychiatry and Alternate Therapies* (pp. 250–258). Hawaii: University of Hawai'i Press.

Kora, T. (1955). Principes et pratique de la therapeutique de Morita. (Principles and practice of Morita's psychotherapeutic method.) *L'Hygiène Mentale*, 44(2), 41–53.

Kora, T. (1965). Morita therapy. *International Journal of Psychiatry*, 1(4), 611–640.

Kora, T. (1968). A method of instruction in psychotherapy. *Jikeikai Medical Journal*, October, 15(4), 315–325.

Kora, T. (1978). In Memorium: Prof Mitsuzo Shimoda. *Seishin Shin Keigaku Zasshi*, 80(11), 605–606.

Kora, T. (1989). An overview of the therapy and practice of Morita therapy (Part 1). *International Bulletin of Morita Therapy*, 2, 70–79.

Kora, T. and Ohara, K. (1973). Morita therapy. *Psychology Today*, 63–68.

Kora, T. and Sato, K. (1958). Morita therapy: A psychotherapy in the way of Zen. *Psychologia*, 1(4), 219–225.

Koren, L. (2008). *Wabi-Sabi for Artists, Designers, Poets & Philosophers*. Point Reyes, CA: Imperfect Publishing.

Krech, G. (2002). *Naikan: Gratitude, Grace and the Japanese Art of Self-Reflection*. Berkeley, CA: Stone Bridge Press.

Krishnamurti, J. (1970). *Think on These Things*. First Perennial Library, New York: Harper and Row.

Kumasaka, Y., Levy, N.J., and DeVos, G.A. (1965). Discussion on Morita therapy. *International Journal of Psychiatry*, 1, 641–645.

Kwee, M. and Ellis, A. (1998). The interface between rational emotive behavior therapy (REBT) and Zen. *Journal of Rational-Emotive & Cognitive-Behavior Therapy*, 16(1), 5–43.

Lad, V. (2007). *The Textbook of Ayurveda: A Complete Guide to Assessment, Volume Two*. Germany: Narayana Verlag, Ayurvedic Press.

Lambourne, L. (2007). *Japonisme: Cultural Crossings Between Japan and the West*. UK: Phaidon.

Lammers, A. (2011). *The Jung-Kirsch Letters: The Correspondence of C.G. Jung and James Kirsch*. (U. Egli and A. Lammers, Trans.) East Sussex, UK: Routledge.

Leibrecht, W. (Ed). (1959). *Religion and Culture: Essays in Honor of Paul Tillich.* New York: Harper & Brothers.

Leonhard, K. (1965). Die Japanische Morita therapie aus der sicht eigener psychothera-peutischer verfahren. *Archiv für Psychiatrie und Nervenkrankheiten,* 209, 185.

LeVine, P. (1991). A comparative analysis of Morita therapy and constructive living (in Japa-nese). *Journal of Morita Therapy,* October, 2(2), 123–133.

LeVine, P. (1993). Case study of Morita inpatient in Melbourne, Australia. Second Interna-tional Congress of Morita Therapy, April, Fukuoka, Japan.

LeVine, P. (1994). Impressions of Karen Horney's final lectures. *Australian Psychologist,* 29(1), 153–157.

LeVine, P. (2000). Use of the 'Trauma Detachment Grid' in assessment and differential diag-nosis. *Journal of Morita Therapy,* Tokyo, 11(1), 1–5.

LeVine, P. (2003). Cultural implications for Morita therapy in the Austral Asia region: Treat-ing anxiety with dissociation related to cumulative trauma. *Psychiatria et Neurologia Japon-ica,* 105(5), 567–575.

LeVine, P. (2008). Morita Therapy in Australia. Paper presented at the International Congress of Psychotherapy, October, Beijing, China.

LeVine, P. (2010). *Love and Dread in Cambodia: Weddings, Births, and Ritual Harm Under the Khmer Rouge.* University of Singapore Press and University of Hawai'i Press.

LeVine, P. (2011). Classical Morita therapy: The power of silence. In R. Bordes (Ed.) *Dire les Maux. Anthropologie de la Parole dans les Médecines du Monde* (pp. 249–275). Ethique et Pratique Médicales. Paris: L'Harmattan.

LeVine, P. (2015). Classic Morita Essentials with Consideration to Treating Anxiety and Trauma. Washburn University, Kansas, regional conference on Morita Therapy for Allied Health (May 21, 2015).

LeVine, P. and Frew, J. (2008). Squaring History: Fritz Perls, Japan, and Morita Therapy in 1962. In Comparative Analysis of Gestalt and Morita Therapy Workshop, International Gestalt Therapy Conference, August, Manchester, UK.

LeVine, P. and Ogawa, B. (2015). Integration of Classic Morita Therapy and Individual Out-patient Counselling as a Sequenced Method. International Symposium (October, 15). The 33rd Annual Meeting of the Japanese Society for Morita Therapy. Kurashiki, Japan.

Liotti, G. (1992). Disorganized/disoriented attachment in the etiology of the dissociative disorders. *Dissociation,* December, V(4), 196–204.

Liotti, G. (1999) Disorganized attachment as a model for the understanding of dissocia-tive psychopathology. In J. Solomon and C. George (Eds), *Attachment Disorganization* (pp. 291–317). New York: Guilford Press.

Liotti, G. (2009). Attachment and dissociation. In P. F. Dell and J. O'Neill (Eds), *Dissociation: DSM-V and Beyond* (pp. 53–65). New York: Routledge.

Long, A. (1982). Soul and body in Stoicism. *Phronesis,* 27(1), 34–57.

McCaskill, D. and Kempe K. (1997). *Redevelopment or Domestication: Indigenous Peoples of Southeast Asia.* Chiang Mai: Silkworm Books.

McCown, D., Reibel, D., and Micozzi, M. (2010). *Teaching Mindfulness: A Practical Guide for Clinicians and Educators.* New York: Springer.

McNally, R.J. (2007). Betrayal trauma theory: A critical appraisal. *Memory,* 15, 280–294.

Macfie, J., Cichetti, D., and Toth, S.L. (2001). The development of dissociation in maltreated preschool-aged children. *Development and Psychopathology,* 13, 233–254.

Main, M. and Hesse, E. (1990). Parents' unresolved traumatic experiences are related to infant disorganized attachment status: Is frightened and/or frightening parental behav-ior the linking mechanism? In M. Greenberg, D. Cicchetti, and E.M. Cummings (Eds). *Attachment in the Preschool Years: Theory, Research and Intervention* (pp. 161–184). Chicago: University of Chicago Press.

Malchiodi, C. (1990). *Breaking the Silence: Art Therapy with Children from Violent Homes*. New York: Brunner/Mazel.

Malchiodi, C. (2007). *The Art Therapy Sourcebook*. New York: McGraw-Hill Professionals.

Manicavasaga, V., Silove, D., and Curtis, J. (1997). Separation anxiety in adulthood: A phenomenological investigation. *Comprehensive Psychiatry*. 38(5), September–October issue, 274–282.

Mann, B.J. and Sanders, S. (1994) Child dissociation and the family context. *Journal of Abnormal Psychology*, 22, 373–388.

Maritain, J. (1955). *Creative Intuition in Art and Poetry*. New York: Meridian Books. (First published in 1953 by the Trustees of the National Gallery of Art, Washington DC.)

Marra, M. (1999) *Modern Japanese Aesthetics: A Reader*. Hawaii: University of Hawaii Press.

Martin, A.R. (1972). The dynamics of insight. In J. Rubins (Ed.), *Developments of Horney Psychoanalysis: The Karen Horney 20th Anniversary Volume*. Huntington, NY: Krieger Publishing Company.

Masten, A.S. (2001). Ordinary magic: Resilience processes in development. *American Psychologist*, 56, 227–238.

Masuda, N. (1986). Sleep-wake rhythms for those with neurosis under the absolute bedrest stage in Morita therapy (in Japanese). Tokyo *Jikeikai Ika Daigaku Zasshi*, 101, 467–492.

Matsubara, T. (1973). Japanese psychotherapy: Morita therapy and its relationship to Zen Buddhism. *Journal of the National Association of Private Psychiatric Hospitals*, 5(1), 9–14.

May, R. (1958). The origins and significance of the existential movement in psychology. In R. May, E. Angel, and H. Ellenberger (Eds), *Existence: A New Dimension in Psychiatry and Psychology*. New York: Simon and Schuster.

May, R., Angel, E., and Ellenberger, H. (Eds) (1958). *Existence: A New Dimension in Psychiatry and Psychology*. New York: Basic Books.

Menninger, K., Mayman, M., and Pruyser, P. (1963). *The Vital Balance: The Life Processes in Mental Health and Illness*. New York: Viking Press.

Mercer, J. (2016). An Inquiry into the Nature & Extent Of Operational Zen Principles in Classic Morita Therapy. PhD Thesis at University of Melbourne, School of Global and Population Health.

Michelson, L. and Ray, W. (Eds) (1996). *Handbook of Dissociation: Theoretical, Empirical, and Clinical Perspectives*, New York: Plenum Press.

Miller, A. (1981). *The Drama of the Gifted Child*. New York: Basic Books.

Miller, A. (1984). *Thou Shalt Not Be Aware: Society's Betrayal of the Child*. NY: Meridian Printing.

Miller, A. (1990). *The Untouched Key, Tracing Childhood Trauma in Creativity and Destructiveness*. New York: Anchor Books, Random House, Inc.

Miller, D. (Ed., Trans.) (1995). *Goethe, Volume 12: Scientific Studies*. New Jersey: Princeton University Press.

Miller, M. (2002). Zen and psychotherapy: From mutuality, through relationship, to the emptying place. In P. Young-Eisendrath and S. Muramoto (Eds), *Awakening and Insight: Zen Buddhism and Psychotherapy*. East Sussex, UK: Brunner-Routledge.

Mitchell, J. (1986). *The Selected Melanie Klein*. London, UK: Penguin.

Miura, M. and Usa, S. (1970). A psychotherapy of neurosis: Morita therapy. *Psychologia*, (13), 18–34.

Mohr, M. (1998). Japanese schools and the transition to Meiji: A plurality of responses in the nineteenth century. *Japanese Journal of Religious Studies*, 25(1–2), 167–213.

Mollica, R., Brooks, R., Ekblad, S., and McDonald, L. (2015). The new H5 model of refugee trauma and recovery. In J. Lindert and I. Levav (Eds), *Violence and Mental Health*. New York: Springer.

Montessori, M. (1909). Montessori method: Scientific pedagogy as applied to child education. In *The Children's Houses* (A.E. George, Trans). New York: Frederick Stokes.

Mori, A. and Kitanishi, K. (1989). *The Study of Morita Therapy*. Tokyo: Kongo Shuppan.

Mori, A., Komatsu, J., and Masuda, N. (1986). Sleep-wake rhythms in absolute bedrest in Morita therapy (in Japanese). *Rinsho Noha*, 28, 468–475.

Morita, S. (1998). *Morita Therapy and the True Nature of Anxiety-based Disorders: Shinkeishitsu.* (Kondo, Trans.; LeVine; Ed.) (1928 translation.) New York, NY: State University of New York Press.

Murase, T. and Johnson, F. (1974). Naikan, Morita and Western psychotherapy: A comparison. *Archives of General Psychiatry*, 31(1), 121–128.

Nakamura, K. (1995). Social Anxiety Related Syndromes: Their Universality and Cultural Diversity. Paper presented at the Third International Congress of Morita Therapy and the First International Symposium on Scientific Studies of Psychotherapies in Asia. Beijing, China 1995 (April).

Nakamura, K. (2002). The neurotic versus delusional subtype of *taijin-kyofu-sho*: Their DSM diagnoses. *Psychiatry and Clinical Neurosciences*, 56, 595–601.

Nakamura, S. (1974). A study of the similarities between life in Zen monasteries and Morita therapy-special emphasis on human relationships and experience process. *Practice and Theory of Psychotherapy*, Tokyo, 5(2), 42–45, 78–79.

Nietzsche, F. (1872). *The Birth of Tragedy: Out of the Spirit of Music.* (First published in 1872 as *Die Geburt der Tragodie aus dem Geiste der Musik.*) Leipzig: Verlag von E.W. Fritzsch.

Nijenhuis, E. (2009). Somatoform dissociation and somatoform dissociative disorders. In P.F. Dell and J. O'Neill (Eds), *Dissociation: DSM-IV and Beyond* (pp. 259–275). New York: Routledge.

Nishida, K. (1950). *Zen no Kenkyu (A Study of the Good).* Tokyo: Iwanami Shoten.

Nishida, K. (1958). *Intelligibility and the Philosophy of Nothingness.* (R. Schinzinger, Trans.) Tokyo: Maruzen.

Nishida, K. (1990). *An Inquiry into the Good.* (M. Abe and C. Ives, Trans.) New Haven, CT: Yale University Press.

Nishitani, K. (1989). Encounter with Emptiness. A Message from Nishitani Keiji (Taitetsu Unno, Trans.) In *The Religious Philosophy of Nishitani Keiji* (pp. 3–4). Berkeley, CA: Asian Humanities Press.

Nishitani, K. (1990). *The Self-overcoming of Nihilism.* (G. Parks and S. Aihara, Trans.) Albany, NY: State University of New York Press.

Noll, R. (2001). *American Madness: The Rise and Fall of Dementia Praecox.* Cambridge, MA and London: Harvard University Press.

Nomura, A. (1963). *Morita Therapy: A Therapy Developed in Japan.* Proceedings of a joint meeting between the American Psychiatric Association and the Japanese Society of Psychiatry and Neurology.

Nomura, A. (1974). *Critical Biography of Shoma Morita* (Japanese). Haruyo-sha Publications.

Ogawa, B. (1988). Counseling victims of sexual assault. *International Bulletin of Morita Therapy*, 1, 19–25.

Ogawa, B. (1989). *Walking on Eggshells: Practical Counseling for Women In or Leaving a Violent Relationship.* California: Volcano Press.

Ogawa, B. (2007). *A River to Live By: The 12 Life Principles of Morita Therapy.* Bloomington, IN: Xlibris/Random House.

Ogawa, B. (2013). *Desire for Life: The Practitioner's Introduction to Morita Therapy for the Treatment of Anxiety Disorders.* Bloomington, IN: Xlibris/Penguin.

Ogawa, J.R., Sroufe, L.A., Weinfield, N.S., Carlson, E.A., and Egeland, B. (1997). Development and the fragmented self: A longitudinal study of dissociative symptomatology in a normative sample. *Development and Psychopathology*, 9, 855–879.

Ohara, K. (Ed.). (1987). *Morita Therapy: Theory and Practice.* Tokyo: Kanehara Shuppan.

Ohara, K. and Reynolds, D.K. (1968). Changing methods in Morita psychotherapy. *International Journal of Social Psychiatry*, 14(4), 305–310.

Ohara, K., Aizawa, S., and Iwai, H. (1970). *Morita Ryōhō* (Morita Therapy). Tokyo: Bunkodo.

Ohnuki-Tierney, E. (1987), *The Monkey as Mirror; Symbolic Transformations in Japanese History and Ritual*. Princeton, NJ: Princeton University Press.

Okamoto, S. (2007). *La thérapie de Morita inconnue: Trace de vingt années d'échanges*. Franco-Japonais. Tokyo: Hokuju-Shuppan.

Onda, A. (1962). Zen and creativity. *Psychologia: An International Journal of Psychology in the Orient*, 5, 13–20.

Onda, A. (1967). Zen, autogenic training and hypnotism. *Psychologia: An International Journal of Psychology in the Orient*, 10, 133–136.

Onda, A. (1992). Zen, self-control and creativity. *Japanese Health Psychology*, 1, 97–102.

Onuma, H. (1993). *Kyūdō: The Essence and Practice of Japanese Archery*. Tokyo: Kodansha International.

Ozawa-de Silva, C. (2006). *Psychotherapy and Religion in Japan: The Japanese Introspection Practice of Naikan*. London: Routledge.

Ozecetin, A., Belli, H., Ertem, U., Bahcebasi, T., Ataoglu, A., and Canan, H. (2009). Childhood trauma and dissociation in women with pseudoseizure-type conversion disorder. *Nordic Journal of Psychiatry*, November, 63 (6), 462–68.

Parsons, W. (2009). Psychoanalysis meets Buddhism: The development of a dialogue. In J. Belsen (Ed.). *Changing the Scientific Study of Religion: Beyond Freud? Theoretical, Empirical and Clinical Studies from Psychoanalytic Perspectives* (pp. 179–209). Netherlands: Springer Science.

Paulson, D.S. (2004). *Walking the Point: Male Initiation and the Vietnam Experience* (2nd Edn). New York: Paraview Press.

Paulson, D. and Krippner, S. (2007). *Haunted by Combat*. Connecticut: Praeger Security International.

Perls, F. (1969). *In and Out of the Garbage Pail*. California: Real People Press.

Perry, B.D. (2006). The neurosequential model of therapeutics: Applying principles of neurodevelopment to clinical work with maltreated and traumatized children. In N.B. Webb (Ed.), *Working with Traumatized Youth in Child Welfare*. New York: Guilford Press.

Perry, B. D., Pollard, R.A., Blakley, T.L., and Vigilante, D. (1995). Childhood trauma, the neurobiology of adaptation, and 'use-dependent' development of the brain: How 'states' become 'traits'. *Infant Mental Health Journal*, 16(4), Winter.

Peters, E. (1989). *Inquisition*. Berkeley, CA: University of California Press.

Philip, N. (2001). *The Great Mystery: Myths of Native America*. New York, NY: Clarion Books.

Polster, E. (1966) A contemporary psychotherapy. *Psychotherapy: Theory, Research & Practice*, 3(1), February, 1–6.

Putnam, F. (1997). *Dissociation in Children and Adolescents: A Developmental Perspective*. New York: Guilford Press.

Quinn, S. (1988). *A Mind of Her Own: The Life of Karen Horney*. New York: Summit Books.

Rank, O. (1907). Der Künstler (The Artist). In *The Artist: Towards a Sexual Psychology (Der Künstler: Ansätze zu einer Sexual-Psychologie)*. Leipzig und Wien: Hugo Heller.

Rank, O. (1989). *Art and Artist: Creative Urge and Personality Development*. (C.F. Atkinson, Trans.) New York: Agathon Press.

Ram Das, B. (1971). *Be Here Now*. San Cristobal, New Mexico: Lama Foundation.

Rappard, J. F. H. van (1976). *Psychologie als zelfkennis*. Amsterdam: Academische Pers. [Psychology as self-knowledge (1979)]. (L. Faili, Trans.), Assen, Netherlands: Van Gorcum.

Roszak, T. (1975). *The Unfinished Animal: The Aquarian Frontier and the Evolution of Consciousness*. New York: Harper and Row.

Reivich, K.J., Seligman, M., and McBride, S. (2011). Master resilience training in the U.S. Army. *American Psychologist*, 66(1), 25–34.

Reynolds, D.K. (1969). Directed behavior change: Japanese psychotherapy in a private mental hospital. Doctoral Dissertation, University of California, Los Angeles.

Reynolds, D.K. (1976). *Morita Psychotherapy*. Berkeley: University of California Press

Reynolds, D.K. (1980). *The Quiet Therapies: Japanese Pathways to Personal Growth*. Honolulu: University of Hawai'i Press.

Reynolds, D.K. (1984a). *Constructive Living*. Honolulu: University of Hawai'i Press.

Reynolds, D.K. (1984b). *Playing Ball on Running Water: Living Morita Psychotherapy*. New York: Quill.

Reynolds, D.K. (1992). A reply to Ives. *International Bulletin of Morita Therapy*, 5(1&2), 18–21.

Rhyner, B. (1987). Morita therapy, Mitchell's Rest Treatment and Otto Binswanger's 'geregelte Lebensführung': A methodological comparison. *Psychologia: An International Journal of Psychology in the Orient*, 30(2), 70–74.

Rhyner, B. (1988). Morita psychotherapy and Zen Buddhism: A comparison of theoretical concepts. *Psychologia*, 31, 7–14.

Richardson, C.R., Faulkner, G., McDevitt, J. et al. (2005). Integrating physical activity into mental health services for persons with serious mental illness. *Psychiatric Services*, 56(3), 324–31.

Rosen, G., Spitzer, R., and McHugh, P. (2008). Problems with the post-traumatic stress disorder diagnosis and its future in DSM-V. *The British Journal of Psychiatry*, 3(4), 192.

Roszak, T. (1975). *Unfinished Animal: The Aquarian Frontier and the Evolution of Consciousness*. New York: Harper and Row.

Roszak, T. (1992). *The Voice of the Earth*. New York: Simon and Schuster.

Sartre, J.P. (1936). *La transcendance de l'ego: Esquisse d'une description phénoménologique*. France: Librairie Philosophique J.Vrin. Sartre, J.P. (1960) English version. *The Transcendence of Ego: An Existentialist Theory of Consciousness*. (F. Williams and R. Kilpatrick, Trans.) New York: Hill and Wang.

Sartre, J.P. (1939). *Esquisse d'une théorie des émotions* (Sketch of a Theory on Emotions). Paris: Hermann & Cie.

Sartre, J.P. (1940). *L'imaginaire: Psychologie phénoménologique de l'imagination*. Paris: Gallimard.

Sartre, J.P. (1948). *The Emotions: Outline of a Theory*. (B. Frechtman, Trans.) New York: Philosophical Library.

Sartre, J.P. (1956). *Being and Nothingness: An Essay on Phenomenological Ontology*. (H.E. Barnes, Trans.) New York: Philosophical Library.

Sartre, J.P. (1957). *The Transcendence of the Ego: An Existentialist Theory of Consciousness*. (F. Williams and R. Kirkpatrick, Eds and Trans.) New York: Noonday Press.

Sartre, J.P. (1962). *Imagination: A Psychological Critique*. (F. Williams, Trans.) Ann Arbor: University of Michigan Press.

Sartre, J.P. (2004). *The Imaginary: A Phenomenological Psychology of the Imagination*. (J. Webber, Trans.) London and New York: Routledge.

Sato, K. (1959). How to get Zen enlightenment: On Master Ighiguri's five days intensive course for its attainment. *Psychologia*, 2, 107–118.

Sato, K. (1964). Death of Zen masters (Posture of death). *Psychologia*, (7), 143–147.

Sayers, J. (2000). *Kleinians: Psychoanalysis Inside Out*. Cambridge, UK: Polity Press.

Scaer, R. (2005). *The Trauma Spectrum: Hidden Wounds and Human Resiliency*. New York: Norton Press.

Schore, A. (2009). Attachment trauma and the developing right brain: Origins of pathological dissociation. In P.F. Dell and J. O'Neill (Eds), *Dissociation: DSM-V and Beyond* (pp. 107–144). New York: Routledge Press.

Schneider, R. and Wieczorek, V. (1991). Historical aspects of neurosciences. Otto Binswanger (1852–1929). *Journal of Neurological Sciences*, May, 103(1), 61–64.

Seligman, M. (2011). *Flourish: A Visionary New Understanding of Happiness and Well-being*. New York: Free Press.

Semenova, N. (2016). On teaching Morita therapy: The applicability and validity of the Moritian model on foreign soil. Abstract in *Japanese Journal of Morita Therapy*, 27(2), 172–173.

Shapiro, F. (2001). *EMDR: Eye Movement Desensitization of Reprocessing: Basic Principles, Protocols and Procedures* (2nd edn). New York: Guilford Press.

Shibata, M. (1981). The diary of a Zen layman: The philosopher Nishida Kitarō. *The Eastern Buddhist Society*, 121–131.

Shimoda, M. (1942). *Seishin Eisei Kōwa* (Lectures on Mental Health). Tokyo: Iwanami Shoten.

Shugg, H., Richards, D., and Frost, J. (2016). Morita therapy for depression and anxiety (Morita Trial): Study protocol for a pilot randomised controlled trial. *Trials* (pp. 1–13). UK: BioMed Central.

Smith, G. (2014a). Revisiting formulation: Part 1. The tasks of formulation: their rationale and philosophic basis. *Australasian Psychiatry*, 22, 23–27.

Smith, G. (2014b). Revisiting formulation: Part 2. The task of addressing the concept of the unique individual. Remediating problems with formulation. *Australasian Psychiatry*, (22), 28–31.

Smith, K. (1981). Observations on Morita therapy and culture-specific interpretations. *The Journal of Transpersonal Psychology*, 13(1), 59–67.

Smith, L.T. (1999). *Decolonising Methodologies*. New Zealand: University of Otago Press.

Smith, P. (1997). *Japan: A Reinterpretation*. Toronto, Canada: Harper Collins.

Spates, C. R., Tateno, A., Nakamura, K., Seim, R., and Sheerin, C. (2011). The experiential therapy of Shoma Morita: A comparison to contemporary cognitive behavior therapies. *Annals of Psychotherapy and Integrative Health*, 14(1), 14–25.

Stadlen, A. (2003). A poor model for those in training: The case of Thomas Szasz. *Existential Analysis*, 14(2), 213–244.

Stadlen, A. (2013). Thomas Szasz obituary. *Existential Analysis*, 24(1), 7–18.

Stadler, A. (1977). Morita psychotherapy. *Horizons*, 4(2), 275–276.

Stavrakakis, Y. (1999). *Lacan and the Political*. London: Routledge.

Stein, G. (1993). Sacred Emily. In *Geography and Plays*. Madison, WIS: University of Wisconsin Press. (First published in 1922 with The Four Seasons Company in Boston, Massachusetts.)

Stern, D. (2003). *Unformulated Experience: From Dissociation to Imagination in Psychoanalysis*. Hillsdale, NJ: Analytic Press.

Storr, A. (1988). *Solitude: A Return to Self*. New York: Random House.

Suzuki, D.T. (1949). *A Miscellany on the Shin Teaching of Buddhism*. Kyoto: Shinshu Otaniha Shumushi.

Suzuki, D.T. (1959). *Zen and Japanese Culture*. New York: Random House.

Suzuki, D.T. (1963). *Zen Buddhism and Psychoanalysis*. New York: Grove Press.

Suzuki, D.T. (1964). *An Introduction to Zen Buddhism*. New York: Grove Press.

Suzuki, D.T. (1971). *Living by Zen*. Tokyo: Sanseido Publishing Company.

Suzuki, D.T. (1975). Zen and psychology. *The Eastern Buddhist*, Vol. VIII, No 1, Kyoto, 1–11.

Suzuki, D.T. (1977). Reality is act. *The Eastern Buddhist*. Vol 111, No 2. October 1975, Kyoto, 1–6.

Suzuki, D.T. (2002). *Buddha of Infinite Light*. Boston and London: Shambhala Publications.

Suzuki, D.T. (2005). *Zen and Japanese Culture*. (K. Momo, Trans.) Tokyo: Kodansha.

Suzuki, D. (2007). *The Sacred Balance: Rediscovering Our Place in Nature*. St Leonards: Allen and Unwin.

Suzuki, T. (1969). *Noiroze no Taiken Ryoho* (Experiential Treatment of Neurosis). Tokyo: Seishinshobo.

Suzuki, T. (1989). The concept of neurasthenia and its treatment in Japan. *Culture, Medicine, and Psychiatry*, June, 13(2), 187–202.

Suzuki, T. and Suzuki R. (1973). A follow-up of neurotics treated by Morita therapy. *Proceedings of the 5th World Congress of Psychiatry,* Honolulu, Hawaii.

Suzuki, T. and Suzuki, R. (1977). Morita therapy. In E. D. Wittkower and H. Warnes (Eds), *Psychosomatic Medicine: Its Clinical Application.* New York: Harper & Row.

Suzuki, T. and Suzuki, R. (1981). The effectiveness of inpatient Morita therapy. *Psychiatric Quarterly,* September, 53(3), 203–213.

Suzuki, Y. (1987). Expanded application of Morita therapy: Alcohol dependency. In K. Ohara (Ed.), *Seishinka Mook* No. 19: *Morita Therapy: Theory and Practice* (pp. 133–138). Tokyo: Kanehara Shuppan.

Szasz, T. (1961). *The Myth of Mental Illness.* New York: Harper and Row.

Tamai, K., Takeichi, M., and Tashiro, N. (1990). The possibility of applying Morita Therapy to borderline cases. *Journal of Morita Therapy* (in Japanese), 1, 224–230.

Tamai, K., Takeichi, M., and Tashiro, N. (1991). Morita therapy for treating borderline personality disorder: The utility of treatment structuredness and limit-setting. *International Bulletin of Morita Therapy,* 4(1&2), Spring/Fall.

Tedeschi, R. and McNally, R. (2011). Can we facilitate posttraumatic growth in combat veterans? *American Psychologist,* 66(1), 19–24.

Tillich, P. (1952) *Courage To Be.* New Haven, CT: Yale University Press.

Tummala-Narra, P. (2001) Asian trauma survivors: Immigration, identity, loss and recovery. *Journal of Applied Psychoanalytic Studies,* 3(3), 243–258.

Tuttle, J. (2000). Letters from Elizabeth Stuart Phelps (Ward) to S. Weir Mitchell, M.D., 1884–1897. University of Nebraska Press. *Legacy: A Journal of American Women Writers,* 17 (1), 83.

Triana, R. (1978). Zen and Morita Therapy. Master degree thesis in Department of Religious Studies. Charlottesville: University of Virginia.

Tro, R. P. (1993). Karen Horney, psychoanalysis and Morita therapy: A historical overview of the Zen connection. *International Bulletin of Morita Therapy,* 6(1–2), 30–46.

Ueda, Y. (1978). *Letters of Shinran: A Translation of Mattōshō.* (D. Hirota, Trans.) Shin Buddhism Translation Series. Kyoto: Hongwanji International Center.

Usa, S. (2002). Morita Therapy: Its Transcendence of History. Symposium on 'Transcultural Psychotherapy' at the 12th World Congress of Psychotherapy, 26 August. Yokohama, Japan.

van der Hart, O. and Friedman, B. (1989). A reader's guide to Pierre Janet on dissociation: A neglected intellectual heritage. *Dissociation,* 2(1), 3–16.

van der Hart, O. and Nijenhuis, E. R. S. (1999). Bearing witness to uncorroborated trauma: The clinician's development of reflective belief. *Professional Psychology: Research and Practice,* 30(1), 37–44.

van der Hart, O., Nijenhuis, E.R.S., Steele, K., and Brown, D. (2004). Trauma-related dissociation: Conceptual clarity lost and found. *Australian and New Zealand Journal of Psychiatry,* 38, 906–914.

van der Hart, O. and Steele, K. (1997). Time distortions in Dissociative Identity Disorder: Janetian Concepts and Treatment. *Dissociation,* 10(2), 91–103.

Van der Kolk, B. (1996). The body keeps the score: Approaches to the psychobiology of posttraumatic stress disorder. In B.A. van der Kolk, A.C. McFarlane, and L. Weisaeth (Eds), *Traumatic Stress* (pp. 214–241). New York: Guilford Press.

Velten, E. (Ed.) (2007). Chapter Seven, Hard Facts for ACT to Follow: Morita Therapy, General Semantics, Person-Centered Therapy, Fixed-Role Therapy, Cognitive Therapy, Values Clarification, Reality Therapy, Multimodal Therapy, and – yes, of course – Rational Emotive Behavior Therapy. *Under the Influence: Reflections on Albert Ellis in the work of Others.* Arizona: Sharp Press, LLC.

Vernon, J. (1963). *Inside the Black Room: Studies of Sensory Deprivation.* Harmondsworth, UK: Pelican Books.

Walborn, F. (2014). *Religion in Personality Theory*. Oxford, UK: Elsevier.

Watkins, G. and Watkins, H. (1996). Overt-covert dissociation and hypnotic ego state therapy. In L.K. Michelson and W. Ray (Eds), *Handbook of Dissociation: Theoretical, Empirical, and Clinical Perspectives* (pp. 431–448). New York: Plenum Press.

Watts, A. (1953). Asian psychology and modern psychiatry. *The American Journal of Psychoanalysis*, 1(1), 25–30.

Webster, N. (1927). *Webster's New International Dictionary,* Merriam series. Springfield, MA: Cambridge version.

Weglyn, M. (1976). *Years of Infamy: The Untold Story of America's Concentration Camps*. Seattle: University of Washington Press.

Weintraub, S. (1974). *Whistler: A Biography*. New York: Weybright & Talley.

Weisenfeld, G. (2001). *MAVO: Japanese Artists and the Avant-Garde, 1905–1931 (Twentieth-Century Japan: The Emergence of a World Power)*. Berkeley, CA: University of California Press.

White, M. (2007). *Maps of Narrative Practice*. New York: W.W. Norton.

White, M. (2004). Working with people who are suffering the consequences of multiple trauma: A narrative perspective. *The International Journal of Narrative Therapy and Community Work*, (1), 45–76.

Wiener, P. (1956). G.M. Beard and Freud on 'American Nervousness'. *Journal of the History of Ideas*, 17(2), 269–274.

Williams, W.M. and Yang, L.T. (1999). Organizational creativity. In R.J. Sternberg (Ed.), *Handbook of Creativity* (pp. 373–391). Cambridge, UK: Cambridge University Press.

Wilson, C. (2001). *The Outsider*. London: Orion Books Ltd.

Wilson, E.O. (1984). *Biophilia*. Boston: Harvard University Press.

Wood, E. (1990). *Zen Dictionary*. Tokyo: Charles Tuttle Company.

Wood, R. (1961). Tillich encounters Japan. *Japanese Religions,* 2, 48–71.

Woolf, V. (1925). *The Common Reader*. New York: Harcourt, Inc.

Wray, I. A. (1986). Buddhism and psychotherapy: A Buddhist perspective. In G. Claxton (Ed.), *Beyond Therapy: The Impact of Eastern Religions on Psychological Theory and Practice* (pp. 153–172). London: Wisdom Publications.

Wright, P.A. (1997). History of dissociation in Western psychology. In S. Krippner and S.M. Powers (Eds), *Broken Images, Broken Selves: Dissociative Narratives in Clinical Practice* (pp. 41–60). Washington, DC: Brunner/Mazel.

Yalom, I. (1980). *Existential Psychotherapy*. New York: Basic Books.

Yamada, M. (n.d.). (Nishimura, E., Trans). Publication by the Kyoto Institute for Zen Studies with no date listed. *How to Practice Zazen*. (Taken from Lectures on the Zazen-gi.) Kyoto: Institute for Zen Studies [Hanazono College 8-I Tsubonouchi-cho, Nishinokyo, Nakakyo-ku, Kyoto, Japan].

Yamakage, M. (2006). *The Essence of Shinto: Japan's Spiritual Heart*. Tokyo: Kodansha International.

Yokoyama, K. (1968). Morita therapy and seiza. *Psychologia*, 11(3–4), 179–184.

Yusa, M. (2002) *Zen and Philosophy: An Intellectual Biography of Nishida Kitarō*. Hawaii: University of Hawai'i Press.

Zubek, J. (1969) *Sensory Deprivation: Fifteen Years of Research*. New York: Appleton-Century-Crofts Publisher.

INDEX

When the text is within a figure, the number span is in **bold**.
Eg, bonsai xx, 13, 16, **20–1**, 124n1
When the text is within the glossary, the number span is <u>underlined</u>.
Eg, *arugamama* (isness, suchness) <u>129</u>
When the text is within a note, this is indicated by page number, 'n', note number.
Eg, Abe, Masao 48–9, 65n28
Single names denote a case study.
Case studies are also listed under that heading.
Eg, Kevin (case study) 112–15, 115–17, 119, 120, 123, 125n18

For Product Safety Concerns and Information please contact our EU
representative GPSR@taylorandfrancis.com
Taylor & Francis Verlag GmbH, Kaufingerstraße 24, 80331 München, Germany